KU-020-499

ABSOLUTE
BEGINNER'S
GUIDE

(TO)

Security, Spam, Spyware & Viruses

Andy Walker

que®

800 East 96th Street
Indianapolis, Indiana 46240

Absolute Beginner's Guide to Security, Spam, Spyware & Viruses

Copyright ©2006 by Que Publishing

All rights reserved. No part of this book shall be reproduced, stored in a retrieval system, or transmitted by any means, electronic, mechanical, photocopying, recording, or otherwise, without written permission from the publisher. No patent liability is assumed with respect to the use of the information contained herein. Although every precaution has been taken in the preparation of this book, the publisher and author assume no responsibility for errors or omissions. Nor is any liability assumed for damages resulting from the use of the information contained herein.

International Standard Book Number: 0-7897-3459-1

Library of Congress Catalog Card Number: 2005905788

Printed in the United States of America

First Printing: November 2005

08   07   06   05   4   3   2   1

Trademarks

All terms mentioned in this book that are known to be trademarks or service marks have been appropriately capitalized. Que Publishing cannot attest to the accuracy of this information. Use of a term in this book should not be regarded as affecting the validity of any trademark or service mark.

Warning and Disclaimer

Every effort has been made to make this book as complete and as accurate as possible, but no warranty or fitness is implied. The information provided is on an "as is" basis. The author and the publisher shall have neither liability nor responsibility to any person or entity with respect to any loss or damages arising from the information contained in this book.

Bulk Sales

Que Publishing offers excellent discounts on this book when ordered in quantity for bulk purchases or special sales. For more information, please contact

U.S. Corporate and Government Sales
1-800-382-3419
corpsales@pearsontechgroup.com

For sales outside the United States, please contact

International Sales
international@pearsoned.com

Associate Publisher
Greg Wiegand

Executive Editor
Rick Kughen

Development Editor
Rick Kughen

Managing Editor
Charlotte Clapp

Project Editor
Seth Kerney

Production Editor
Heather Wilkins

Indexer
Aaron Black

Technical Editor
David Eytchison

Publishing Coordinator
Sharry Lee Gregory

Interior Designer
Anne Jones

Cover Designer
Anne Jones

Page Layout
Toi Davis

Reviewers
David Eytchison
Brian Knittel
Will Schmied

Contents at a Glance

Table of Contents

About the Author

Andy Walker is one of North America's top technology journalists. Since 1995, he has written about personal computer technology for dozens of newspapers, magazines, and websites. His personal technology advice column was syndicated across the Southam Newspaper chain and today the body of work is published at Cyberwalker.com where more than 5 million unique visitors read the advice annually. Andy has appeared as a tech expert on hundreds of TV and radio broadcasts and co-hosts the internationally syndicated TV show *Call for Help* with Leo Laporte and Amber MacArthur. He has also worked with some of the biggest luminaries in technology publishing. Between 2002 and 2004, Andy was the executive editor of Berkeley-based *Dig_iT* magazine, a publication focused on the digital lifestyle. It was founded by David Bunnell and Fred Davis, the publishing pioneers behind *PC Magazine*, *PC World*, *MacUser*, and *MacWorld*. Andy was born in the United Kingdom, educated and raised in Canada, and now lives in Toronto with two cats and a really secure personal computer.

Foreword

What if you forgot to lock your front door when you left the house today? In all likelihood, you'd come home and everything would be untouched, just as you left it. But what if that just happened to be the day an evildoer chose to wander down your street rattling door knobs? When he came to your door, he'd find it open. Now depending on his nerve and his evil intent, he might just open the door and leave it at that. Or he might come inside and start rummaging around. Other evildoers, seeing the door open, might stop in, too. Some would be looking for valuables. Others would be more interested in snooping into your personal business. Still others might use this as an opportunity to start doing business out of your house. You'd come home that night to a house full of strangers, each doing his own thing, all oblivious to the fact that you're the rightful owner, and getting rid of them would be quite a chore.

Sounds like locking your front door is a pretty good idea.

I think you probably know where I'm going with this. Your computer is just like that house. If you leave it unprotected when you venture onto the Internet, all sorts of bad guys can move in, take it over for their nefarious needs, and you'll have a devil of a time getting rid of them.

That's what this book is all about: Locking your system down to keep out the bad guys—and how to exterminate them if they've already managed to sneak in.

Computer invasion is no fanciful threat. There are well over 30,000 Windows viruses itching to get into your machine. Antivirus vendor Trend Micro recorded 10 million infections during the second quarter of 2005. It's more than likely that you were one of the victims. And if not, you can't rely on your good luck to hold.

You need to take action to protect yourself right now. Fortunately, you have everything you need to know in your hands.

In this book, Andy Walker will take you on a tour of the entire zoo of malware: viruses, Trojan horses, worms, spyware, zombies, BHOs, spam, root kits, and keystroke loggers. You'll learn what they are, how they work, and what to do to keep them off your computer. And you couldn't find a better tour guide. Andy has been helping computer users for years, both on his website, cyberwalker.com, and on radio and TV. Most recently he and I have worked together on a TV show named *Call for Help*. I've never worked with anyone better able to explain complex technology topics in a way in which anyone can understand them.

If you own a PC, you need this book. Read it and follow its instructions. It's not hard to lock your computer down tight. In fact, it's a lot easier to do that than to get rid of the bad guys after they've moved in. As my old grandmother used to say, an ounce of prevention is worth a pound of browser hijacker objects. Well, she would have said it, if she had had a computer.

If you have a computer, you need this book. Put it to work, and you can get to work knowing your PC is locked up safe and sound.

Leo Laporte

Petaluma, California

August 29, 2005

Dedication

For Greg and Dorothy, my parents, who taught me that anything is possible.

Acknowledgments

This book would not have been possible without the hard work, faith, and talents of some remarkable people.

To Sarah Hammond, the best assistant a writer could want. If you work in publishing, hire her. Sarah is more talented that I thought possible.

I'd like to thank my researchers Sean Carruthers and Maurice Cacho for working to make some of the hard parts of this book easy. Sean, you are a godsend. Maurice, you have a fantastic career ahead of you.

Thanks to Sam Hiyate, my agent and friend, for believing in me early on and being a tireless advocate for my career.

To Rick Kughen, my acquisitions and development editor. Thank you for your faith, guidance, professionalism, and most of all, good humor. Let's go fishing some time.

To Matt Harris, for being there when I needed you most. I couldn't have a better friend.

To JJ Dugoua, for your imaginative care and healing.

To the gang at *Call for Help*, especially Amber, Katya, and Mike, all who put up with my fatigue, grumpiness, and multiple personalities.

To Simon, Nick, and Joanna, my brothers and sister, for your lifelong cheerleading.

To Steve Gibson, for your generosity of mind and spirit.

To Leo Laporte, my friend, my mentor, and my guide; without you this book would never have happened.

And finally, to Roo, who traveled with me so many miles.

Andy Walker

August 9, 2005

We Want to Hear from You!

As the reader of this book, *you* are our most important critic and commentator. We value your opinion and want to know what we're doing right, what we could do better, what areas you'd like to see us publish in, and any other words of wisdom you're willing to pass our way.

As an executive editor for Que Publishing, I welcome your comments. You can email or write me directly to let me know what you did or didn't like about this book—as well as what we can do to make our books better.

Please note that I cannot help you with technical problems related to the topic of this book. We do have a User Services group, however, where I will forward specific technical questions related to the book.

When you write, please be sure to include this book's title and author as well as your name, email address, and phone number. I will carefully review your comments and share them with the author and editors who worked on the book.

Email: feedback@quepublishing.com

Mail: Rick Kughen
Executive Editor
Que Publishing
800 East 96th Street
Indianapolis, IN 46240 USA

For more information about this book or another Que Publishing title, visit our website at www.quepublishing.com. Type the ISBN (excluding hyphens) or the title of a book in the Search field to find the page you're looking for.

Introduction: Ignore This Book at Your Own Peril!

Viruses.

Spyware.

Spam.

Phishers.

War drivers.

Snoops.

Hackers.

Salad cream.

And identity thieves.

These are eight good reasons why you should buy this book, plus one arbitrary reference to a British salad condiment from Heinz that I love, just to keep the list interesting.

If you run Windows XP, the most insecure computer operating system ever invented, these eight nasty threats will rob you blind and torment you within an inch of your digital life and make your glorious and shiny minivan existence starkly miserable and mud splattered.

These computer nasties are a big fat plague. Good thing salad cream was invented.

And the worst of it is that very few computer owners know how bad it really is. No salad cream jokes here. In all seriousness, the state of computer security today is just ugly.

Here's the good news, however. I can help. And not only will I help, but I'll do it without forcing you to spend much more money than you already have spent on your computer. Almost everything I'll teach you in this book is done using mostly free software, easy-to-understand techniques, and analogies that often use small furry, chittering creatures.

Not convinced? Okay, put this book down if you haven't bought it already, go home, download the free Microsoft AntiSpyware from www.microsoft.com/spyware/, and run it on your computer. If you don't find at least one nasty program that shouldn't be on your computer, come back and buy Danielle Steele's latest novel over in the romance section because you don't need my help.

In this book, I'll show you how to cleanse your computer, halt further infections, do major damage control, and lock down the most insecure computer operating system you have ever seen. I know I said that earlier, but XP is just awful. You'll also enjoy 1,329 other really good bits of information that will be equally compelling.

When you're done with this book, you'll want to dance until you wear out your pants. And in fact I encourage it often in these pages. Then you'll want to go help your grandma because you'll know that if you're at risk, she's in deep grandma trouble with her computer. Then I want you to tell your neighbors and help them. And become the gal or guy who everyone goes to for help on home computer security. And here's the kicker: You don't even have to be a geek. Nope, you can continue to dress fashionably; eat good, wholesome food; and hold eye contact with handsome men and pretty women in elevators. Geeks are actually cool. But you don't have to become one to learn about personal computer security.

All I ask is that you read one chapter at a time. Start with the first seven, which detail the key threats you'll face in computer security. I'll scare the socks off you and then make it all better with easy-to-understand, geek-free help.

How This Book Is Organized

Chapter 1—Viruses: Attack of the Malicious Programs

In this first and vividly exciting chapter, I tell you what viruses are, why they are a problem, and how to get rid of them. Plus learn secrets, such as the real reason people write them in the first place.

Chapter 2—Spyware: Overrun by Advertisers, Hijackers, and Opportunists

This is a modern day computer pandemic. Your computer is probably rife with this malware. Bad companies are making money with it learning what you do on your computer. At the same time, spyware is also slowing your computer down. Most people experience a 30%–50% performance boost when they get rid of spyware for the first time. How's that for an upsell?

Chapter 3—Hackers: There's a Man in My Machine

Who are these people? Why do they want to get on to your computer? I tell you why and then show you how to shut them out. And I make a good joke about cheese in this chapter.

Chapter 4—Identity Thieves and Phishers: Protect Your Good Name and Bank Account

These people are going to suck your bank account dry. And they trick you into helping them do it. I show you how to stop them.

Chapter 5—Spam: Unwanted Email from Hell

Junk mail is a deluge, but like a Shop Vac on spilled ketchup, it's easy to clean up. I'll show you how in only a few pages.

Chapter 6—Wireless Network Snoops: Lock Down Your Wi-Fi Network

Let's pretend you're free of all the other nasties in this book, but I bet if you have a wireless home network, your neighbors are using your Internet connection and maybe even snooping in places they shouldn't be inside your computer. I help you stop them.

Chapter 7—Privacy Snoops: Cover Your Tracks and Your Reputation

Do you surf places on the Internet that are naughty? Do you plan birthday presents for nice people in your home? Do you keep exciting secrets on your computer? Keep the snoops out of your personal business. I'll show you how.

Chapter 8—Let's Smash-Proof Windows: Tweak Windows XP Nice and Tight

In the second part of this book, I'll walk you through how to lock down Windows XP so tight that you'll think it's the most secure operating system ever. All with freebie software!

Chapter 9—Starting from the Beginning: Wiping a Hard Drive and Rebuilding from the Ground Up

And if you are really ambitious, I'll also show you how to wipe your computer clean and start fresh (it's like gallivanting among tulips the first time you do it) and then I'll show you how to lock down Windows XP so it's more secure than a bucket of Brussels sprouts at a birthday party.

Chapter 10—Ongoing Maintenance: Fend Off Future Threats!

Of course it's fine to be safe now, but what about tomorrow and the next day? Well, clever me, I've thought of that. I show you how to keep your computer secure tomorrow, next week, next month, but not next year because I want to sell you another book.

Chapter 11—Selecting Software: Steals, Deals, and Software Duds

Next, I'll go over what the story is with lots of different security software. Do you have to buy it or can you get it all free?

Chapter 12—Tools of the Trade: Security Products You Should Own

And in the final chapter I'll tell you what software is really good and where to get it.

Glossary

Also, my talented assistant Sarah Hammond has written the best and most exciting glossary you have ever read. It's really scintillating and has been nominated for glossary of the year.

Special Elements Used in this Book

You'll also see a lot of help in the margins of this book. Here's how it looks and what it means.

note

This is stuff that I figured I should tell you when it popped in my head. Notes aren't essential reading, but I urge you not to skip them as you'll learn a lot of extra stuff here that you might not find elsewhere.

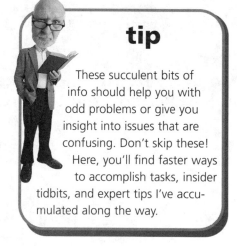

tip

These succulent bits of info should help you with odd problems or give you insight into issues that are confusing. Don't skip these! Here, you'll find faster ways to accomplish tasks, insider tidbits, and expert tips I've accumulated along the way.

caution

These blurbs keep you out of trouble. I hope. If you don't read these, you're asking for trouble. Security is risky business. I've done my best to point out common pitfalls, gotchas, and other assorted nasties.

SIDEBARS

Occasionally, I've added some additional information that's ancillary to the main topic, but still worth reading. Think of these as important stuff that didn't fit anywhere within the confines of the chapter you're reading, but are too important to skip.

Reader Competition...of Sorts

If you are one of the first 10 people to tell me by email what page the Monica Lewinsky reference is on and whether it's a note, tip, or caution, I'll send you a Cyberwalker T-shirt or a Cyberwalker thong—your choice. Both are nice and if you don't believe me, ask Rick Kughen, my editor at Que. He wears his fishing. Pictures (of the garments, not Rick) are on www.cyberwalker.com.

When you email me at monica@cyberwalker.com, include the answer and your full name, and put either *thong* or *shirt* in the subject line. Size (of the thong or T-shirt) is also helpful.

Finally, if you want to contact me and say nice things, tell me about how you saved your grandma with advice from this book, or send me chocolate cake (which I also love), email me at andy@cyberwalker.com.

And if you've read this far, go buy this book. I am almost out of salad cream.

PART

I

SECURITY BASICS: SOME VERY REAL THREATS

1

VIRUSES: ATTACK OF THE MALICIOUS PROGRAMS

We all know computer viruses are bad. This chapter explains what they are, what they do, and where they come from. It examines all the types that can potentially infect your computer and make your life a living hell. It also covers specialty viruses called worms and Trojan horses. And it looks at how viruses exploit programming bugs in your computer and what to do about it. Of course, the best part is that it shows you how to use the computer equivalent of a sledgehammer to squish them before they leap into your computer and delete your prom photos, the dog's prescription, and your patent for a better spatula.

What Is a Computer Virus?

A decade or so ago, viruses were pretty simple. They got into a system and infected a file or two. It was a basic as ordering coffee when coffee was easy to order. "One coffee please—black."

Today, the catalog of viruses you have to defend yourself against is frighteningly complex. In fact, it's become as complex as, well, ordering coffee.

"Looks like you've been infected by a dropper that's put a Trojan on your system, which deployed a multi-partite that opened a backdoor and also infected the master boot record."

Sounds like an order at Starbucks, don't you think?

These days a discussion about a virus can actually occur without using the word *virus* because sometimes viruses are worms or Trojan horses, which are virus-like nasties that act a little different than their infectious cousins.

Don't let all this frighten you, though. It's not that hard to figure out and defending your computer against viruses is pretty straightforward. Still, if the idea makes you queasy, skip ahead to the part of the chapter about how to easily protect yourself from viruses. But I hope you stick around because the more you know, the geekier you will be. Okay, not really. But understanding them makes them much less scary.

> **note**
>
> Why are they called computer *viruses*? Well, because they have similar characteristics to biological viruses that infect humans—in at least one way. The computer variety jumps from computer to computer much like a cold virus jumps from your kids to you and from you to your spouse.

Viruses were one of the first real security threats people had to deal with when personal computers started appearing in homes a couple of decades ago. The first computer viruses were written in the 1980s; however, they really didn't become a big threat until the late 1990s when everyone who owned a personal computer started connecting to the Internet.

Before then viruses spread via floppy disks or CDs. They would ride on the back of files stored on a disk or in the boot area of the floppy and replicate when the disk was inserted into the computer.

The Internet's popularity has also become the chief reason that security on personal computers has become such a hot topic. A Net connection is the off-ramp from the Internet into your computer for all data. And guess what? For viruses it's an express lane.

Before we go any further, let's define what a computer virus is because it's important to understand that before we start smacking them with a hammer. Here's a basic definition:

A *computer virus* is a malicious computer program that, when executed by an unsuspecting human, performs tasks that primarily include replicating itself and in some cases deploying a payload.

Not so hard, right? Let's break it down into easy-to-chew pieces.

What Is It?

A computer virus is a malicious computer program...

A virus is just a program, but it's written by a person of questionable character who wants to do harm. It's made up of lines of programming instructions and runs like any other program.

Who Triggers a Computer Virus?

...an unsuspecting human...

For a virus to be successful, it has to be executed on a computer by a human. That means a file has to be opened, a program has to be run, or a computer has to be booted. In other words, programming code has to be run by a human action. That could be you, me, friends, or family—anyone who uses a computer. This is not to say that anyone executes a virus on purpose. Usually we're tricked into it. But a virus requires a human's help to proliferate. Remembering this fact goes a long way to preventing viruses from ever running amuck on your computer.

note

Interestingly, viruses were first conceived in 1949, when computer pioneer John von Neumann wrote a paper theorizing that programs could become self-replicating. Von Neumann's theories came to life in the 1950s at Bell Labs where programmers created a game called "Core Wars" in which two players could unleash software "organisms" into the mainframe computer and watch as they competed for control of the machine. It would take more than 30 years for computer viruses to become a threat, but when PCs started becoming commonplace in homes and schools in the early 1980s, computer viruses could replicate and move from computer to computer—first by infected floppies, and later via networked PCs.

Now you know...

How Does It Spread?

(It) performs tasks that primarily include replicating itself...

To steal a little lingo from Star Trek, replicating is a virus's prime directive. For a computer virus to be successful by any definition, it must clone itself, make its way into other computers, and repeat the replication cycle. This is how it spreads. Of course, it uses many tricks to do this, including riding on other programs' backs, moving in email as a file attachment, and even downloading from a web page. Virus writers use many methods to move a virus between computers, but you can categorize them into two types:

- **External media**—Any storage device that can contain a computer file, such as a floppy disk, DVD, or CD, and be connected or inserted into a computer.

- **A network connection**—A network is a group of computers connected so they can exchange data. The Internet, which is the most common source of viruses these days, is a large network. Viruses can use the connection to move in chat, in email, via the Web, and via specialty computer-to-computer connections.

note

In 1984, University of New Haven professor Fred Cohen first used the term *computer virus* in a research paper "Experiments with Computer Viruses." Although Cohen is sometimes credited with coining the term, he credits theoretical computer scientist Leonard Adleman with inventing the term.

DON'T SNEEZE ON MY PC AND GIVE IT A VIRUS!

In the early 1990s, when people started buying personal computers for the home, a very concerned woman stopped me in the hall at work one day in a bit of a tizzy. Her home computer had been infected by a virus and her husband was blaming her. But she couldn't understand how that might have happened. "I didn't sneeze on the computer," she said, puzzled. "I had a cold, but I was very careful. How did it jump from me and get into the computer?"

Of course, a computer virus and a human virus are not the same thing. The virus that gives you the sniffles is a tiny living organism that gets inside your body and makes you sick.

A computer virus, on the other hand, is a program. It's designed to find its way inside a computer, often without your permission or knowledge, using a very specific set of instructions.

I explained that to her, and calmer, she later when home to tell her husband, who refused to believe the explanation and continued to keep sick people away from his precious virus-free computer.

What Damage Can It Do?

...in some cases (it can) deploy a payload.

This last piece of the definition is the scariest part. A virus can be (and often is) programmed to do bad things. This part of the virus is called a *payload*, or sometimes referred to as a *bomb*. Here are the most common payloads:

- **Jokes or vandalism**—Sometimes virus writers just want you to know they have succeeded in getting a virus into your computer. So they post messages or alerts to your computer. It's the equivalent of writing "Andy has a cute bum" on a bus shelter. It might not be true, but it's slightly amusing (at least to its author).

- **Data destruction or corruption**— Viruses can infect files and damage them or make them unusable. They can also wipe out entire hard drives.

> **note**
>
> There's an exception to this rule—computer worms. They are a type of virus that self-executes and can spread without human intervention. Worms are discussed in more detail later in "Worms: Network-Savvy Viruses," p. 18.

- **Spam distribution**—Some virus writers engineer their viruses to send spam from your computer. This takes the heat off them when angry spam recipients trace unwanted email back to its source. Spam gets sent from *your* computer and *you* get the blame. Or a virus can also open up a door so someone can come along later to take control of your computer and use it remotely for their purposes. The mass-mailing worm known as Sober.P sends an email enticing people to open an email attachment. The worm then steals email addresses from the victim and blasts spam at the victim's contacts.

- **Data or information theft**—Viruses can monitor and steal data or personal information from your computer or open up security holes so malicious people on the Internet can remotely connect and snoop around inside your computer and steal information themselves.

- **Hijacking**—Your computer can be turned into what is called a *zombie* by a virus. If your computer is zombified, it can later be used to bombard another computer with nonsense data. When thousands of computer zombies are harnessed simultaneously, they can crash major web servers. CNN, Yahoo!, and Amazon.com have all been victims of an attack like this, which is called a Distributed Denial of Service (DDoS) attack. It can also be hijacked for use as a file server (storing pirated software) or do tasks for someone who remotely controls it from the Internet.

- **Ransomware**—A new nasty payload has been detected that holds your data ransom. It encrypts (scrambles) part of your hard drive so you can't get at it without typing in a password. The virus leaves a ransom note for you that says the data will be unlocked if you pay a ransom. So far this technique was an isolated incident discovered in May 2005, but it's feared that it could become more widespread as virus writers figure out how to perfect the extortion and cover their tracks so the ransom payment can't be tracked to them.

■ **Virus distribution**—Your computer can be harnessed to redistribute the virus to your friends, family and business contacts.

Viruses: As Many Kinds As Sniffles in Kindergarten

So far I've been using the word *virus* fairly liberally. And for sheer practicality, it's handy to have a catch-all word that more or less covers what we're talking about. Some self-righteous sticklers, however, will poke you with a pointy stick if you use the term *virus* too broadly.

If you start ranting across your Corn Flakes about how viruses spread on their own, inevitably a stickler will pipe up.

"Actually, that's not a virus."

"Yes, it is," you might say indignantly.

"No, it's not," he'll say as he spoons his Cheerios. "That's a worm."

A worm?

Yeah, bad news here. Not all viruses are viruses.

I know that's confusing, but so is a man in a clingy dress. Bear with me a sec—we'll get to the bottom of this.

To say "I have a *virus*" is sort of like saying "I am having *meat* for dinner" as opposed to "I am having quail with a tasty pistachio butter." The word

tip

A worm called the KakWorm embeds itself in an HTML email (an email that works like a web page to display pictures and layout). All you need to do to execute it is to preview the email in either Microsoft Outlook or Microsoft Outlook Express. The security hole that allowed this has now been patched, so if you have all your Windows security patches installed you won't get Kakked. But should you turn off your email preview feature just in case? I'll leave that up to you to decide. Personally, I've left mine on because it is such a handy feature. But then again, I am fastidious about keeping my security patches and virus signatures up to date.

note

Some people will tell you that viruses can purportedly overheat and damage computer hardware by turning off cooling systems. If it's been done, its success has been limited. I think this is a myth.

virus is often used as a generic term to describe all malicious computer files that do bad stuff to your computer, but note that the word *virus* is specific to malicious programs that need human intervention to run.

So let's talk about the different types and all their trimmings, and then I'll cover viruses' evil cousins: worms, Trojan Horses, and virus hoaxes.

Macro Viruses

A *macro* is a computer programming language built into a larger program. It's used to automate tasks. For example, a Microsoft Word macro can be written to format an entire document or share the contents of a Word file with other Microsoft Office programs. Windows has a few built-in macro languages (sometimes called scripting languages) as do the various programs in Microsoft Office, WordPerfect, and other productivity software programs.

A macro can be as short as a few lines of programming code or it can be a massive program that contains zillions of instructions. And it can be designed to run as soon as a file is opened. It's not surprising that virus writers saw this technology as a great opportunity to deploy their malicious software. And sure enough, they have been exploiting this feature in the last few years with great zeal.

The basic strategy has been to generate a virus in a macro and then send a file with a macro embedded as an email attachment. The secret to making this work is, once again, people. A virus writer has to also convince someone to start the macro so the virus can execute and proliferate.

> **tip**
>
> One good way to defend against macro viruses is to turn off the capability to open them by default and have a document warn you if a macro is present and give you the option to turn it on. It's annoying to get bugged like that, but it's a good and easy way to defend against macro viruses. To change the macro security level in Office 2003 programs, click Tools, Options, and then the Security tab. Under Macro Security, click the Macro Security button. Click the Security Level tab, and then select the security level you want to use. The medium setting is a good choice.

I DON'T LOVE YOU, BUT MY VIRUS DOES

The best viruses are ones that convince people to help spread them. This is a form of what security experts call *social engineering*. It's a term used to describe a technique of tricking people into revealing information or compromising computer security voluntarily. Social engineering is used by virus writers to convince people to deploy viruses. If I sent you an email that said "I love you," you'd open it, if only to satisfy your curiosity. Or maybe you are secretly in love with me. (Okay, maybe not, you only bought my book. What was I thinking?) Anyway, that's what the I Love You worm (dubbed the Love Bug) did back in 2000. And many love-starved people opened the "love letter" attached to the email only to infect their computers. They had been socially engineered.

One of the most famous macro viruses is called Melissa, purportedly named after an exotic dancer the virus writer was rather taken with. The virus became famous because of the speed with which it spread. Within three days of its release, Melissa (the virus, not the woman) had infected 100,000 computers.

Melissa spread by arriving as an email with an infected Word document attached with the message "Here's the document you asked for…don't show it to anyone else ;->." When it was opened the virus code executed and sent an email to the first 50 entries in a victim's Outlook email address book.

The Scary Stuff

Unlike other viruses, macro viruses infect documents or document templates. Still, they can do substantial damage to a system including turning off security programs, including antivirus applications. It can generate unusual system behavior including random beeping and rude or cryptic messages. It can also modify the Windows Registry or destroy data.

The Windows Registry is a filing cabinet in Windows that keeps track of a zillion settings that makes Windows what it is. It's so important that in case it gets damaged or deleted, Windows keeps a backup. However, if both get corrupted, Windows will not start.

Perhaps the worst impact of a macro virus is the annoyance factor. It wastes your time and, in widespread outbreaks, can force companies to shut down their systems and networks until the problem is dealt with.

Webopedia.com suggests that 75% of the world's active viruses are macro viruses. It's the virus you are most likely to come into contact with because macro viruses spread as attachments to email.

> **caution**
>
> You can look in your Windows Registry by clicking Start, Run, typing **regedit**, and clicking OK. This opens a registry editor. I'll warn you now: Do not mess with it unless you know exactly what you are doing. This cautionary tip is brought to you by the slogan, "Look, but don't touch."

PAYLOAD HAS A 13-POINT SCORE IN SCRABBLE

The Melissa virus had a curious payload that executed every hour. When the day of the month equaled the minute value, the following text was typed at the computer's cursor:

"Twenty-two points, plus triple-word score, plus fifty points for using all my letters. Game's over. I'm outta here."

The quote, which refers to the game of Scrabble, is taken from a Simpsons episode.

Memory-Resident Viruses

A *memory-resident virus* gets into a computer's random access memory (RAM). This is where files and programs are loaded when a computer runs them. For example, when you edit a photo or document, it is loaded into the RAM. From its privileged perch in the RAM, the virus gets access to all key operations carried out on the computer and it can corrupt files and programs with great ease as they are accessed, modified, or manipulated. When the computer is turned off, all data in the memory is purged, including the virus. However, when it infects a system it ensures it is activated in memory every time a computer turns on.

The Scary Stuff

Memory resident viruses can slow down your computer by stealing system resources. They can damage data and system files that could stop your computer from running correctly.

File Infector Viruses

There are many types of files on a computer, but the files that do the heavily lifting are program files. Document files have file extensions such as `.TXT` or `.DOC`. A letter to Grandma might be called `grandma.TXT` or `letter to grandma.DOC`. Program files, however, are identified with the extensions `.EXE` and `.COM`. A program like this appears as `MyProgam.EXE` or `time wasting game.COM`. It's these program files that are vulnerable to *file infector viruses*. They attach themselves to the file, making them slightly bigger, and execute when the file is run.

The Scary Stuff

File infector viruses can damage program or data files. They can be disinfected or replaced from original installation disks but there's a possibility they can damage your crucial files and either cripple your computer or eat your data.

Boot Viruses

A *boot virus* affects the boot sector of a floppy or hard disk. The boot sector is an area on a disk that contains a program that starts the computer up when it is first switched on. A boot virus swaps itself for the program that boots the computer and spreads to other disks when it is active. You can get a boot virus from a floppy disk, which, in turn, infects your hard drive.

The Scary Stuff

This kind of virus infects any disk with which it comes in contact. It can render a computer unbootable. That means that if you turn the computer on, it won't start.

Multi-Partite Viruses

These complex viruses are cleverly designed. They can infect a computer several times using a whole toolbox of techniques. The idea is to attack a computer at several vulnerable spots including files, programs, disk drives, and macros. For example, the multi-partite virus called Tequilla infected the master boot record of a hard disk and then tried to infect program files with .EXE file extension.

The Scary Stuff

Multi-partites can do all the usual kinds of nasty things that viruses do, including making computers unbootable and files unusable. The tough part is that they are good at hiding and just as you think you've cleaned one infection up, you discover another.

Worms: Network-Savvy Viruses

A *computer worm*, quite simply, is a virus that moves from computer to computer across a network. It's a traveling virus. Many worms email themselves to email addresses found on the infected computer. They arrive as attachments and when the attachment is opened by a human, the replication cycle starts all over again (see Figure 1.1).

FIGURE 1.1

A variant of the Bagle worm arrives via email pretending to be a come on from a pretty girl.

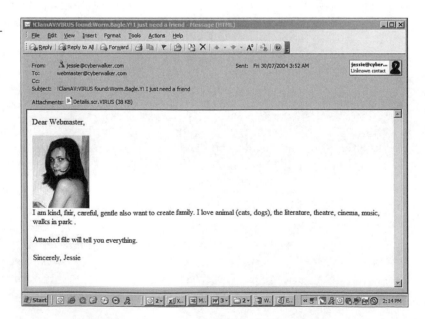

Some are designed with no need for human intervention to execute. They worm their way from computer to computer over a network connection employing techniques that are normally used to move files or information between computers.

During a bad worm outbreak, you might notice the Internet or your company network responding very slowly. Two famous examples were Sasser and Blaster. In 2004, Sasser hit hundreds of thousands of Windows XP and Windows 2000 computers globally, including computer systems at American Express and Delta Airlines. The slower-moving Blaster worm hit a year earlier than Sasser and crawled across the Internet infecting computers with Windows XP, Window NT, Windows 2000, and Windows Server 2003. It caused infected systems to either freeze or reboot repeatedly every few minutes. It also initiated a denial of service (DoS) attack against the Windows Update server at Microsoft. A denial of service attack is an effort to overwhelm a server by flooding it with data requests across the Internet.

> **note**
>
> Viruses and worms are known to be seeding bots—software that can seek out and infect themselves on vulnerable computers. They then work quietly in the background without the owner of the system knowing they are there. They wait for commands from a remote attacker through chat servers and peer-to-peer networks.

The Scary Stuff

Worms can do a lot of damage, but their most famous threat is network congestion. Because they travel between computers across networks (such as the Internet) they can clog all the networks connections, much as a 2-year-old, an open toilet lid, and a 12-pack of Charmin clogs the toilet. Network traffic builds to such an extent that it can crash computers and clog networks so they are unusable.

Trojan Horses: Hey Helen, the Achaeans Left Us a Present!

You have probably heard of the story of how the Achaeans (also known as the Greeks) rolled up a great big wooden horse to the gates of Troy (see Figure 1.2). When the delighted Trojans found it, they figured it was a peace offering from their sworn enemies and brought it inside the city. But in the middle of the night, a bunch of sneaky Achaeans hopped out of the horse's hollow belly, let their friends through the gates of Troy, and then attacked the somewhat dim Trojans and burnt and ransacked their city.

FIGURE 1.2

Trojan horses appear to be fun or useful programs that you need. After you have been tricked into installing them on your computer, they do bad things such as deploy viruses.

Guess what? A computer virus called a *Trojan horse* works in a similar way. You find (or are sent) a fun, maybe useful computer program and install it on your computer. While you're jumping up and down with delight, bad stuff comes out of the file's belly, opens the door for other bad guys to come into the computer, and then proceeds to ransack its contents.

A Trojan horse is sometimes deployed by a *dropper*. That's a file that conceals a Trojan horse (or a virus) so it evades antivirus programs (see Figure 1.3).

FIGURE 1.3

This dropper is detected by Norton AntiVirus as it tries to dump a virus or Trojan horse into a Windows XP computer.

The Scary Stuff

Actually, a Trojan horse cannot only ransack your data and files, but it can cause lots of other mayhem. It can vandalize your desktop, delete files, or create what's known as a *backdoor*, which gives bad guys on the Internet an easy way in to snoop around and inflict further mayhem on your computer. Sometimes Trojan horses deploy viruses on your system.

Virus Hoaxes: Fake Viruses that Scare the Heck Out of You

Virus hoaxes are almost as annoying as the actual thing. They arrive as emails from a well-meaning friend who thinks they are doing you a favor by forwarding on an email they think is a virus alert (see Figure 1.4). The email comes in various forms, but typically contains details about a rampant virus that is wiping out hard drives or doing similarly awful things to people's computers. Of course it's all fiction, but it's written in a convincing way, urging recipients to send the warning to all their friends. The irony is that the act of forwarding a hoax is the key to the hoax's success. It's how it replicates.

FIGURE 1.4

The Life Is Beautiful hoax was first circulated in Portuguese and later in English, French, German, and Chinese.

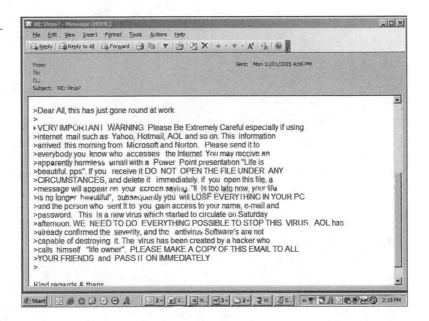

The Scary Stuff

A virus hoax is scary to those who don't know better because they think there's a nasty out-of-control virus that is about to eat their computer. It's not a real threat, though. It's also a big annoyance to those who know they are hoaxes but receive them on a regular basis. Mostly it results in embarrassment for the naïve sender when they are outed as fools by their angry in-the-know buddies.

How to Spot a Virus Hoax

The email message goes something like this: "If you receive email titled Win A Holiday—Do Not Open It. It will erase everything on your hard drive."

caution

Some virus hoaxes tell you to search for and delete specific files on your system that it claims are viruses. When you look for the specified file to see if it's on your system, you always find it. That's because its part of Windows! Deleting the file can damage your system.

These types of email chain letters are a plague to email users because they waste time and cause unnecessary panic. The truth is that they are hoaxes. But how do you know for sure? By applying a little bit of knowledge and common sense. Here are some telltale signs of an email hoax.

They all reference a technology authority. Sometimes it's IBM or Microsoft or America Online. Sometimes the author claims that several sources have verified the threat.

The author also promises that the catastrophic virus will arrive as email and wipe out a computer's hard drive or do some other awful damage.

They also encourage the recipient to spread the word about the impending evil that's about to descend by forwarding the message to all their friends. That line is the giveaway to the hoax. It is the reason for the email's existence and the mechanism by which the hoax is spread. Sometimes the request to forward to the message is urged more than once in the hoax.

The best way to see if an email warning is a virus hoax is to copy a sentence or two from it and search for it on Google.com or your favorite search engine. For example, the first line of the Win a Holiday virus hoax says

If you receive an email titled Win a Holiday—Do Not Open It. It will erase everything on your hard drive.

If you cut and paste this into Google.com, you see dozens of websites that tell you it's a hoax. You can also look up viruses hoaxes at www.f-secure.com/virus-info/hoax/.

> **tip**
>
> Your best bet when it comes to emails you receive about viruses is to consider the source. If the email comes from a friend or co-worker and has been forwarded like a chain letter, chances are that it's a hoax. That's not to say that your friend or co-worker is in on the sham. Rather, that person—like all the others in the email trail—has been duped into believing the virus is real. If you receive an email regarding a virus *directly from* your Internet Service Provider, *directly from* your system administrator at work, or some other extremely reliable source, you should consider the threat real. A hoax often refers to the source of the hoax as a reliable source, but it never comes straight from one of those sources. In any case, forwarding virus warning emails doesn't help anyone and only serves to clog inboxes and create unnecessary panic.

Who Creates Computer Viruses?

Computer viruses are written by a variety of perpetrators. Historically they have been brilliant teenage kids or desperate people in search of attention. They are typically male and in their teens (see Figure 1.5) or early 20s. However, David L. Smith, author of the famous Melissa virus, was 30 when the FBI caught up with him.

FIGURE 1.5

An excerpt from
an email com-
munication with
a 13-year-old
who had
attacked
GRC.com, a web-
site run by famed
security expert
Steve Gibson,
using zombie
computers in a
DDoS attack.

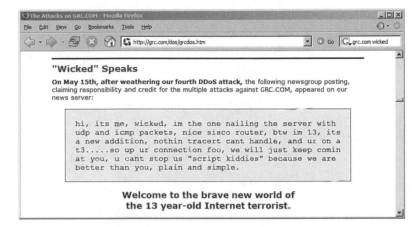

> **"Wicked" Speaks**
>
> **On May 15th, after weathering our fourth DDoS attack,** the following newsgroup posting, claiming responsibility and credit for the multiple attacks against GRC.COM, appeared on our news server:
>
> hi, its me, wicked, im the one nailing the server with udp and icmp packets, nice sisco router, btw im 13, its a new addition, nothin tracert cant handle, and ur on a t3.....so up ur connection foo, we will just keep comin at you, u cant stop us "script kiddies" because we are better than you, plain and simple.
>
> **Welcome to the brave new world of
> the 13 year-old Internet terrorist.**

Still, I like how Jack Sebbag, a vice president at the antivirus software company McAfee, characterizes virus writers: "They're 14-year-old kids who can't get a date, but have incredible talent and are looking for a challenge to bring (millions of) computers down just to get a little notoriety."

And some, as it turns out, are looking for work. In one variant of the MyDoom worm, there was a message to the antivirus software industry that said, "We [sic] searching 4 work in AV industry."

It's an ill-conceived strategy, of course. No one in the antivirus industry will go near them. Graham Cluley, senior technology consultant for Sophos, an antivirus company, said in a posting to the company website, "It's hard to tell if the creators of these new versions of the MyDoom worm are being serious, but there is no way that anybody in the anti-virus industry would touch them with a bargepole," adding, "It's very simple—if you write a virus, we will never ever employ you. Not only is it unethical to write malicious code, but it raises issues as to whether you could ever be trusted to develop the software which protects millions of users around the world from attack every day."

Nowadays, virus writers don't need much programming savvy to write a decent virus. They just modify existing viruses creating what are called *variants*. The pro-gramming code is widely available on the Internet. Virus writers, hiding behind pseudonyms, even meet anonymously in chatrooms and swap tips, tricks, and brag-ging rights.

Ultimately, most motivations behind virus writing these days are financial. The virus turns your computer into a zombie, which is a computer that can be remotely controlled by a hacker or virus writer to do malicious tasks such as send spam or to attack another computer by sending a flood of data at it across the Internet in what are called distributed denial of service (DDoS) attacks.

Spam makes money for the virus writer by distributing massive volumes of junk email. DDoS attacks work via extortion. A wealthy corporation receives an email that demands a lump sum payment in return for protection. If the demand isn't paid, the perpetrator remotely commands all the zombies to attack and crash the company's server. Gambling web sites are often targets of these schemes.

What Not to Do!

When it comes to computer security, it's often as important to learn what not to do as it is to learn what you should do to protect yourself. If you have a family computer used by children, your spouse, or other family members, this is the section you should review with them. Good computer security habits are as critical as good security software.

Here's what not to do:

- The majority of viruses come via email attachments these days, so don't open attachments you are not expecting, especially if they arrive from someone you don't know.

- Be cautious of attachments from people you do know, especially if you are not expecting something from them. If your friend's computer is infected with a virus, it can send an email to you that looks like it's from your friend. Your virus scanner should scan all inbound attachments, but if it doesn't, right-click suspicious attachments and save it to your Windows desktop. Then use the file scanner feature in your antivirus program to scan it before opening it. Or better yet, call your friend and ask him if he sent a file via email to you.

- Don't use peer-to-peer (P2P) programs for downloading music, software, or other files. Teens like to download files from P2P services such as Kazaa. The company says it scans for viruses on its P2P network and has built-in antivirus protection in its software, but suggests you should use an antivirus program on your computer as well.

- Never turn off your antivirus protection for any length of time. You will be instantly vulnerable. If you need to turn it off to service the computer, consider disconnecting it from the Internet first.

- Although less common these days, infections from floppy disks and home-burnt CDs and DVDs can still contain infected files. Don't copy files from disks, CDs, DVDs, and other external sources without your antivirus program running on your computer.

- Make sure your computer is protected with a software or hardware firewall. It will help protect you against worms. Learn more about firewalls on **p. 90**.

■ Don't accept unsolicited files from people you don't know when using Internet chat programs such as MSN Messenger, AOL Instant Messenger, and Yahoo! Messenger. Infected files can also be transmitted via Internet Relay Chat (IRC), an open type of chat service on the Internet.

When Viruses Attack!

When you're hit by a bad virus attack, it becomes pretty obvious, pretty fast. Your computer starts to behave oddly. Here are a few symptoms you might see individually or in combination:

■ Frequent crashes or system restarts.

■ Very slow or erratic performance.

■ No Internet connection

■ Email in Sent Items folder of your email program that you personally didn't send.

■ Missing or corrupt data or system files.

■ The computer fails to start and displays errors.

As soon as you think you might be infected with a virus, immediately use your antivirus program to update its virus signatures—these are snapshots of viruses used by the program to identify an infection (see Figure 1.6). All antivirus programs have this feature built in. You click an update button in the software and the updates are fetched from the Internet.

FIGURE 1.6

Your antivirus program probably missed the virus your computer is infected with because its signatures were out of date.

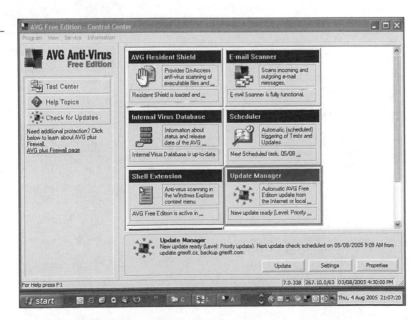

Then use the antivirus program to run a system scan (see Figure 1.7). Choose to run a deep or thorough scan, if possible, as opposed to a quick scan.

FIGURE 1.7

Scan your hard drive for viruses as soon as you think you are infected.

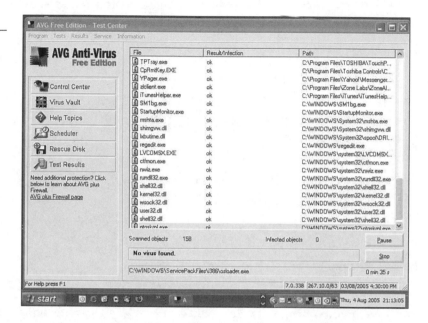

Disconnect As Soon As Possible

One of the first things most malware tries to do when it creates an infection—and this especially includes viruses—is to make contact with the outside world. So one of the first things you should do after detecting an infection (after updating your virus and spyware signatures via the Internet) is to disconnect your computer from your home network, if you have one, and get off the Internet.

- If you use a dial-up account where your computer dials a number using the phone line, unplug the phone line from the computer.

- If you use a high-speed Internet service such as cable, DSL or satellite, turn off your high-speed modem.

- If your computer shares a high-speed Internet connection with other computers in the house, turn off your router. This is the little box (sometimes with an antenna) that is connected to your high-speed modem.

tip

If you don't have an up-to-date antivirus program, go out right now—leave the book open on the table and I'll wait—and buy one at the store. Or if it's storming outside, download one. I recommend the free AVG Free Edition program from free.grisoft.com. It's as good as any commercial program and it's free for personal use. After you have it, install it and run it.

■ If your computer is wireless, disable the Wi-Fi adapter by physically switching it off, or by right-clicking the connection icon in the Windows system tray (bottom right of your screen) and choosing Disable (see Figure 1.8).

FIGURE 1.8
Right-click the wireless icon in your Windows system tray in the bottom right and choose Disable to turn off your Wi-Fi connection.

Virus Infection Found! How to Cleanse Your System

When the antivirus program finds a virus, it alerts you immediately and asks for a decision. Make a note of the virus's name and have it removed.

If your antivirus program fails to remove the virus, all is not lost. It could be that infected files are running and so they can't be deleted by Windows. Try scanning the computer in Windows Safe Mode. This is a special emergency mode in which Windows starts up in a raw state and loads only the bare necessities into memory.

To get into safe mode, shut down and restart the computer. When the screen is black (and before the Windows logo appears), hit the F8 key. You might have to press the F8 key a few times to trigger it. A menu appears. Use the arrow key to choose Safe Mode, and press Enter.

If you are presented with a choice of Windows logins (one for you, your spouse, and your hairy little children, perhaps), choose the administrator login. If it's your computer, chances are that you are the administrator.

When the Windows desktop appears in safe mode, run your antivirus program and scan the system for viruses. Because safe mode loads only the necessary processes in memory, the virus is not loaded unless it has infected one of the system files that makes Windows run. In safe mode, you should be able to easily kill the virus.

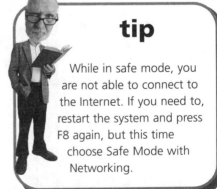

tip

While in safe mode, you are not able to connect to the Internet. If you need to, restart the system and press F8 again, but this time choose Safe Mode with Networking.

Your antivirus program might ask if it should quarantine the virus or delete it. If you quarantine the files, they are put in the computer equivalent of jail, an electronically walled-off area where they can't cause any further damage. From the quarantine area, they can be submitted to the antivirus maker for analysis, if you choose to do this. If you choose to delete the snared virus, it is wiped from your computer.

My Antivirus Program Won't Update!

If your antivirus program fails to fetch the latest virus signatures, a virus might have stomped on your Internet connection. Some viruses modify the Windows HOSTS file, a holdover from the early days of computer networking that helps a system find other computers on the Internet. The HOSTS file on your computer is normally found in the following folders:

tip

The big antivirus software publishers offer free virus removal programs for specific virus threats. These tools can be downloaded from the company's websites. See Symantec's removal tools at http://www.sarc.com/avcenter/tools.list.html and McAfee's tools at http://us.mcafee.com/virusInfo/default.asp?id=vrt.

- In Windows XP, the HOSTS file is at
  `C:\WINDOWS\SYSTEM32\DRIVERS\ETC`.

- In Windows 2000, the HOSTS file is at
  `C:\WINNT\SYSTEM32\DRIVERS\ETC`.

- In Win 98\Me, the HOSTS file is at `C:\WINDOWS`.

The file can be opened with Notepad or another text editor. It contains comments that begin with the character #—these can be left alone (see Figure 1.9).

FIGURE 1.9

The HOSTS file can be modified by malware to block access to websites. Pictured is a healthy HOSTS file.

Lines beginning with # should be left alone

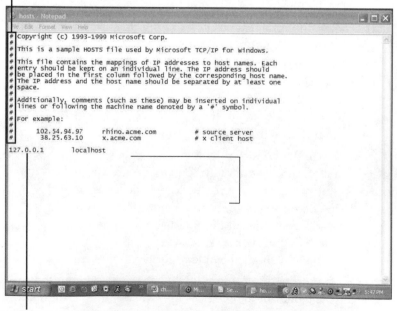

This is the only other entry that should be in your HOSTS file

The HOSTS file should contain only one other line:

```
127.0.0.1 localhost
```

Any other lines of text can be removed. After editing it, save the file and close it. Now try to update your anti-virus program. You should have no problem.

Now I Have Your Attention...

Let's say I have made you a little worried (a little fear can be a good thing, right?) and you want to ensure your computer never gets infected with a virus. To help with this, I've divided the virus protection help into two sections.

The first gives you a list of easy-to-do defense strategies that thwarts most virus attacks. The steps should only take about 10 minutes.

That's not all you'll have to do, however. The 10-minute strategies are like putting a screen door on a castle. It'll keep the local peasants out, but if you really want to fortify your keep against the angry pointy helmeted hordes, you'll need to spend a little more time. That's where the second part of the section comes in. It requires more time, perhaps a couple of hours in an afternoon.

Here's your to-do list:

- Be sure to update Windows with security patches from Microsoft.
- Update your virus signatures if you have an antivirus program installed.
- Install an antivirus program, or upgrade if your program is old.
- Install Service Pack 2 if you have Windows XP and turn on key SP2 features.

As you can see, we have lots of work to do, so let's get to it.

Antivirus Checkup: 10-Minute Tactics

Here are your 10-minute virus protection strategies that quickly make your computer safer from viruses if you only have a few minutes.

Install Windows Security Updates

At the click of a button you can be almost instantly safer from viruses by installing security updates issued by Microsoft. These can be downloaded from the Internet and installed to your computer in a matter of minutes.

tip

If you run Windows Update and it offers to download SP2, choose not to download it. It takes longer than 10 minutes. We'll deal with this issue more in the next section called "Fortify Your Computer: Strong Virus Defense in a Few Hours" that starts on **p. 32**.

Virus writers exploit software bugs (mistakes made by programmers) in programs and operating systems such as Windows. When these are discovered, patches or fixes are issued by the maker of the software that can be downloaded free from the Internet. If you can imagine an operating system as if it were a house, think of a software patch as a toolbox that is used to fix a loose window, a wonky door lock, or a hole in a wall.

To take advantage of these fixes all you need to do is run the Windows Update feature, a service that has been around since Windows 95 was released. This can be found by clicking the Start button, clicking Programs or All Programs in Windows XP, and looking at the top of the menu for Windows Update. You can also open the Internet Explorer web browser and go to the Windows Update site directly by typing http://windowsupdate.microsoft.com (see Figure 1.10). Choose Express Install from the menu to get all the latest critical updates. You can go back later and get the noncritical optional updates when you have more time.

For noncritical updates, Microsoft makes you download a program called `genuinecheck.exe` to validate your Windows XP system to ensure it's not a pirated copy before you can get at the updates. This slows you down by about five minutes, so leave the noncritical updates for another time. To learn more about the Windows validation process, see Chapter 8, "Let's Smash-Proof Windows: Tweak Windows Nice and Tight."

FIGURE 1.10

The Microsoft Windows Update feature downloads updates, including security fixes, for your operating system.

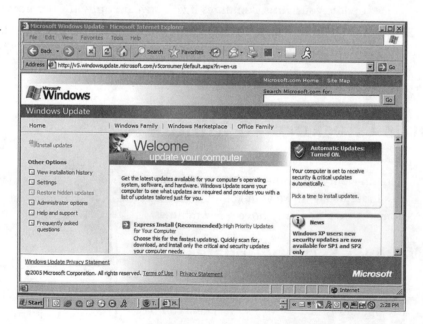

These security updates are available for all supported versions of Windows. If you have Windows XP, it is possible that these updates are turned on already and download automatically if you have a security update called Service Pack 2 (SP2) installed. SP2 was issued in the fall of 2004, so if you computer is newer than that, SP2 is likely installed. If you have done a Windows Update before, SP2 is likely installed already.

Update Your Virus Signatures

Another critical step you can do in a few minutes is to update the virus signatures in your antivirus program on your computer. (You do have one installed, don't you? If not, immediately see the next section on how to fortify your computer.)

Virus signatures are, in effect, digital mugshots of what each virus looks like. Imagine if a security guard had pictures and descriptions of all the known bad guys that could possibly come

tip

Some antivirus companies, such as Trend Micro, recommend updating hourly. Look for this option where you set a program's update schedule.

into the building he guards. As people arrived, he'd compare the profiles to each person and if they turned out to be a crook, he'd stop them. That's what an antivirus program uses virus signatures for. The antivirus software publishers issue signatures for download as new viruses are discovered, often within hours of their very first infection.

To update your virus signatures, take the following steps:

- Open your antivirus program and look for a feature either under the Tools menu or a configuration menu of some sort. There is likely to be a feature called Update, Update Virus Signatures, or Internet Update (see Figure 1.11).

FIGURE 1.11

Norton AntiVirus updates virus signatures through its LiveUpdate feature.

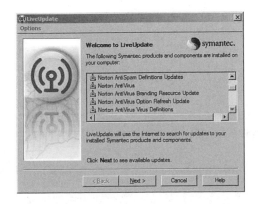

- Ensure that your computer is connected to the Internet and run this option. The program looks for virus signature updates on the website run by the antivirus software maker and downloads and installs them. You should do this daily if you have time and weekly at a minimum. It only takes a few minutes.

- Some programs, such as McAfee VirusScan and Norton AntiVirus, automatically look for updates and install them as they become available. If your program has an auto-signature update feature like this, it is probably turned on but you should double-check.

note

Some programs have an added feature called *heuristics*. This is a kind of artificial intelligence that allows the software to learn as it goes and can detect virus-like behavior without knowing what the virus is. Unfortunately, it can generate what's called a false positive. That's when the software erroneously flags a file as virus-laden even though it's not.

Fortify Your Computer: Strong Virus Defense in a Few Hours

So let's say you have a bit more time on your hands. Maybe it's early Saturday morning before the cartoons start—and the kids are still dozing in their beds. Maybe you have an hour or two to yourself. Here's what you can do to really protect your computer from viruses.

Install or Upgrade an Antivirus Program

Most people have heard of an antivirus program, but amazingly many don't even have one installed on their computer.

An antivirus program watches what comes into your computer and checks it against a library of known viruses. Some antivirus programs also look for virus-like behavior and stop it before it starts.

There are many antivirus programs to choose from. The two you have probably heard about are Symantec's Norton AntiVirus and McAfee VirusScan. Although no antivirus package is completely foolproof, having an up-to-date antivirus program installed drastically reduces the risk of being infected by a virus.

So how do you get one? Well, you can run out to the store and buy a boxed antivirus product from your local software dealer. Or you can download one from the Internet. For a list of antivirus programs and where to find them, flip to **p. 328** for tips on what to buy and an overview of some key titles.

If you don't already have an antivirus program installed, let me show you how to install a free antivirus program called AntiVir.

First you'll need to visit AntiVir's website and download the Personal Edition of its antivirus program (see Figure 1.12). It's free and very good! Note that its license allows for private individuals to use it free. If you use it for business purposes, the company asks you to pay for its commercial product.

Okay, let's get started. Here is what you need to do to install AntiVir:

1. Connect to the Internet and open your web browser.

2. Browse to the web page www.free-av.com.

tip

Many computers come with a free 30-day starter antivirus program that continues to run after the trial period expires. It does not continue to download virus signatures, however. Don't rely on a program like this to protect you. If you haven't updated your virus signatures in years, you are extremely vulnerable to new infections. Dump the program and replace it with an up-to-date antivirus program.

FIGURE 1.12

AntiVir is a great antivirus program that's free to download.

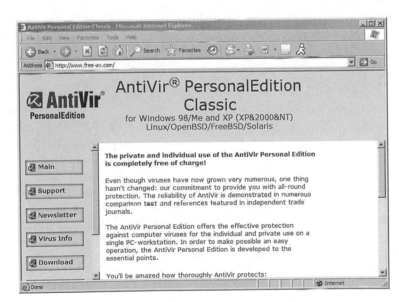

3. Look for the Download button, click on it, and on the ensuing page look for a link to AntiVir Personal Edition for Windows 98/Me & NT/2000/XP.

4. If your web browser is Microsoft Internet Explorer, right-click on the download link on the page and choose Save Target As and then be sure to save the file to a place you can find it later. I like to drop downloaded files into my desktop.

5. When it is downloaded, close all programs on your system that don't need to be open and double-click on the AntiVir installation file and follow the installation steps.

6. During the installation, AntiVir scans your computer for viruses (see Figure 1.13). Let it run to completion. This might take a while, especially if you have a big hard drive. You can also stop it and run the scan later if you want, though it's best to let the scanner run until it's completed. After the program is installed, you're much more protected from viruses than you were 10 minutes ago!

Scan Your Computer for Viruses

Your antivirus program has the ability to scan your computer for viruses in case a clever piece of code has slipped past your defenses.

I recommend that you run this scan once a week. Some programs have a quick scan feature, which checks the likely places on your computer where viruses like to hide.

It also has an intensive scan that looks at every file on the system and in every nook and cranny. Run the intensive scan once a week. Sometimes this can be scheduled to run automatically. If you leave your computer on, it's a good idea to schedule the intensive scan overnight; maybe on a Friday night so you can deal with any results Saturday morning, if your schedule permits.

---

tip

Why buy a commercial antivirus product when you can get one free? Many smart people are asking the same question and using their hard-earned money to buy nicer bed linen and more flowerpots. I quite like McAfee, so there's no argument there if you want to spend the money. Norton, on the other hand, suffers from bloat-itis. In recent years it has grown unruly and become buggy. However, both companies have kick-butt virus detection groups that write antivirus signatures. A commercial product updates your virus signatures automatically when new signatures are available and certainly more often than once a day as the free version of AVG does. If you buy a commercial antivirus program, you also get telephone support. In a crisis it can be valuable to have someone helpful at the other end of the phone when a virus is gorging on your data.

FIGURE 1.13

During installation AntiVir the program does an initial scan of your hard drive to look for viruses.

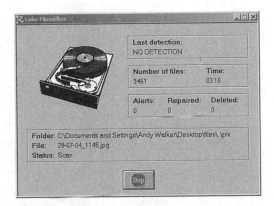

Install Service Pack 2 and Enable Virus Protection

As I mentioned earlier, Microsoft issued a major security update called Service Pack 2 (SP2) for Windows XP in the fall of 2004. If your computer was bought since, it likely has this update installed.

Microsoft issued SP2 via Windows Update, its software update service. If you have been religious about using this download service, you probably have already received it and installed it. If not, please visit (and I am begging you!) http://windowsupdate.microsoft.com right now and download and install it. You can also order a CD with SP2 onboard from Microsoft for free from http://www.microsoft.com/windowsxp/downloads/updates/sp2/cdorder/en_us/.

tip

I love Grisoft's AVG. It's the best free antivirus program on the market. I show you how to install it in Chapter 8 on **p. 223**. So in this section I decided to show you how to install another freebie called AntiVir. It's quicker and easier on system resources, but it does not scan your email for viruses.

DO I HAVE SP2?

Not sure if you have Windows XP's SP2 installed? To figure it out, click your Start button, and then click Run. In the Run dialog box, type **winver** and click OK. A box displays the Windows version you are running and any service packs that are installed. If you are running Windows XP, look for a notation that says Service Pack 2.

There's always more than one way to do stuff in Windows, so if you don't like that trick because it's too geeky, try this alternate method: To find out which version of Windows is running on your PC, open any folder on your hard drive (My Documents is an easy choice), click on the Help menu, and then select About Windows. A dialog box appears showing the version of Windows running on your PC, as well as any Service Pack updates.

Also, be sure to check my SP2 installation tips on **p. 236** because it can sometimes be a little quirky to install.

SP2 has some critical virus-repelling features that are discussed in Chapter 8, but the key feature you should pay attention to is the Security Center applet (see Figure 1.14). It is turned on for you when you install SP2. It's a dashboard that enables you to know about three key security systems and their status.

You can check it out by clicking Start, Control Panel, and double-clicking on the Security Center icon. It's also represented by a little colored shield in the Windows XP System Tray, which is the row of icons at the bottom right of your screen.

The Security Center has three key areas.

tip

If your antivirus package allows you to schedule virus scans, try to schedule the scans to occur late at night or while you're at work. The trick is to find a time to scan your drive while you're not busy on the computer. Many antivirus programs give you the option to scan your hard disk when you boot up the system, but if you're anything like most users, you'll find this annoying.

FIGURE 1.14

SP2 adds the Security Center applet to Windows XP. It enables you to know the status of key security features on your computer.

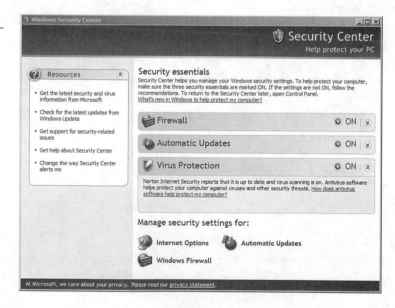

Firewall

I talk more about firewalls in Chapter 3, "Hackers: There's a Man in My Machine," but for now all you need to know is that you should turn the Windows firewall on because it gives you added protection against worms. There would be two scenarios where you wouldn't bother:

- If you were running a third-party software firewall, such as ZoneAlarm or Sygate, because these programs do a better job than the Windows Firewall.

- If you have a home network and use a router that shares the Internet connection among several computers. Home Internet routers (sometimes called gateways) have a built-in firewall mechanism called Network Address Translation (NAT) that acts as a firewall. I will teach you how NAT works in Chapter 3. For now, if you have one, you can turn Windows Firewall off.

Automatic Updates

When this feature is turned on it automatically seeks the latest Windows updates and downloads and offers to install them. Turning this on is a must.

Virus Protection

This feature monitors your antivirus program and alerts you when it is out of date so you can download the latest virus signatures.

No Worm in My Apple?

If you own an Apple Macintosh computer, should you worry about viruses, worms, and Trojan horses? Yes, but not to the same extent as on a PC. Viruses have been written for Apple computers, but they haven't proliferated to epidemic proportions in the same way they have on Windows-based PCs.

So why not? Well, for one, Apple has designed its operating systems really well, especially the latest one called Mac OS X.

Before the operating system came along, there were about 60–80 Mac viruses in the wild that threatened Mac computers. Since, there's been none that have been able to assault Macs running OS X. Apple has had to fix security holes in the operating system and issue patches, however.

By comparison, McAfee reports there are more than 100,000 viruses that can attack PCs.

Arguably, contrarians would say there are far fewer Macs in the world than there are Windows-based PCs. The impact of a Mac virus wouldn't have the same cachet for a virus writer looking for attention, so they don't bother.

Ultimately, it doesn't matter. Arguing either way will inevitably deteriorate into an angry, futile debate. The reality is that viruses are not currently a problem on Mac computers, but that could change if a virus writer exploited a newly found security hole.

There is one exception Mac users should be aware of. A PC virus can still live inside a file stored on a Mac or if a Mac is running Windows emulation software. If an unsuspecting Mac user sent an infected file to a PC-using friend, she might not be a friend for much longer.

Antivirus programs are available for the Mac. Symantec, Sophos, and MacAfee all make them. And there's a free Mac antivirus program called ClamXav that can also be downloaded from http://www.clamxav.com (see Figure 1.15).

FIGURE 1.15

ClamXav is a free antivirus program for Apple computers.

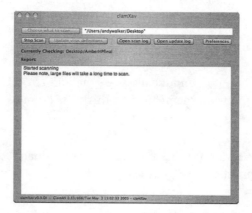

Is That a Virus in Your Pocket?

Mobile gadgets, such as smart phones and personal digital assistants (PDAs), are vulnerable to viruses written for them, but the threat is still relatively small. No mobile gadget virus has run rampant through the world's pockets in any notable way—yet.

The current crop of viruses attack Nokia's Series 60 smartphones that run the Symbian operating system, which is the world's most dominant mobile operating system. However, it is installed on only 2%–3% of mobile phones worldwide.

One virus, called Cabir, jumps between devices using Bluetooth, a short range wireless technology designed for gadget-to-gadget data transfer. The virus Commwarrior uses multimedia messaging service (MMS) to transfer the virus. Normally MMS is used to send pictures and audio between phones. And the Skulls virus spreads into a Symbian smartphone inside another program.

The upshot is that you really have to work hard to infect your gadgets with a virus. That might change as gadgets evolve and get more powerful, like computers, but for the time being your devices are mostly safe from viruses.

THE ABSOLUTE MINIMUM

■ Computer viruses are programs written by malcontents that do bad things to your computer. These days most new viruses are written to earn their authors money through sending spam or extortion rackets.

■ Viruses are triggered by an action you take. You have to execute a virus for it to infect your computer.

■ Specialty viruses, known as worms, can deploy without your intervention. Worms travel across networks.

■ Viruses can destroy data, vandalize your computer, take control of it, or use it as a spam sender.

■ Your best defense is to run an up-to-date antivirus program and scan your computer with it once a week.

■ You should download Windows security updates as they become available.

■ The most important security update for Windows XP is Service Pack 2 (SP2).

2

SPYWARE: OVERRUN BY ADVERTISERS, HIJACKERS, AND OPPORTUNISTS

Spyware and adware, its rude sister, are two of the most prolific threats to the privacy and the security of your computer today. This chapter explains what they are, how they spy on you, and what methods they use to sneak onto your computer. It also covers the many flavors of spyware and a snoop profile for each type. Of course, no chapter on spyware would be complete without tips on how to remove infections and defend against future threats. By the end of the chapter you will have a license to kill (spyware, that is). Just don't drop your gun in your breakfast milk, okay?

What Is Spyware?

Cue the spy theme music. Pulse-pound music plays over the scene of a Cold War era suburb. Outside a row of cookie-cutter houses, a devastatingly handsome man and his mysterious and shapely cohort (who has a Luger in her fishnets) sneak up on a lit window. Inside, the room is warm, cozy, and full of minivan dads. And wait, there *you* are, mousing away on a computer.

That's what spyware is all about, right? International intrigue!

Sadly, it's not that exciting. No one is interested in the soccer-league spreadsheet on your Dell or whose turn it is to bring the orange slices to next Sunday's game.

Spyware is software. And it's not written and distributed to pursue some fancy spy agency agenda, such as finding out the color of Fidel Castro's shower curtain. It's mostly written so its authors can find out about you, where you live, what you like to do on your computer, and where you go on the Web. Why do they care? Because they can make money from that information.

Now there's nothing wrong with earning a living, but spyware makers do it in a nasty underhanded way that is generally immoral, sometimes illegal, and definitely annoying.

I like the way that my friend (and famed security guru) Steve Gibson, president of Gibson Research Corp. and owner of www.grc.com, once described spyware:

> Spyware is "uninvited, unwanted, stealthful, invasive, annoying, exploitive, and potentially privacy-compromising PC add-on software whose ongoing presence in millions of PCs worldwide benefits not the computer's owner and operator, but the interests of the publishers of this troubling new class of software."

Steve is the guy who coined the term *spyware* when he first caught a program chattering from his computer back to a server on the Internet. He's a notorious James Bond character in the geek world. And while Steve's spy wear is jeans and a T-shirt most days, he probably would look great in a tux.

What Does Spyware Do and Why Is It Bad?

Spyware is considered malware (malicious software) because it installs itself on your computer without your knowledge. Then it watches your computer habits, compromising your privacy.

Spyware is also annoying because it pushes unwanted advertising at you. Pop-up ads appear out of nowhere on your desktop. And because it is spying on you, it pushes ads at you that it thinks you'll click on.

If that's not enough, spyware can clog your system's memory and use space on your hard drive, causing performance slowdowns. It can get so cloggy that it'll make your computer unusable.

Some spyware programs can even capture your keystrokes and send them to a third party. This can potentially expose your user IDs and passwords to thieves.

It can also allow installation of an electronic back door that allows bad people to log into your computer remotely and use it for their own purposes, such as sending spam or launching malicious attacks on other computers on the Internet.

Spyware can change settings and hijack your web browser so a rogue homepage is loaded every time you surf the Web.

On top of all this, some spyware embeds itself so cleverly and deeply into your system that removing it requires a lot of computer expertise. You almost have to be as computer-savvy as a nine-year-old.

How Does Spyware Sneak onto My Computer?

Spyware gets onto your computer through a variety of sneaky techniques:

- It arrives as an automatic download from a website you are surfing. This is called *drive-by downloading*. If you visit naughty websites, those sites are probably your chief source of spyware.

- You can be tricked into clicking on a link that downloads spyware from a website. Those browser windows that pop up telling you that you've won a prize are a prime example.

- Spyware can be embedded in the installation process of a free or pirated piece of software you download. File sharing programs, such as Kazaa, are known for including a variety of spyware programs with their installers.

- Spyware can also get on your computer via an email attachment you shouldn't have opened. It often comes as an attachment to commercial email, also called *spam*.

INTERNET DOWNLOADS THAT MIGHT CONTAIN SPYWARE

Here are the kinds of files that you can download from the Internet that might contain spyware:

- Toolbars for your desktop or web browser
- Free games, puzzles, or other interactive entertainment
- Free screensavers or animated characters (see Figure 2.1) for your computer's desktop
- Free pop-up blocker programs
- Files downloaded from file-sharing services

Note: Not all free downloads contain spyware. Many programmers release their programs free for the good of the Internet community and they are spyware-free.

FIGURE 2.1
Bonzi Buddy is an animated monkey that can act as a fun talking virtual helper. The software, however, is a well-known piece of spyware.

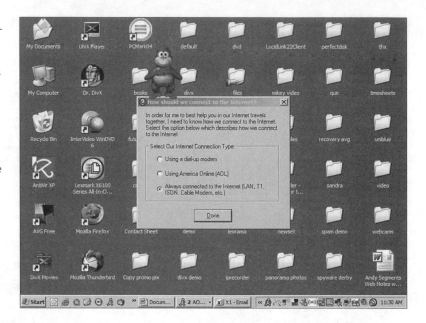

Types of Spyware: Snoops, Adware, Cookies, and More

Like the term *virus*, which is often used as a generic term for all malicious attack software, the term *spyware* has a similar catch-all usage. It encompasses a family of malware that all has some snoop capability. Let's have a look at the various types.

Spyware: I Spy with My Little App

Spyware includes programs that can record what you do on your computer and share that information with a stranger via an Internet connection. Some can watch and record your web-surfing habits. Some log everything you type. Spyware can also capture user IDs and passwords. It might have the ability to see where you have been on the Web. If there's information on your computer that is of interest to someone and can make them a little money, there's probably a spyware program to capture it.

The motivation to spy this way can be criminal (capturing information for identity theft, perhaps) but most often it's commercial in nature. A company wants to understand you better so it can trigger customized ads or analyze your behavior and sell that marketing data.

Adware: Attack of the Pop-ups

Adware is equally annoying because it not only spies on you, but then it shows you ads. Some adware spies on you because its mission is to show you ads customized to your tastes, usually via pop-up ads on your computer's desktop.

Sometimes adware is a legitimate part of a free program. Software publishers often bundle adware in with free programs they offer, using it as a revenue source. Many warn you of the adware during installation in the End User License Agreement, also referred to as an EULA. (That term always make me think of a slightly portly aunt that you hate to kiss but who makes good cupcakes.)

In a computer, the EULA is that scrollable box of soporific text (which probably earned some lawyer a Jacuzzi) that we all have to agree to before we can install a software package.

The EULA's legalese often says that in return for use of the program for free, you must allow the installation of the adware (see Figure 2.2).

FIGURE 2.2

The End User License Agreement (EULA) for Weatherscope warns you that in return for giving you use of the software, information about you will be gathered.

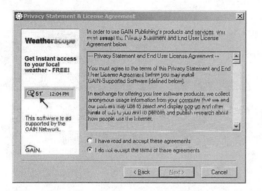

Marketing companies that publish and distribute adware often take offense if their products are called spyware. Then again they take offense if you call it anything but install-this-now-because-it's-really-good-ware.

To thwart any potential legal action, computer security companies sometimes call these products potentially unwanted programs or PUPs. Security company McAfee—famous for its antivirus software—coined the term.

In any event, it pays to at least skim the EULA before just clicking the Next button. If you see anything suspicious, cancel the installation and do a Google search on the software you're installing. Chances are that if it contains spyware, adware, or any other undesirables, someone will be railing about it on the Internet somewhere.

Snoopware: I Wanna Know What You're Up To!

Snoopware watches your computer habits on behalf of someone else, usually someone you know. This can include parental monitoring software—programs designed to track children's computer habits.

Employers might install snoopware to keep an eye on employee computer habits to ensure they're not spending too much time on ineedanewboyfriend.com.

One of the most popular uses of snoopware is to track the behavior of a spouse. Usually it's purchased by wives who suspect their husbands are up to no good on the Internet, though it can equally track wives who might be sending the pool boy spicy emails.

The software can grab screen captures (snapshots of a screen) and record email, chat conversations, and other computer communications. In some cases it can deliver that information in real-time across a computer network.

I'll skip any moral judgments on snoopware and leave that for the nice ladies over at the garden club. Needless to say, it creates lots of controversy.

One of the most famous snoopware software companies is called SpectorSoft at www.spectorsoft.com (see Figure 2.3).

FIGURE 2.3
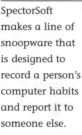
SpectorSoft makes a line of snoopware that is designed to record a person's computer habits and report it to someone else.

Browser Hijackers: Turn This Browser Around, We're Going to Cuba.com

Browser hijackers are perhaps the most malicious spyware programs because they are so hard to remove. When you first open your web browser your home page pops open. Most people set this to Google.com, a news site, or their favorite web page.

Browser hijackers override this setting and reset a browser's homepage to one of their choosing, usually a commercial web page. Why? Well, the link to the web page they set can be something called an *affiliate link.* The hijacker's author makes money when you are sent to the affiliate link.

Sometimes the web page you are directed to contains further affiliate links. Money is earned from affiliate links if you click and buy something or sometimes if you simply just click the link.

Browser hijackers are a legitimate way for many web content publishers to make income. Unfortunately, it's also a revenue source for spyware makers as well.

Often browser hijackers direct you to a webpage that looks like search sites such as Google or Yahoo!. The most famous browser hijackers are ones that redirect to a website called Cool Web Search (see Figure 2.4). The owners of the Russian-based site say they terminate affiliate arrangements with anyone who writes a browser hijack. Still, lingo has been born from the practice. The worst hijacker offenders are referred to generically as *CWS hijacks.*

note

Many affiliate links are 100% legitimate. For example, when surfing the Web, you'll often come across a link to a product that takes you to the manufacturer's or third-party reseller's site to purchase the item. The website placing the link on its site earns a kickback. These links generally aren't malicious, but they are capitalistic. The point here, however, is that all affiliate marketing isn't bad. It's just a shame that browser hijackers and the like ruin the party for everyone.

FIGURE 2.4

Many browser hijacker programs set Internet Explorer home pages to open to the website Cool Web Search.

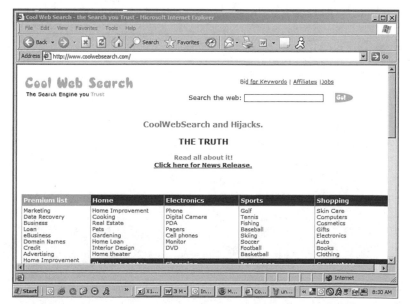

Why the notoriety? Because this type of spyware can be extremely difficult to remove. Meanwhile, Webroot, an anti-spyware software maker, lists CoolWebSearch (CWS) as its top spyware threat on the Net.

The hijacker program works by initially setting your browser to the homepage it wants. If you reset it, the hijacker's code runs and resets the homepage again the next time your computer restarts or your browser is opened. It's as frustrating as cleaning doorknobs at a finger-painting festival. And worse, removing a browser hijacker requires some serious tinkering behind the scenes in Windows.

tip

I show you how to rid yourself of a browser hijack on **p. 71**. Make sure you bring your happy face, though. It ain't pretty.

Key Loggers: Snooping on Your Typing Skills

Key loggers can either be hardware or software. The software versions run secretly in a computer's memory and capture everything typed into the computer. It then saves it for later analysis by a third party. A key logger can also be a piece of hardware that is attached between a computer's keyboard and its keyboard port.

Sometimes Trojan horses install software key loggers and then give access to the computer to someone on the Internet so they can fetch the log file containing the captured data remotely.

Dialers: Dial In, Dial Out, Dial Often

Dialers are programs that initialize a computer's modem and call out silently to a toll line and connect to a web page.

It's the computer equivalent of one of those psychic help lines they advertise on TV. The longer you are connected the more you pay. The one difference is the "psychics" on the destination site you're connected to by dialers are not so psychic and they seem to have forgotten their clothes.

Victims can find themselves on the hook to pay a huge phone bill for a lengthy long distance call. Typically it's the charges to a toll number that cause the most pain, however.

tip

You might have already surmised this, but cookies are an excellent way for others to easily see what kinds of sites you've visited lately. If you don't clean these out, your spouse, buddies, or co-workers can easily open the Cookies folder (in Windows XP, navigate to Documents and Settings/Username/Cookies) and see what you've been up to lately. If you have any particular proclivities that you'd rather others not know about, keep the incriminating cookies weeded out. See the "Clean Cookies" section later in this chapter to learn how to deal with unwanted cookies.

The good news is dialers are ineffective if your computer's modem is not connected to a phone line with a dial tone.

Trojan Horses: Pretty Ponies with Deadly Insides

I list Trojan horses here because anti-spyware programs often detect and issue spyware signatures for them. A *Trojan horse*, named after the famous hollow wooden horse that got the Greeks secretly into Troy, is an innocent-looking innocuous program that contains a virus or some other nasty malware in its belly (for more on Trojan Horses, see Chapter 1, "Viruses: Attacks of the Malicious Programs").

Even though Trojan horses are classified as a form of virus, they are also spyware because they can allow malicious people to connect remotely to your computer over the Internet. These are sometimes called backdoor Trojans because after they are installed on your computer, they can open an electronic backdoor so someone bad can sneak in from the Internet.

Cookies: Does My Oreo Have a Tape Recorder in It?

Cookies are tiny text files stored on your computer (see Figure 2.5) to help websites track your movements through their pages. They also record sign-in data and other site logon information that allows easy access to the site when you come back later. Web shopping baskets also use cookies to keep track of what you have selected to buy as you move from page to page on a shopping site.

FIGURE 2.5

Cookies are stored as tiny text files on your computer for access by the websites that put them there.

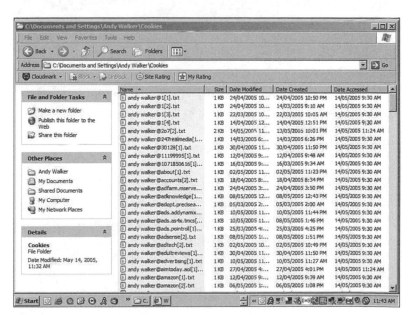

Some anti-spyware programs classify these cookies as spyware. They can be because they do deliver information about your web surfing habits to someone else. But they are not all bad. In fact, some computer cookies are helpful.

Although it might seem objectionable to have your movements tracked on your own computer, it's not as insidious as you might think. Web programmers that code their sites to put cookies on your computer are the only entities that know the cookies are there. And they are the only ones that can access the information.

But cookies should be the least of your worries. Be more concerned about spilling guacamole on the cat.

tip

Some anti-spyware scanners might freak you out because they include cookies in their scans. It might look like you have hundreds of spyware infections, but if they are browser cookies they are mostly harmless, though purists will want to clean their cookies on a regular basis.

If you visit, let's say, www.drunklazyhusbands.com, and it gives you a cookie to store on your computer, www.annoyedwiveslookingfortheirhusbands.com won't know about that cookie.

There have been circumstances where some browsers have had security vulnerabilities around cookies. For example, Microsoft issued a security patch when it was discovered that Internet Explorer 5 and earlier browsers would allow malicious website operators to gain access to cookies generated by another site and read, add to, or change them.

If you are worried, you can delete cookies from your computer. (See the "Clean Cookies" section on **p. 64** to learn how to do that.) If you do, some sites you visit regularly won't know who you are. If you have provided a site with preferences, the deletion of your cookies destroys that information. Shopping sites use cookies frequently, so if you delete your cookies, you will have to re-enter information you have provided previously. And deleting cookies as you buy stuff on a website would empty your shopping basket.

Cookies that are considered spyware are issued by web ad networks (see Figure 2.6). These keep track of the kind of ads you respond to so they can provide more targeted material to you.

And in case you were wondering, if you visit keebler.com or oreo.com, you do get sent cookies, but sadly, not the delicious kind.

FIGURE 2.6

The anti-spyware program Spybot Search & Destroy earmarks the cookies on your computer that it considers to be spyware.

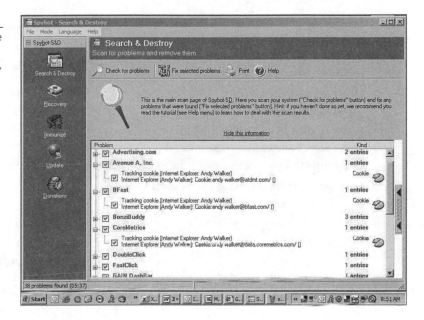

Who Is at Risk?

Spyware is the most widespread security threat to Windows-based computer users today. Depending on who you talk to, and how they define spyware, the vast majority of PC-users have some form of spyware on their computer. If you include cookies, we all do.

Now you're probably thinking almost everybody, but not me! Let me reiterate. If you have never switched your computer on and you live alone, you don't have any spyware on your computer. Everyone else pretty much does.

And a word to those people (men: pay attention) that spend time on free websites that feature pictures of naked people—that's a great place to get spyware, especially the drive-by download kind.

How Do I Know If I Have Spyware?

Spyware is easy to spot, especially when there's a lot of spyware installed on a computer. Here are some symptoms:

- **Sluggish PC performance**—Spyware takes up computer memory and can bog down performance.

- **Weird pop-up ads**—If lots of pop-up ads start to appear on your computer even if you are not surfing the Internet, chances are you have adware on your computer.

- **New toolbars you can't delete**—If a strange toolbar appears on your desktop or in your web browser and won't go away, it's probably spyware.

- **Unexpected changes to your home-page settings**—If your web browser starts opening to a web page you've never seen before, your computer is likely infected with a browser hijacker.

- **Internet connections go awry**—If one day you can no longer connect to the Internet, it could be because spyware has been messing with your connection settings.

- **Unusual search results**—When you search for something on the Internet, a strange or unexpected search site produces results. Your web browser has probably been redirected by spyware to a search engine of its choosing.

- **Software malfunction**—If a program you use was working fine and then one day it won't start or it produces weird errors, it could be that spyware has corrupted files it requires to run or messed with the way it works.

- **Frequent computer crashes**—Spyware can cause a computer to crash either because a system is overwhelmed or because the spyware programming is badly written and causes the crashes.

> **tip**
>
> Macintosh computers don't have the same problem with spyware as PCs. Each software install on newer Macs (which run the operating system called OS X) requires a user to type a password for the installation to continue, so self-installing spyware is stopped. That said, there has been spyware created for the Mac and it can find its way on to your Mac when you install legitimate software. It's safe to say that spyware is not a problem on the Mac, while on PCs it's a plague. But do note that snoopware for the Mac does exist. Cookies are also a feature of web browsers on the Mac, too.

Defend Yourself Against Spyware

Spyware is more annoying than scary, though you do have to be on your guard against the worst of its ill effects. Luckily, it is relatively easy to defend against. In this section I'll show you how to scan, cleanse, and defend your system against it. For the more advanced spyware infections, please see **p. 66**. Okay, let's get busy.

Spyware Countermeasures: 10-Minute Tactics

Here are a series of tasks that should take no more than 10 minutes each. When complete you'll be a lot less vulnerable to spyware.

Download a Free Anti-spyware Program

Spyware can be detected and cleansed with an anti-spyware program. It works similarly to an antivirus program except that its purpose is to keep your system free of spyware and adware.

The good news is there are many anti-spyware programs out there. The bad news is there are many anti-spyware programs out there. It's hard to choose the good from the bad. Some are great, some are not, and some are really awful and don't do much except find your cookies and flash overanxious alerts at you. So what to do?

The three products I recommend you use to protect your system are

- Microsoft AntiSpyware
- Spybot Search & Destroy
- Ad-Aware SE Personal Edition

All three are free. In the case of Microsoft AntiSpyware (see Figure 2.7), it used to be called Giant AntiSpyware until Microsoft bought it. The happy news is it's one of the best products out there. (Say what you want about Microsoft, they never cheap out when it comes to key acquisitions.)

FIGURE 2.7

Microsoft AntiSpyware is an easy to use, highly effective anti-spyware tool for Windows XP and 2000 that's free.

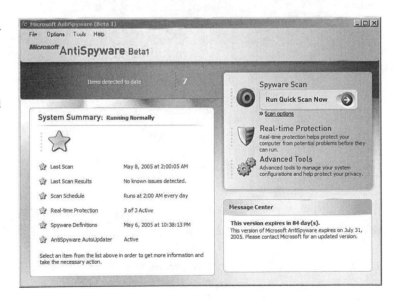

Microsoft said it will build the program into future versions of Windows. In the meantime, the company has made it available free from its website. Note that it's designed for use with Windows XP or Windows 2000 (and won't work on older versions of Windows).

If you use either of these operating systems, the best thing you can do right now is download and install it. That should take you about 10 minutes. Do a quick scan to cleanse your system of most of the pressing spyware threats and then go back to your regularly scheduled life, until you have more time to think about the problem.

To download Microsoft AntiSpyware, follow these steps:

1. Open Internet Explorer, and visit www.microsoft.com/spyware/.

2. Find the Download Microsoft AntiSpyware link and follow it until you get to the page with the Validation Required box and click the Continue button (see Figure 2.8).

tip

If you have an older copy of Windows such as Windows 95, 98, or Me, I suggest you get yourself a free copy of Spybot Search & Destroy from http://www.safer-networking.net or Ad-Aware SE Personal Edition from http://www.lavasoft.de.

FIGURE 2.8

Before you can download Microsoft AntiSpyware, you have to go through the Windows validation process to ensure you have a legal copy of Windows XP.

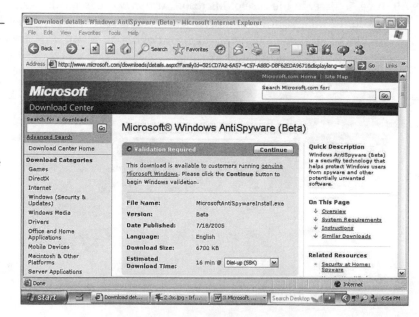

3. The program takes you to a page where you can start a Windows validation check to make sure you own a legal copy of Windows XP prior to downloading Microsoft AntiSpyware software (see Figure 2.9).

FIGURE 2.9

The validation process analyzes the copy of Windows XP on your computer to ensure it is a legitimate copy before it lets you download Microsoft AntiSpyware.

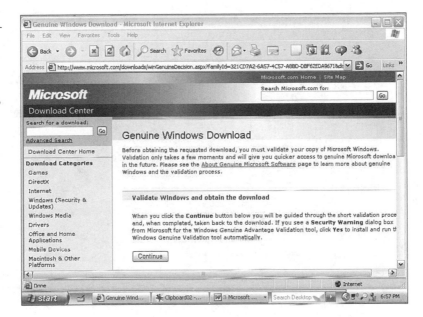

4. When the validation process is finished, the MicrosoftAntiSpywareInstall.exe program downloads. Click Download (see Figure 2.10) and when the download box appears, click Run (see Figure 2.11).

5. If you get a security warning, click Run (see Figure 2.12). It's safe to run the downloaded software in this case.

FIGURE 2.10

After your Windows version is validated, you may download Microsoft AntiSpyware.

FIGURE 2.11

When the installer program for Microsoft AntiSpyware downloads, choose Run to install it.

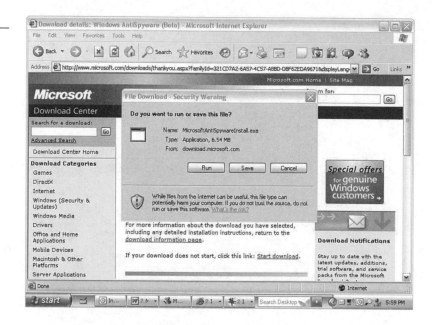

FIGURE 2.12

You might get a security warning when you download the installer for Microsoft AntiSpyware. It's okay to run it.

6. Microsoft AntiSpyware begins to install. When you see a license agreement, read it and click the option beside I Accept the Terms in This License Agreement (if you agree).

7. Click Next twice and click Install. Installation is quite speedy unless your computer is old and pokey or filled with spyware.

8. When the installation process completes, tick off the box that reads Launch Microsoft AntiSpyware and click Finish.

9. When the program launches, you'll see the Setup Assistant (see Figure 2.13). Click Next to get started.

note

If you do the validation with the Firefox web browser, the process has a few extra steps. This is outlined on **p. 230**.

FIGURE 2.13

After installation, Microsoft AntiSpyware runs the Setup Assistant. Be sure you don't ignore this crucial step.

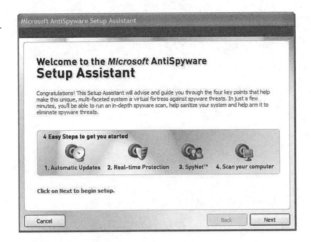

10. The program asks you if you'd like to configure it so it automatically updates itself. Select the Yes option, and then click Next (see Figure 2.14).

FIGURE 2.14

Be sure to turn on AutoUpdates in Microsoft AntiSpyware when prompted during configuration so you get the latest spyware signature updates.

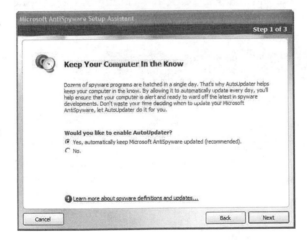

11. You'll then be asked if you want to enable Real Time Security Protection (see Figure 2.15). This is important—select the Yes option and click Next. Real Time Protection is a mechanism that watches for spyware trying to sneak on to your system from a variety of sources. If a spyware program is a cockroach, Real Time Protection is the guy with fat-heeled boots and good aim.

FIGURE 2.15

Be sure to turn
on Real Time
Protection in
Microsoft
AntiSpyware. It
keeps watch on
your computer to
ensure spyware
doesn't sneak
onto the
machine.

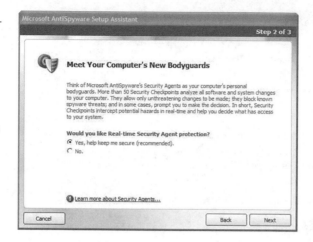

12. Next you'll be asked if you want to join SpyNet and help fight against spyware (see Figure 2.16). This is up to you. If you agree, the program submits new spyware it finds on your computer via the Internet to the Microsoft database to help the developers learn about new infections.

FIGURE 2.16

Joining the
SpyNet commu-
nity allows the
software to send
suspected
spyware back to
Microsoft to help
develop spyware
signatures.

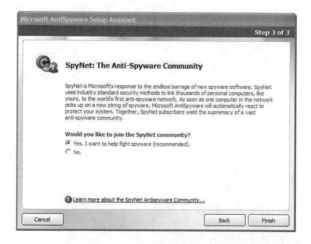

13. When you've made your selection, click Next. During this installation process, you may receive a notice that you're running NetBIOS, a service used to send alerts to a computer (see Figure 2.17). NetBIOS is to computers what those electronic alert boards are to a highway. Imagine if an advertiser hijacked one of those and used it to sell you soft drinks. So it doesn't hurt to let Microsoft AntiSpyware switch NetBIOS off.

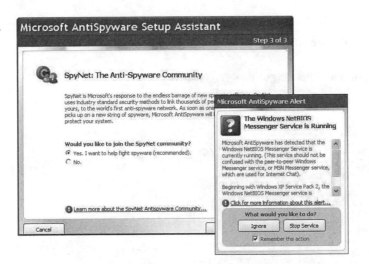

FIGURE 2.17

Microsoft AntiSpyware switches off NetBIOS, which is a computer messaging mechanism that can be hijacked to broadcast ads at you.

14. When you've finished with all of these options, you'll see the final screen, which suggests you run a spyware scan now. Click the big fat button in the middle of the screen that says Run Quick Scan Now.

15. When it asks you if you'd like to update your spyware signatures, click on Update Now. These signatures help the program recognize known spyware. They are like electronic mugshots of the bad guys.

16. Wait for the update to complete and click Close. Your first scan begins. Allow the program to clean up any spyware it finds. Learn more about spyware removal on **p. 66**.

Increase Browser Security Settings

In Internet Explorer set your security settings to medium or high. This provides you with a reasonable amount of security as you surf the Web and you'll see a warning if anything tries to download to your computer without your permission. To set this up follow these steps:

1. Open Internet Explorer.

2. Click the Tools menu and select Internet Options.

3. Choose the Security tab.

4. Click the Internet icon in the Web Content Zone box.

caution

If you fail the validation test, you are not able to continue with the download. Microsoft gives you two options. If you send in your CD, show proof of ownership, and fill out a piracy report, the company replaces the CD with a free valid copy. If you don't have the CD, you can fill out a piracy report and get a discounted full version of Windows XP.

5. Click the Default Level button and a vertical slider appears (see Figure 2.18).

6. Move the slider to the Medium or High setting.

FIGURE 2.18

Set your security settings to medium or high in Microsoft Internet Explorer. This alerts you to unwanted downloads from the Web that could be spyware trying to get onto your system.

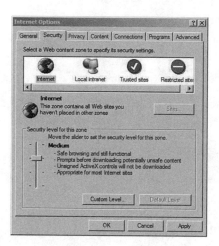

ANTI-SPYWARE WEB-SURFING TIPS

If you remember these three tips you'll be on your way to preventing spyware from getting on to your computer:

- Only download files or programs from websites you trust.

- Read a website's privacy statement and software license agreements. These provide you with clues to any misuse of your personal information when using these sites or about programs you download.

- If you can't close a pop-up window, never click OK, Agree, or Close inside the body of the window. Only close the window by clicking the X in the top-right corner of the window.

Run Windows Update Frequently

You'll see this recommendation a lot in this book. Run Windows Update every week. This service downloads all the latest security fixes for Windows to your computer. If you have Windows XP, ensure you download and install Service Pack 2 and turn on automatic updates so your computer automatically downloads the critical fixes for you.

caution

To curtail software piracy, Microsoft requires you to run the Windows validation process each time you download an XP add-on. The exception is Windows security updates.

Update Your Spyware Signatures

If you already have an anti-spyware program installed, be sure to update its spyware signatures regularly. These are like mugshots of bad guys. The anti-spyware program compares the spyware signatures to potential threats as they arrive on your computer. If there's a match, the program stops the spyware. Some anti-spyware programs update these signatures automatically. On others you have to do it yourself. For example, Microsoft AntiSpyware automatically updates its signatures, while Spybot Search & Destroy does not (see Figure 2.19).

tip

If your computer has Windows XP, the most critical fix available is a huge security update from Microsoft called Service Pack 2 (SP2). Learn more about installing SP2 on **p. 281**.

FIGURE 2.19

To keep Spybot Search & Destroy up to date, you need to check for new spyware signatures using the program's update feature.

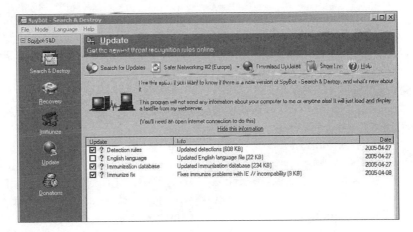

Ban All Spies: Strong Spyware Defense in an Afternoon

Here are a few techniques you can employ to make your system more resistant to spyware and safeguard it further.

Run a Full System Scan

Most anti-spyware programs offer both a quick scan feature and a full system scan feature (sometimes called a *deep scan*). When you have more time, be sure to run a full system scan (see Figure 2.20). The program digs deeper into your system to look for less obvious spyware.

FIGURE 2.20

Microsoft
AntiSpyware has
a full system
scan that should
be run occasion-
ally when you
have time to
check every
nook and
cranny of your
computer for
spyware.

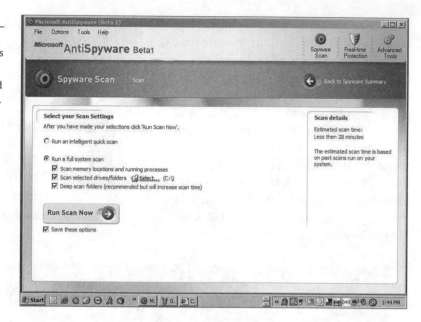

Install a Second Anti-spyware Program

The anti-spyware program you choose will not stop and clean all spyware infections. There are so many kinds of spyware that many anti-spyware programs only
capture a portion of them. So to be vigilant it's advisable to use two anti-spyware
programs on your computer. I've had good luck with using both Microsoft
AntiSpyware and Spybot Search & Destroy together (see Figure 2.21). I also
like PestPatrol, a commercial anti-spyware product available from http://www.
pestpatrol.com that is very effective at catching more spyware than the freebies. A
third free anti-spyware tool is Ad-Aware SE Personal Edition available from
http://www.lavasoft.de.

Inoculate Your System

Microsoft AntiSpyware comes with a feature called Real-time Protection (see Figure
2.22). This feature watches 100 key areas of your computer looking for spyware
behavior. If a setting is changed or an Internet connection is made, it alerts you to
the behavior with an information pop-up box. If the alert is deemed severe, it asks
you for a decision.

Spybot Search & Destroy also has a similar feature. It's called Immunize. It tweaks
settings in Internet Explorer to block installation of known spyware.

FIGURE 2.21

I recommended using two anti-spyware programs on your computer. Besides Microsoft AntiSpyware, I like to use Spybot Search & Destroy, another excellent free anti-spyware tool.

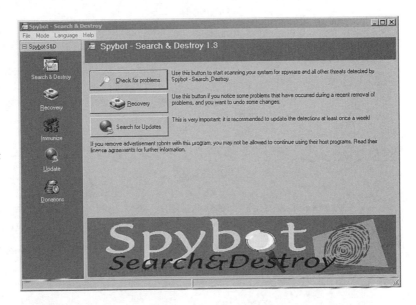

FIGURE 2.22

Microsoft AntiSpyware has a feature called Real-time Protection that watches over 100 key entries points used by spyware to get onto a computer.

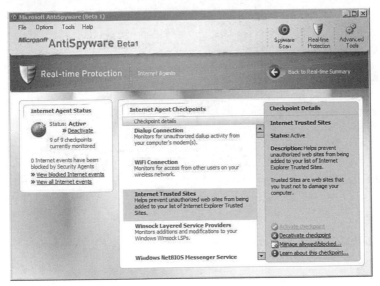

Use Firefox

If anyone is to blame for the spyware problem, it's Microsoft. That's because the great big software company produced operating systems that are full of security holes. At particular fault is Microsoft's web browser Internet Explorer (IE). It has all kinds of functions that are exploited by spyware writers. These include software called Browser Helper Objects (BHOs) which are add-ons for the browser that can auto-install from the web. IE also uses something called ActiveX which allows mini-programs to self-install on a computer.

Many people quit using IE as their browser. Instead they install Firefox (see Figure 2.23), a really nice alternative from Mozilla.org that doesn't have the security holes that plagues IE. I recommend this as well.

FIGURE 2.23

Using Firefox as your primary web browser closes one door on spyware on your system because its mechanisms won't allow spyware to come onto your system automatically.

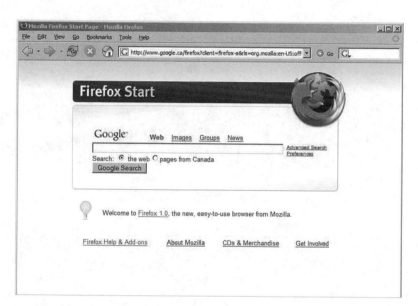

You can't totally abandon IE because some sites, including Microsoft's own Windows Update, won't work without it. However, installing and using Firefox most of the time is a good stopgap against getting your machine chuck full o' spyware.

Clean Cookies

If you'd like to clean browser cookies in the Internet Explorer web browser (see Figure 2.24), take the following steps:

1. Open Internet Explorer.
2. Click the Tools menu, and then click Internet Options.
3. Click the Delete Cookies button on the General Tab in the Temporary Internet Files section.
4. To selectively delete cookies, click the Settings button instead. Then click View Files.
5. A box opens with a list of your cookies files and other temporary browser files. You can selectively delete them from here.

FIGURE 2.24

In Internet
Explorer's
Internet Options
box you can
clean all your
cookies with
one click.

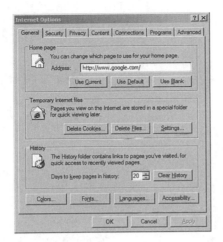

If you'd like to clean your cookies in Firefox (see Figure 2.25), do the following:

1. Start Firefox.

2. Click the Tools menu, and then click Options.

3. On the left menu, click the Privacy icon.

4. Next to the cookies entry, click Clear. Or to selectively delete them, click the +
   sign next to Cookies and a submenu opens.

5. Click View Cookies to look at the cookies in Firefox and delete the ones you
   don't want.

FIGURE 2.25

In the Firefox
Options menu
you can wipe
out many tem-
porary Internet
files, including
cookies.

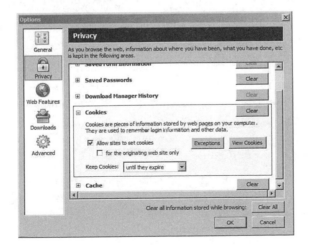

Spyware Infection Found! How to Scrub Your System

Despite your best efforts, you might still get infected by spyware or adware. In fact, because of the pernicious nature of this kind of malware, it's almost a certainty. So this section will come in handy. Here's how to clean spyware and adware from your system.

Clean, Yes! Spyware, No!

I am going to show you how to use Microsoft AntiSpyware to remove threats. The process that most other anti-spyware software use is not that different.

First, you'll want to run a system scan to detect infections. When you do this, the software does the following:

caution

If you clean your web browser's cookies, you could wipe away the good with the bad. Cookies can be used to remember user IDs, passwords, and other settings you use to log on to membership-based websites. So be aware that if you wipe your cookies clean, you'll have to re-enter this info the next time you visit a membership-based website such as your online bank.

- It examines all the files on your computer looking for traces of spyware.
- It scours your computer memory looking for active spyware.
- It rakes through the Windows registry, which is a massive storehouse of settings and data used to run your computer.
- It examines web browser and system settings as well as the startup areas of Windows.

Anti-spyware programs usually offer two kinds of scans:

- **Quick scan**—This kind of scan checks the likely hiding places that spyware set up camp in, but doesn't delve too deeply into the deep dark areas of your hard drive. A quick scan catches most active spyware on your system, but misses the ones that are dormant or that have cleverly obscured themselves. This is handy to run once a day or when you think your system might have recently been compromised.
- **Deep scan**—This looks at the same areas the quick scan looks at but also deeply combs the hard drive seeking any sign of spyware. It checks every nook and cranny, every bit and byte. As a result, it takes a while to complete. This should be done weekly.

Microsoft AntiSpyware has both modes. Let me take you through a deep scan. Before you start, check to see if there are any spyware signature updates.

1. Make sure you are connected to the Internet either via your broadband connection (cable, DSL, or satellite) or dialup. (If you can check email or surf the Web, you are connected.)

2. Start Microsoft AntiSpyware.

3. Click the File menu.

4. Choose Check for Updates.

5. The program checks to see if there are any new updates on the Microsoft server and downloads and installs them.

6. Now click Scan Options under the big Run Quick Scan Now button. You'll see two options: Run an Intelligent Quick Scan and Run a Full System Scan (see Figure 2.26).

7. Choose the full system scan. When you do this the grayed out check boxes become active.

8. You want to keep them all checked. If you want to target a second hard drive or removable storage device, you want to click Select and choose the drive or folder to scan (click the + sign to pick specific folders).

FIGURE 2.26

Microsoft AntiSpyware can do either a quick scan that takes a few minutes or a thorough deep scan that takes a half hour or more, depending on the size of your hard drive.

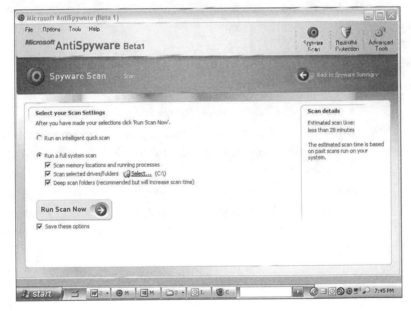

9. After you've decided on the options, click the Run Scan Now button. As the scan runs, it starts to display the threats it finds and the number of files associated with the threat (see Figure 2.27).

FIGURE 2.27

Microsoft
AntiSpyware
alerts you as it
finds threats
during the scan.

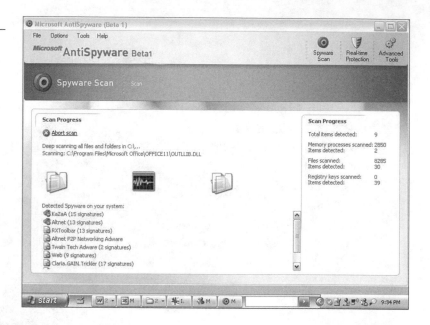

When the scan is complete, Microsoft AntiSpyware lists all the threats it found and
rates its severity as follows:

■ **Severe**—Severe-risk items have an extreme potential for harm, such as a
security exploit, and should be removed.

■ **High**—High-risk items have a large potential for harm (allowing someone
to take control of the computer), and should be removed unless you know-
ingly installed them.

■ **Elevated**—These programs have potential for harm and should be removed.

■ **Moderate**—These items have some potential for harm, but may be needed
to make a program run. Often adware that is part of a free program is rated
this way.

Microsoft AntiSpyware also recommends an action to take when you click the
Continue button to clean the threats from the system:

■ **Always Ignore**—When selected, the threat will be permanently ignored by
the program in all future scans.

■ **Ignore**—The threat is ignored this time but will be detected next scan.

■ **Quarantine**—This removes the program and places it in a safe area (called quarantine) where it can't do any harm. It can be removed from quarantine at a later date and restored.

■ **Remove**—This removes every trace of the spyware or adware from the system so it is no longer a threat.

What to Do When an Infection Is Found

When Microsoft AntiSpyware finishes its scan, it gives you the option to remove it (see Figure 2.28). Click Continue. Hum merrily—spyware killing can be fun. Be sure to reboot your system after the removal process is done to stop spyware from regenerating. As long as it's in memory, some spyware and adware can re-install, self-repair, and download new infections from the Internet.

FIGURE 2.28

When a scan is done, Microsoft AntiSpyware rates the threat and makes a recommendation as to what you should do with it.

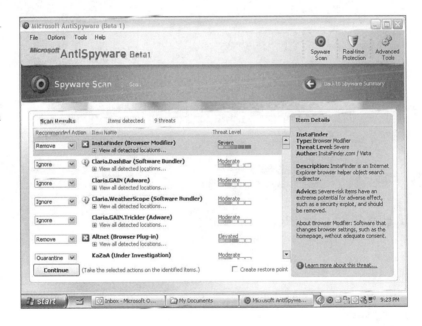

LOOK WHAT I FOUND! PLEASE IGNORE IT

If Microsoft AntiSpyware finds software from Claria, formerly Gator, on your computer (such as GotSmiley, Weatherscope, or DashBar) it recommends that you ignore these products (see Figure 2.29).

It's been a highly controversial issue. That's because Gator/Claria has been a notorious producer of spyware and adware even though it vehemently defends its practices.

Rumor has it that Microsoft has been sniffing around Claria looking at it as a possible acquisition. Rumors about a possible Microsoft acquisition of Claria began around the same time Microsoft began to recommend that Claria software be ignored when Microsoft AntiSpyware detected it.

It appears to be part of a larger picture as Microsoft downgraded some other adware company products, but the anti-Microsoft conspiracy theorists went bonkers when this happened.

To be fair, Claria has cleaned up its act a lot. When you install its free programs, it declares that its software collects information on you and pushes ads at you. However, it does give you an option to buy a version without these sneaky features.

FIGURE 2.29
Microsoft recommends that you ignore programs from Claria, a company with a history for releasing software that snoops.

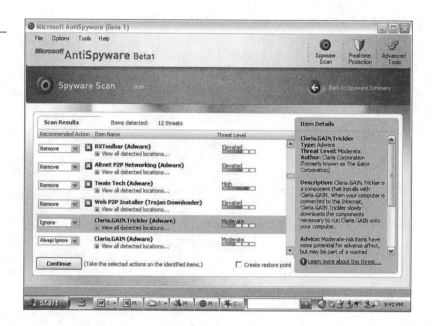

If the Removal Routine Fails

If an anti-spyware program has a problem removing a threat, you may want to do a scan with it in Windows Safe Mode.

Safe Mode is a Windows troubleshooting mode that allows you to run Windows without loading anything unnecessary in memory. You can get into it by restarting your computer and hitting F8 repeatedly as the computer starts. This takes you to a menu where you choose Safe Mode and boot into Windows in a raw state. This is useful to remove spyware and viruses because in Safe Mode nothing extraneous is loaded into memory, except key Windows components. Since program components spyware uses are not in memory in this state, they can be easily removed. Think of it like this: You can't put a ladder in the garage if you're standing on it. And you can't delete a program if it's running.

Running a scan in Safe Mode increases your chances of successfully removing the threat completely. Before going into Safe Mode, don't forget to update your spyware signatures first, by using the Update button in the program (see the previous section).

How to Fix a Browser Hijack

The infections you'll have great difficulty removing is a category of spyware called *browser hijackers*.

As mentioned earlier in this chapter, it's a kind of malware that takes over your Internet Explorer home page and switches it to another web page. (A home page is the website that loads when a browser is first opened.) If you try to reset the home page, the browser hijack switches it back the next time you start your computer or open Internet Explorer again.

Spybot Search & Destroy, Ad-Aware SE, and Microsoft AntiSpyware all have capabilities to cleanse some browser hijackers, but they are not always successful.

I highly recommend you run all three free anti-spyware programs first before resorting to the following procedures. Fixing a browser hijacker problem can be an extremely difficult task and you'll likely want to recruit some help.

Browser hijackers are very clever at making themselves difficult to remove. They insert themselves in obscure places deep inside your operating system and cling to your computer like an amorous dog on your leg. There are, however, a couple of tools that can help you rid yourself of the more insipid browser hijackers.

note

Booting in Windows Safe Mode causes Windows to start using only its most basic components (mouse, monitor, and keyboard drivers, for example). When in Safe Mode, Windows doesn't load a bevy of other drivers, startup applications, and the like, meaning any spyware lurking on your PC will be peacefully snoozing when you take the wood stake to it. Think of Safe Mode as Windows Unplugged, if you will. It's still Windows, just without all the frills. Here, you are better able to nix spyware. After you're done squishing spyware, reboot your computer in Normal Mode and enjoy your spyware-free computer.

HIJACKER KILLERS WORTH PAYING FOR

There are a few anti-spyware products—which you have to pay for—that I recommend because they are easy to use, remove infections well, and have a high detection rate.

They are also good at removing many browser hijackers. I always suggest running two anti-spyware software programs on a computer. You'll do well to run one of these along with one of the free programs I recommend:

- PestPatrol from Computer Associates (www.pestpatrol.com)
- Webroot Spy Sweeper (www.webroot.com)
- CounterSpy from Sunbelt Software (www.sunbeltsoftware.com)

HijackThis: An Introduction

One way to fix a browser hijack is with a diagnostic program called HijackThis (see Figure 2.30) written by a clever Dutch student called Merijn Bellekom. It's available free from his website at www.merijn.org.

When you type www.merijn.org in your web browser, be sure you spell it right (see Figure 2.31). A slight misspelling can take you to an incorrect web page where there will be misleading links and lots of ads.

FIGURE 2.30

Make sure you type Merijn.org correctly when you go to download HijackThis (the correct site is shown). Misspellings of the site address take you to ad-laden websites.

That said, here's a piece of bad news. HijackThis is about as do-it-yourself as a 747 jet. It's not a tool that beginners should use on their own because you can really bung things up if you make a wrong move. Let me say that again:

You + HijackThis + cavalier attitude = computer goes BOOM!

HijackThis is like that pull catch in your car that opens the hood. Anyone can use it, but it exposes inner workings that can be intimidating, and if you blindly mess around in there, you can get a limb caught in the fan belt.

The program shows you the settings that relate to the guts of Internet Explorer, other web browsers, items that activate during the Windows start up, and other key system settings. It can also remove those settings. The problem here is finding the right items to remove and that takes a trained eye and a steady mouse finger.

So big neon caution here: Your best bet is to find an expert to help. But don't worry, I'll show you where those dastardly hijackers hide and how to lure them out into the sunlight.

FIGURE 2.31

HijackThis is a good but complicated tool that helps you remove a browser hijacker from your computer.

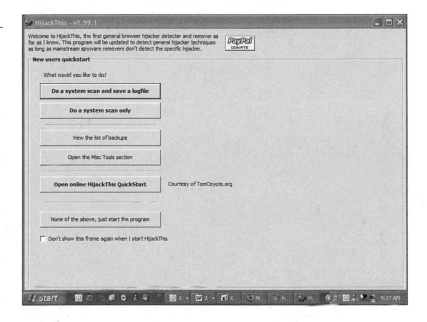

HOW TO CREATE A RESTORE POINT

If you decide to work with HijackThis, you should set a system restore point first in case you make a nasty mistake.

This utility is only available if you have Windows Me or XP (see Figure 2.32). It allows you to reset the system to the way it was in the event that something goes horribly wrong after you start to tinker.

You can set a System Restore Point as follows:

1. Click Start, All Programs.
2. Next click Accessories and choose System Tools.
3. Now choose System Restore.
4. Choose Create System Restore Point and click Next.
5. Name the restore point with a description you will remember later, such as Before I Messed with the System.

If you run into problems and want to go back to the way things were, start up System Restore again, choose Restore My Computer to an Earlier Time, click Next, and find the Restore Point you set earlier. Click Next again and follow the wizard through until the system is restored. Note that it requires a reboot to finish the process.

FIGURE 2.32
Before you start
working with
HijackThis, set a
system restore
point so you can
undo everything
if something
goes horribly
wrong.

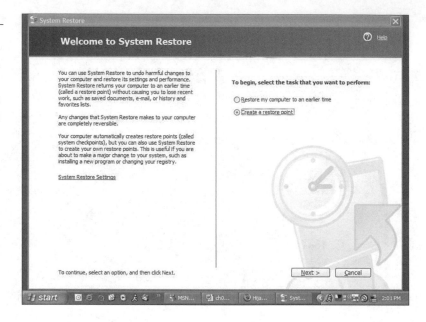

Recruit a HijackThis Expert

Because HijackThis is a very advanced tool, a lot of eager experts on the Web are willing to help you diagnose a spyware problem with it. You just have to find one. Here's how to get an expert to help you.

Close Internet Explorer and any other browsers that are running. Start HijackThis, and follow these steps carefully:

1. In the opening menu of HijackThis, you'll see an option called Do a System Scan and Save a Log File. Choose it. This scans places deep inside Windows where browser hijackers might have put entries. Then it creates a log of these in Notepad.

2. Ask for help by posting your log on a web forum where HijackThis experts hang out. Be sure cut and paste it into your forum post with your request for help. There's a good list of web forums with experts that will help you diagnose your HijackThis log at www.merijn.org/forums.html. There's also a very good Malware Removal forum at Spywareinfo.com (see Figure 2.33).

3. The expert diagnoses your log and walks you through procedures on how to fix the problem using HijackThis and other tools and techniques they'll explain.

4. Ask for the expert's mailing address and send them a box of chocolate cookies. Geeks like cookies.

FIGURE 2.33

The Malware
Removal
discussion area
in the forums at
SpywareInfo.
com is a good
place to post
your request for
analysis of your
HijackThis log.

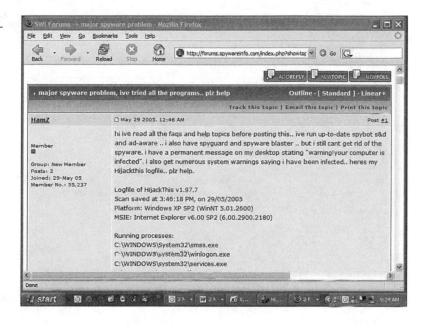

Do It Yourself HijackThis

If you're the kind of person who likes to land the 747 yourself—and really, who doesn't?—you're going to need a few days and an in-depth step-by-step do-it-yourself process to learn HijackThis.

However, how about a quickie course that should both fix most ornery snags that Spybot and Ad-Aware can't fix and at the same time get your feet wet with HijackThis?

Check the Memory First

At the top of your HijackThis log you see a series of programs listed as Running Processes (see Figure 2.34). This is what is in your computer's memory at the time of the scan.

You may see some obvious spyware program running. I helped out one guy who had a nasty spyware infection. Here are five of the 10 things that were running in his system's memory. Pop quiz! Can you guess which program is spyware?

1. `C:\WINDOWS\system32\winlogon.exe`
2. `C:\WINDOWS\system32\svchost.exe`
3. `C:\PROGRA~1\Grisoft\AVGFRE~1\avgcc.exe`
4. `C:\DOCUME~1\s1\LOCALS~1\Temp\nsu1C.tmp\ns1E.tmp`
5. `C:\Documents and Settings\s1\My Documents\Porn stars.exe`

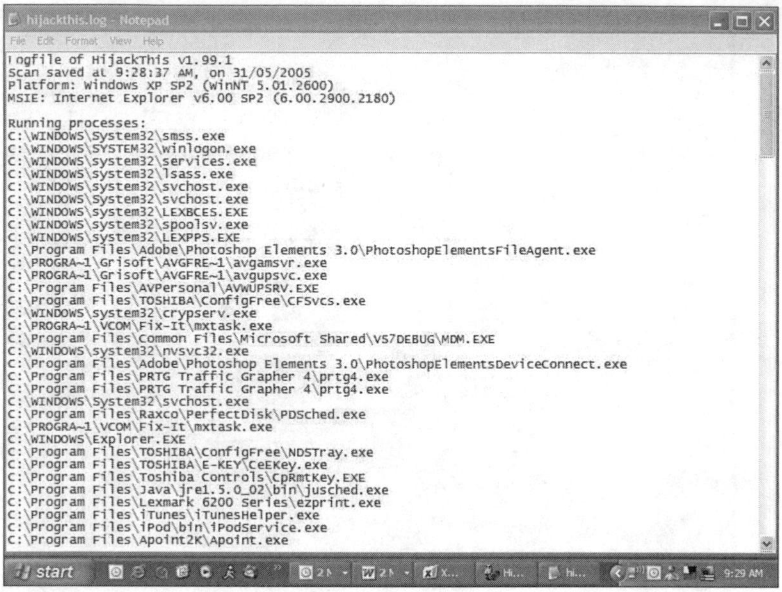

FIGURE 2.34

FIGURE 2.34

At the top of the HijackThis log is a list of processes running in your computer's memory.

If you answered 4 *and* 5, you're right! Number 4 is a giveaway because it an obscure gobbledygook program name with a `.tmp` extension. Very suspicious! Sometimes spyware programs randomize the names of the program they launch to evade detection from anti-spyware programs.

Item 5 is pretty obvious, too. In this sample case, two of these with slight variations to their names were running in memory. Actually, these files had longer names that mentioned actual actors and described the act they were acting, so to speak. I cleansed it for you to keep this book out of the Human Sexuality section of the book store.

So check your HijackThis log for suspicious entries and then do what geeks call the three-finger salute: Hold down the Control and Alt keys and tap the Del key.

The Windows Task Manager opens (see Figure 2.35). If you click on the Processes tab, you'll see all the programs running in memory. Scroll through them and try to figure out which ones are spyware.

To help, check out www.processlibrary.com. You can enter in names of the files you see on that site and it tells you whether it's a legitimate program or spyware. It won't have an answer for everything, though. What it's best for is to help you make a short list of the suspicious programs. Then you can investigate each one.

Use Google.com to help search for program names and be sure to enter them between sets of quotes if there are spaces in the name, as follows:

`"porn stars.exe"`

This tells Google to search for the whole name as a phrase and not pieces of it.

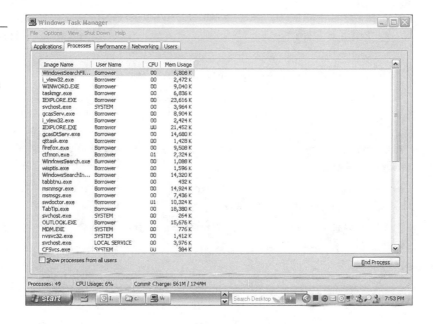

Here Spyware, Spyware. It's Time to Die

With the memory cleansed, you can get down to the business of killing spyware in the system.

Open HijackThis, click the Scan button, and look at the list of entries (see Figure 2.36).

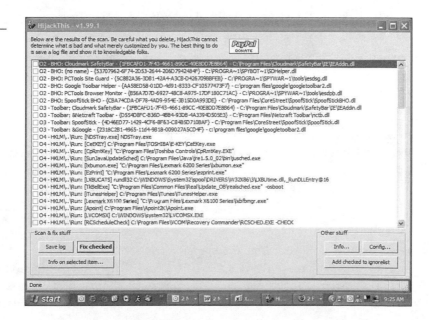

There are lots of entries and they all look like they could be items on a Chinese food menu. But if you study them, you'll start to see stuff you recognize. Let's go through some notable entries you will likely encounter.

R0, R1, R2, R3—IE Start and Search Page

These are addresses of the web pages Internet Explorer uses for the homepage and the default search page. If anything looks funky here and you see web addresses you don't recognize on the right side of each item, the entry is probably a hijack. Check off the boxes to the left of these and click the Fix Checked button. This wipes out the settings.

Congrats, you have just killed your first spyware with HijackThis. I think you are clever! But wait, we are not done.

F0, F1, F2, F3—Autoloading Programs from INI Files

These are autoloading programs from old versions of Windows. F0 references are always bad. Nuke 'em.

F1 items are usually old programs. If you run old Windows programs, you will probably recognize these. Do research on these if you're unsure.

N1, N2, N3, N4—Netscape/Mozilla Start and Search Page

These are Netscape and Mozilla (Firefox) web browser settings for their start and search pages. This look like the following:

```
N1 - Netscape 4: user_pref("browser.startup.homepage", "www.google.com");
➥(C:\Program Files\Netscape\Users\default\prefs.js)
```

These browser settings are usually OK. Malware called Lop.com hijacks these, though. If you don't recognized the web addresses, BBQ them.

O1—HOSTS File Redirections

These are HOSTS file redirects. What that means is the web address on the right will be redirected to the numerical Internet address (called an IP address) on the left when you type it into your web browser. For example

```
O1 - Hosts: 199.181.132.250 google.com
```

In this example, if you typed in Google.com into your web browser, it would be redirected to Disney.com (because that 199 number is an ABC/Disney-related IP address). Unless you put these in your HOSTS file yourself, these are bad. The only one that belongs there is

```
127.0.0.1 localhost
```

O2—Browser Helper Objects

These are called Browser Helper Objects or BHOs. They are programs that install into Internet Explorer that can add new features. They look like the following:

```
O2 - BHO: AcroIEHlprObj Class - {06849E9F-C8D7-4D59-B87D-784B7D6BE0B3}
➥ - C:\Program Files\Adobe\Acrobat 5.0\Reader\ActiveX\AcroIEHelper.ocx
```

For example, you'll see the Google Toolbar here if you have it installed. Of course, BHOs can also be spyware.

If you see something that looks odd or unfamiliar, it could be spyware. Again, it's worth searching Google.com for entries to learn more about them before you nuke them.

O3—IE Toolbars

These items reference Internet Explorer toolbars and look similar to this example:

```
O3 - Toolbar: Yahoo! Companion - {EF99BD32-C1FB-11D2-892F-0090271D4F88}
➥ - C:\Program Files\Yahoo!\Companion\Installs\cpn0\ycomp5_5_5_0.dll
```

If there's an odd toolbar at the top of IE that appears and wasn't there before, chances you'll find it listed as an O3 entry. Torch it.

O4—Autoloading Programs from Registry or Startup Group

These entries reference programs that load automatically when Windows starts. They look like the following:

```
O4 - HKCU\..\Run: [msnmsgr] "C:\Program Files\MSN Messenger\
➥msnmsgr.exe " /background
```

This is where many spyware programs get started. Killing them off here stops them from loading when Windows restarts. Tread carefully here.

Besides these entries listed, there are loads more of esoteric entries that could hide spyware references. Learning them all requires a university course, time, and patience.

For a full compliment of entries and what they do, check out this really good reference page: www.bleepingcomputer.com/forums/tutorial42.html.

If you have the time and the inclination, you can learn tons more about the workings of HijackThis and can make a study of all the critical entries it finds.

I also recommend visiting these web pages to learn more about using HijackThis:

- www.spywareinfo.com/articles/hijacked/
- www.greyknight17.com/spy/hjt.htm

Decimate the Little Suckers with CWShredder

Another free program called CWShredder (see Figure 2.37) might also be able to help you with your browser hijack. It finds and destroys traces of CoolWebSearch, a name given to a wide range of browser hijackers. It's available for free from www.intermute.com/spysubtract/cwshredder_download.html.

FIGURE 2.37
CWShredder is a
free program
that helps defeat
CoolWebSearch
browser
hijackers.

It's a small file so it won't take long to download.
Before you run it, be sure to close Internet Explorer
and Windows Media Player, if they are open.

Now run CWShredder. You'll see four buttons at
the bottom of the initial window. Click Scan Only
if you want to see if there are any CoolWebSearch
hijacks on your system. Click Fix-> if you want to
search for infections and clean them.

Microsoft Mimics HijackThis: System Explorers

Now if all this talk about HijackThis has made
you queasy, you might want to take a step back
and find a tool like HijackThis that doesn't require
a grasp of advanced hamster science to use it.

While it's no HijackThis, Microsoft AntiSpyware
does have a fabulous little function hidden in its
advanced menus that could be termed HijackThis
Lite. It's called System Explorers (see Figure 2.38). The feature exposes key Windows
and browser settings like HijackThis does and identifies those that might be
spyware-related. It's not as comprehensive as HijackThis, but it touches on the key
settings that are frequently changed by spyware.

note

CWShredder was first
written by Merijn Bellekom,
author of HijackThis. He handed it
over to Intermute, makers of the
anti-spyware program SpySubtract
PRO, in October 2004. The company, which was bought by Trend
Micro in May 2005, is responsible
for updating it and continues to
make it freely available.

FIGURE 2.38

System Explorers
is an advanced
feature in
Microsoft
AntiSpyware
that is like
HijackThis
but without the
complexity.

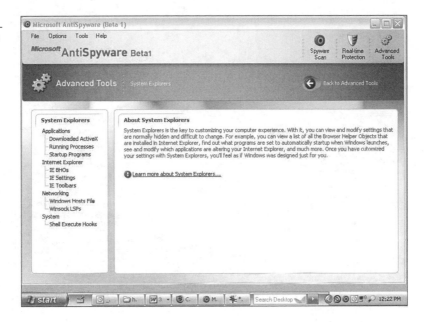

To work with this feature, follow these steps:

1. Start Microsoft AntiSpyware.

2. Click Tools, Advanced Tools, System Explorers.

3. When the System Explorers screen comes up, you see a list on the left that shows a list of key system and browser settings.

4. Click on each one of these to explore them. The programmers have done a good job of explaining what each item does. Simply click on a setting to see a diagnosis of what it is (see Figure 2.39).

5. For each type of setting, customized options help you deal with them, including the ability to disable or remove, if needed (see Figure 2.40).

tip

Some spyware adds itself as Web content on your desktop background. To remove this, follow these steps:

1. Right-click an empty space on the Windows desktop and select Properties.

2. Select the Desktop tab and then the Customize Desktop button.

3. Select the Web tab and delete any content listed that you don't want to be displayed.

FIGURE 2.39

Microsoft AntiSpyware's System Explorers feature can give you a good analysis of each of the Startup Programs that run when Windows XP boots up.

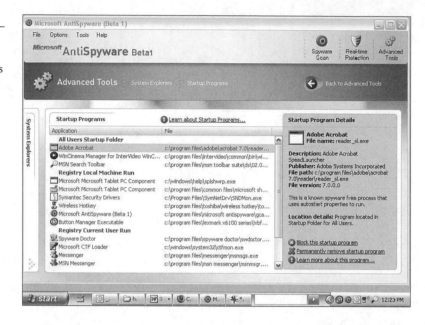

FIGURE 2.40

A problematic toolbar probably left over from a spyware installation is shown in the System Explorers feature in Microsoft AntiSpyware. Note that it can be blocked or removed with controls on the bottom right.

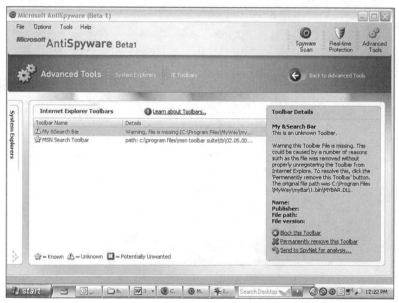

THE ABSOLUTE MINIMUM

- Spyware is software that installs secretly and snoops on you on your computer.

- Adware is like spyware; it snoops, but it also pushes unwanted advertising at you.

- You have to accept some adware if you want to run some free programs.

- Other types of spyware include snoopware, Trojan horses, dialers, browser hijackers, key loggers, and cookies.

- Not all cookies are bad. Some are needed for online shopping and remembering user settings and passwords when you return to a website.

- All PC users are at risk of getting spyware. Spyware is almost non-existent on a Mac.

- Most spyware comes from web pages, free software, and email attachments.

- Spyware compromises your privacy and can put you at risk for identity theft. It can also slow down your computer by using up system resources.

- Your first line of defense against spyware is an anti-spyware program. Three good ones are Microsoft AntiSpyware, Spybot Search & Destroy, and Ad-Aware SE.

- Scan once a week and keep your spyware signatures up to date.

- You should scan with at least two spyware programs because no single program catches all infections.

- SP2 should be installed on your Windows XP computer to help defend against spyware.

- HijackThis and CWShredder can be used to get rid of browser hijackers. HijackThis is an advanced tool, however, and you should seek help on the Web for using it.

- If HijackThis scares you, look at Microsoft AntiSpyware's System Explorer feature.

3

HACKERS: THERE'S A MAN iN MY MACHiNE

If your computer is a fortress, hackers are the interlopers with pointy metal hats who charge the gate, scale the walls, or use stolen keys to get inside. Their mission? To steal your crown jewels or carve graffiti on the walls, such as "The king is a weenie." In this chapter I'll tell you why they want access to your computer, how they gain access to it, and what you stand to lose if they do. There's also a really exciting section on how to stop them and what to do if one of them succeeds. It's like a medieval video game, but scarily, it's real.

What Is a Hacker?

Hacker is one of those terms that has a different meaning depending on who uses it. Among programmers, to be a hacker is to be a star. Hackers are programming code jockeys that can throw together bits of miraculous pieces of programming seemingly at will. They are gurus. People who modify computer and other pieces of electronic hardware are also sometimes called hackers.

Being a hacker can also be a bad thing. A hacker or *hack* can sometimes be someone that has no grace or elegance in his work and throws his projects together haphazardly. Among the general public (thanks to the media and perhaps Hollywood), a hacker is a person who gains illicit access to a computer and steals stuff or breaks into military networks and launches missiles for fun and with no conscience.

To complicate things even further, those that are hackers in the break-and-enter sense consider themselves *crackers* or *black-hat hackers*.

And among people who eat cheese, crackers are savory biscuits.

So you see the problem here. For simplicity's sake, I am going to use the popular mass-media definition of hackers interchangeably with crackers. Both terms refer to bad people who divine access to your computer across the Internet by compromising its defenses or using electronic loopholes.

note

You might hear the terms *white-hat* or *black-hat* in reference to a hacker or cracker. A black-hat is a bad person who gains unauthorized access to a computer or network for nonaltruistic reasons. A white-hat is a security expert who attempts to gain access to a computer or network to detect vulnerabilities so they can be patched. Pink-hats are just fashionable.

Who Are the Hackers?

Hackers and crackers are usually highly intelligent social misfits who tend to have a strong curiosity and often have an anarchist or, at very least, anti-authoritarian bent. They see the Internet as a playground and they tend to believe information should be free. Sometimes they are described as digital joy riders.

In an interview on SafeMode.org, one hacker—who used the nickname xentric—explained why he hacks:

"It's just that feeling when you finally get something done. You put lots of effort into some hacks and I feel a rush of excitement whenever I succeed in doing something. What is the incentive that keeps (me) doing it? Curiosity…"

It's safe to say that the vast number of people who try to gain illegal access to computers are young men. Many high-profile hackers are in their 20s and 30s.

However, many are simply teenagers who have access to publicly available hacking tools that can be downloaded easily from the Internet.

There's a hierarchy in the hacker community. High-status crackers write their own tools and develop their own break-in mechanisms to gain access to computers. Lower down on the hacker food chain are script kiddies. These electronic intruders use freely distributed tools designed by others to engage in computer vandalism, break-ins, or electronic theft.

What Damage Can Hackers Do?

Hackers like to subvert computer security without permission. They are cyber criminals. This can mean gaining access to a computer across the Internet for illicit purposes. They might engage in any of the following activities:

- **Vandalism**—Destruction or digital defacement of a computer or its data for destruction's sake. Sometimes this is ego-driven. They break in and leave their mark to show they've been there.
- **Hacktivism**—A form of vandalism or electronic civil disobedience with a political agenda. Usually hacktivists have altruistic motives.
- **Theft**—Gaining access to intellectual or proprietary technology or information, sometimes for resale.
- **Hijacking**—Many of the financially motivated hackers are interested in using viruses and Trojan horses to hijack your computer so they can remotely control it for their own purposes.
- **Identity theft**—Electronic theft of personal information that can be used to steal financial resources from an individual or corporation.
- **Terrorism**—Some experts believe that terrorists will eventually launch an attack using hacking techniques.

Targets of a Hack Attack

Hacker interests lie in many types of computers on the Internet. Following is a discussion of the types of targets and their appeal to the perpetrators.

Corporate Networks

Corporate computers are often heavily fortified so hacking into one has high cachet. Behind corporate firewalls are repositories of customer information, product information, and sometimes, in the case of a software publisher, the product itself.

Web Servers

Web servers are computers that contain websites. While some contain customer financial information, web servers are usually targets for vandals because they can be defaced to display information the hacker chooses to the public.

Personal Computers

A personal computer by itself has little appeal for the high-profile hacker. However, it has its use in cyber crime. If it can be commandeered, it can be used to engage in hiding the perpetrator's identity. There are several key uses for these hijacked computers, as follows.

Denial of Service Attacks

A hacker can gain control of a computer by planting a program on it, usually by using a virus or Trojan horse. After infected, the hijacked computer, called a *zombie*, can be use as a weapon to attack another computer. It's commanded to blast chunks of data at a target computer in a coordinated effort with thousands of other zombies. This overwhelms the target machine and its stops functioning. This is called a distributed denial of service attack (DDoS). Sometimes a DDoS attack is used against companies who have policies with which the hacker disagrees.

It's also used in extortion schemes. Gambling websites, typically located offshore, regularly receive threats of DDoS attacks unless they pay protection money. These threats are known to intensify around Super Bowl weekend in the United States, when the volume of bets is at an all time high.

Spam, Spam, Spam, Spam, Spam, Spam, Spam

Hackers are also interested in getting their code onto personal computers so they can be turned into spam machines. Sending large volumes of unsolicited email from one computer gets your Internet connection shut down. If you can hijack thousands of other computers to do the spam-sending, however, you retain your anonymity and have a spam network that's hard to shut down because each sending machine has to be blocked one at a time.

Storage

I have had a web server computer hacked before and used as a depository for illegal software or programs that are being shared. Someone used a loophole to get into it and left gigabytes of data on it, presumably for others to fetch as needed.

Hacker Motivation: I Think Therefore I Hack

Hackers' motivations vary. For some, it's economic. They earn a living through cyber crime. Some have a political or social agenda—their aim is to vandalize high-profile computers to make a statement. Others do it for the sheer thrill.

When asked by the website SafeMode.org why he defaces web servers, a cracker replied, "A high-profile deface gives me an adrenalin shot and then after a while I need another shot, that's why I can't stop."

Tools of the Trade: Pass Me a Trojan Horse, Would You?

There are a series of tools that crackers use to gain access to computers:

■ **Trojan horse**—This is a program that looks safe and useful but contains nasty programming inside that does bad stuff. If you are fooled into installing one of these on your computer, it can open what's called a back-door. A *backdoor* is an access point created from inside a computer's defenses that allows outsiders to circumvent security and gain access to the machine from the Internet.

■ **Virus**—A piece of self-replicating programming that infects a computer after being run by a human. It then installs tools that fulfill the attacker's agenda. This could provide access to an outsider, hijack the system to do nefarious tasks, or install tools that can be commanded from afar. People that release viruses aren't traditional hackers, but virus code is one tool in a hacker's toolbox.

■ **Worm**—A self-replicating program that does not need human intervention to spread. It travels across networks looking for computer vulnerabilities and exploits them when encountered. People that release these programs aren't traditional hackers, either. They are virus writers.

■ **Vulnerability scanner**—A program that checks a computer for known weaknesses, such as programming errors or security holes.

■ **Sniffer**—A program that looking for security information such as user IDs and passwords in data as it flows over a network such as the public Internet. This would be like a malcontented postal worker reading postcards as they moved through a sorting facility.

■ **Social engineering**—This is simply the art of fast talking. The easiest way to break security is to have someone give you access. You might have all kinds of security on your computer but if I call you and ask for access (and maybe convince you I am a technician that can help or a co-worker who should have access) and you give it to me, I have used social engineering to gain illicit access by fooling you.

- **Root kit**—This is the equivalent of digital camouflage. It is a programming toolkit that is used to program a virus, spyware, or other piece of malware to keep it from being discovered by a security program.

- **Exploit**—A program that that takes advantage of a known security weakness in a computer.

Firewall: Shut Out the Hackers

This book discusses many of the security tools you can use to defend your computer against digital threats. An antivirus program and anti-spyware programs are critical; however, the third key tool in your defenses should be a firewall, which can be used to keep out intruders and traveling viruses (called worms). A *firewall* is an electronic wall used to keep out an intruder or unwanted communication. It sits between your computer and the Internet (see Figure 3.1).

FIGURE 3.1

A firewall is an electronic barrier between your computer or your home network and the Internet.

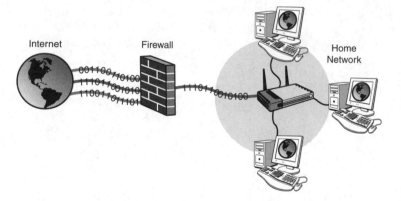

In construction, a firewall is a physical wall that is designed to stop the spread of fire from one part of a building to another. Firewalls are also used in vehicles to separate the engine compartment from the passenger compartment. In the case of a network, a firewall stops unauthorized communication from the public Internet to a computer.

Think of a firewall as a big wall with lots of doors in it. These doors are called ports. When you use your web browser to access a website such as Google.com, you open a port (an electronic door) from inside the firewall and make contact with a server (a computer that sends information on request).

Let's say the server belongs to Google. Now that you have made contact with Google, it is allowed to communicate back to you. So data flows two ways through the port because you have initiated contact first and the firewall knows this.

There are potentially thousands of ports on a firewall. For example, email goes through port 25. Web browsers use port 80, and MSN Messenger uses ports 1863, 6891-6900, and 6901.

You don't have to know what ports are used. Programs on your computer figure that out for you. Some programs, such as file-sharing applications, however, need ports to be specially configured to work.

Crackers use port-scanning software to look for holes in a firewall. These scanners yell out to your firewall on various ports, "Yo dude, are you there?" Your computer would normally respond, "Yep, I am here. Ready to yak." The port scanner then knows that there's an opportunity to exploit a security hole and crawl through that door.

There are two basic types of firewalls at your disposal:

- **Software firewall**—Windows XP comes with its own built-in firewall, but you can also install a third-party software firewall with better features.
- **Hardware firewall**—These firewalls are physical devices. For home users, their home network router has a firewall function, but advanced hardware firewalls are built for businesses.

Software Firewalls: Programs That Stop Hackers

A good software firewall for home users should have the following attributes:

- It's easy to configure.
- It's frugal with system resources so it doesn't bog down the computer.
- It doesn't bug you much.

But not all firewalls are created equal. Let's look at a few.

Windows Firewall: Built-in Defense

The easiest software firewall you can use is the built-in Windows Firewall. It is a feature of windows XP Service Pack 2 (SP2), a great big security fix that was issued in the summer of 2004.

When you install SP2, it turns on the Windows Firewall. It's not a very complex piece of software and it's often criticized for its simplicity. I think it's a decent security tool because

- It's easy to turn on. In fact if you have installed SP2, it is on (provided that you haven't manually turned it off since installing SP2).
- You never hear from it. It silently does its job without needing much user intervention.
- It doesn't slow the system by any perceivable measure.

Now, the Windows Firewall (see Figure 3.2) is not without its critics. It only polices traffic one-way. Inbound traffic is inspected by the software, but data traffic coming from the computer and flowing out to the Internet is not examined. That can be a problem because if there is a virus, spyware, or other malware on your computer trying to communicate with the outside world, Windows Firewall does not catch it on the way out.

Third-Party Software Firewalls

For the best firewall protection possible, install a third-party software firewall. These programs defend a computer in both directions. They inspect data coming into a computer from the outside world and they look at data leaving the computer to ensure it's valid traffic and not coming from spyware, a Trojan horse, or a worm.

These programs also use a question and answer process to learn your habits. They are particularly bothersome when they are first installed because every time a program attempts to move data across the firewall, an alert is generated by the firewall that requires the computer user to respond.

> **tip**
>
> If you have bought a new computer or have bought and installed a copy of Windows XP since the fall of 2004, you probably already have SP2 installed. If you haven't installed SP2 yet, what are you waiting for? Do it. Now. See Chapter 8, "Let's Smash-Proof Windows: Tweak Windows XP Nice and Tight," to learn how to update your existing copy of Windows XP with SP2. See Chapter 9, "Starting from the Beginning: Wiping a Hard Drive and Rebuilding from the Ground Up," if you want to scrap your current Windows installation and start over (recommended if you've been running XP for a long time or suspect that your security has already been compromised).

FIGURE 3.2

The Windows Firewall is included with Service Pack 2 and is easily accessible in the Security Center in the Windows XP Control Panel.

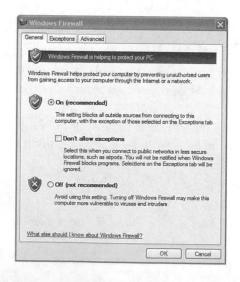

Here are some of the features that third-party firewalls offer over the built-in Windows Firewall:

- **Two-way communication filtering—** For outbound communication, it is particularly annoying when a third-party firewall is first installed. But after a few days of clicking Yes or No on a firewall's dialog boxes (see Figure 3.3), most of the key communication requests have been dealt with and the firewall won't interrupt quite as much.

    Good firewalls offer the user recommendations as to how to respond to an alert when it recognizes the program the communication is coming from. Esoteric processes that need to access the Internet, however, can be hard to deal with because they can be somewhat cryptic for the uninitiated.

caution

Windows Firewall has been drastically improved in Windows XP SP2, so it's important that you upgrade your system to SP2 if you plan to use Windows XP. Learn how to install SP2 in Chapters 8 and 9.

FIGURE 3.3

ZoneAlarm detects that an antivirus program is trying to access the Internet and alerts the user to allow or deny the request.

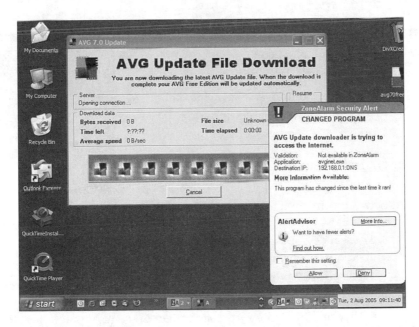

Communication from outside the firewall is less problematic because, unless the user initiates communication with the outside world, the inbound communication is ignored. The firewall can be triggered to alert the user to severe attacks, but you'd be surprised how often your IP address is probed by someone or something on the outside.

■ **Stealth mode**—This mode makes the firewall and the computer behind it invisible. Most good firewalls have this feature available and often it's turned on by default.

Stealth mode works like this: You walk by my house in the middle of the darkest night and you yell, "Is anyone there?" If I turn on the porch light, come out, and say, "Yes, I am here," you know there's a house on the block and you can engage me in a conversation. If you're a bad person, you can find a way into my house by either tricking me or finding an open window or door when I am not looking.

If you yell, "Is anyone there?" as you walk by and I stay in my house and don't respond, you don't know I am there, so you keep going. This is the equivalent of a firewall in stealth mode.

■ **Threat management**—Besides playing traffic cop, a software firewall can also offer other threat management features. It can inspect inbound data and compare it to threat signatures to help block virus and spyware infections. It can also be configured to stop you from sharing personal information with fraudulent websites, helping to defend you against phishing.

Recommended Firewall Freebies

A couple of very good free firewall programs you might consider installing include

■ ZoneAlarm from www.zonelabs.com

■ SyGate from www.sygate.com

Hardware Firewalls

Hardware firewalls are devices that physically sit between your computer and the wire that goes out to the Internet. Although businesses usually use a device that is physically separated from their other network gear, at home you'll find a firewall built into home network routers.

Some of the many advantages to hardware firewalls are

> **tip**
>
> If you really like the idea of a firewall scanning for viruses, spyware, and hackers as they cross the digital threshold, consider the SonicWall TZ 150, a $300 router/firewall hardware combination designed for small business that scans for malware and downloads signatures automatically several times an hour.

■ They are fire and forget. Install them and you are protected. No tweaking needed.

■ They are included in the price of a device that shares your Internet between computers (meaning you can share your Internet connection with other computers in your home). No fees or extra costs.

■ They have no impact on the system performance of your computer.

FIGURE 3.4

The Windows XP Security Center monitors the presence of a software firewall (in this case ZoneAlarm) and, on detection, turns off the Windows Firewalls to avoid redundancy.

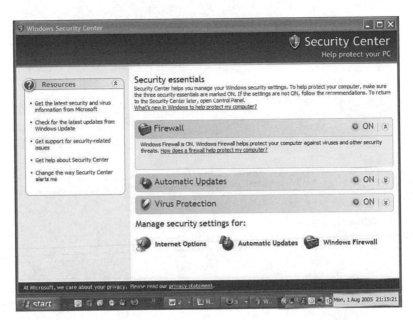

Easy Defense with a NAT Firewall

Home network routers have a firewall feature built in that uses a technology called *network address translation (NAT)*.

It's not a firewall technology itself, but it offers a firewall-like feature that provides natural protection from Internet nasties, such as hackers and worms.

NAT was invented because of a shortage of IP addresses available to the ever-growing Internet population. Sounds complicated but it's not really. An IP address is like a phone number for each device connected to the Internet. Every device on the Internet has an IP number. An IP address is a set of four three digit numbers that can't be any lower than 0.0.0.0 or higher than 255.255.255.255.

If you can surf the Internet on your computer right now, it has an IP address. Because there's a shortage of IP addresses, not everyone can have her own. So NAT devices were invented to help (see Figure 3.5).

note

If you install a third-party firewall on Windows XP, the XP Security Center should detect it and turn off the Windows Firewall (see Figure 3.4) because running two is redundant, could cause conflicts, and can slow down the computer unnecessarily. If for some reason you find that both Windows Firewall and a third-party firewall are running at the same time, simply open the Control Panel, choose Security Center, click on the Windows Firewall button, and turn off the firewall.

FIGURE 3.5

This Netgear
router uses
network address
translation
(NAT) that hides
the identity of
computers
connected to it.

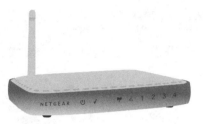

NAT routers work like this: Every large company has
a switchboard. Everyone dials one central public
phone number to talk to the company operator.
When they reach the operator, they ask for an
extension and they are put through.

NAT works like that. The router has an IP address
that everyone on the Internet can call (it's like the
switchboard). Behind the router is a home network. Each computer on the network has a private
IP address (like a phone extension).

When data from the Internet arrives for one of
those computers, it is sent to the NAT router and
the NAT router looks up the computer on its network (in a handy little directory it keeps) and
checks to see which one made the request.

The router hands the data off to that computer.
This is built-in security because no one on the
Internet can send data to a computer behind a
router directly. They always have to go through
the router first.

Stateful Inspection: The Meticulous Traffic Cop

There's one more level of security built into a NAT
router that offers great and easy security. Let's say
your child's computer, your computer, and your
spouse's laptop are all behind a router. Suddenly,
in comes communication from a server on the
Internet that hosts bumfluff.com.

note

Under the current IP
address scheme, called
IPv4, there's only 4,294,967,296
possible addresses in the world
(although not all of those
addresses are available for reasons
that only bona fide, card-carrying
geeks care about). Experts predict
that those addresses could all be
used sometime before 2020 unless
our uber-geek friends come to the
rescue. However, under a new
plan called IPv6 there are 340
undecillion addresses, which is a
really, really, really big number.
According to wikipedia.org, that's
670 quadrillion IP addresses per
square inch of Earth. If that is too
big to fathom, trust me when I say
that if I had that many mallomars,
I'd be fat and probably dead.

The router looks at a list it keeps of all computers attached to it to see who initiated a request with bumfluff.com. When it discovers that none of the computers did, it realizes that bumfluff.com is a bad website that is actually a front for hackersncrackers.com. So it discards the request, and all is right with the world again.

You see, in order to communicate with a computer behind a NAT router, that computer has to first communicate with you (see Figure 3.6).

So if I use my computer to contact bumfluff.com to see the latest news about mallomars (which are tasty marshmallow and chocolate cookies), the router notes that I am making contact. When bumfluff.com comes back to the router with information about mallomars, the router says, "Oh yeah, Andy's computer has been communicating with bumfluff.com, so I'll let it through."

> **note**
>
> The acronym NAT can stand for network address translation or natural address translation. Like a cookie and a biscuit, it's the same thing.

This is called stateful inspection or sometimes stateful packet inspection. All NAT routers engage in stateful inspection.

FIGURE 3.6

In stateful packet inspection, a router only allows information through to a computer if the computer requested it.

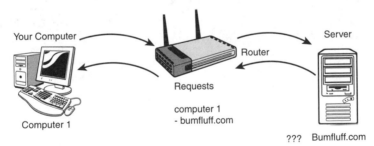

Your Computer — Router — Server

Requests
computer 1
- bumfluff.com

Computer 1

??? Bumfluff.com

How to Detect a Hacker Attack

If a hacker breaks into your computer, just noses around, and makes no changes to your computer, it's not easy to tell he's been there. There's no alert that says, "A hacker was here at 9:16 p.m. He works at the joint where you order your favorite pizza. His phone number is…"

In fact, Windows has no built-in log file that tracks events that occur on your computer. So it's possible that someone can come onto your system, roll around in your data, and leave without your knowledge. If you have a home network router or software firewall, your chances of suffering a hacker attack are massively reduced.

Signs of a hacker can include new odd behavior that suddenly starts to happen on your computer, such as the following:

■ The appearance of strange data, perhaps files or programs stored on your computer. A hacker might be using your computer as a temporary storage area or repository for pirated software.

■ Your computer might start sending spam. A hacker could have added software to send spam from your address.

■ You computer might start sending large volumes of garbage data to another computer. The hacker might have turned the computer into a zombie that can be commanded from afar to attack another computer in a distributed denial of service (DDoS) attack. In these attacks, bad guys harness thousands of computers to attack a single computer to overwhelm it with data and make it crash.

■ The first sign of a hacker could also simply be theft of money from your bank account. If you keep your banking information, including user IDs and passwords, in a file on your unprotected computer, it's entirely possible that someone could sneak on, find this information, and disappear again. However, phishers, key loggers, and other data capture schemes could also be responsible for this.

How to Fix a Hacker Attack

After a computer has been hacked it can never be trusted again. So say the pros, and security expert Steve Gibson, of GRC.com, in particular.

"There is no way to know what might have been altered or changed. Any component could be Trojaned, or TimeBombed, or anything. The only thing to do if you want to *ever* be able to really trust your machine again is to wipe it and start over," says Gibson.

There, you heard it from the man himself. Gibson is one of America's pre-eminent computer security experts.

A Trojan, of course, is a nasty piece of malware that looks harmless but has a program inside that can give someone outside your system remote access or it can contain a virus or spyware. And *TimeBombed*? That's just malware on a timer, set to go off at some future time.

caution

If you've been visited by a hacker, you might wonder if you absolutely have to wipe your computer clean and start fresh. If the computer is just used for games or general recreation and no lifestyle critical tasks, maybe you don't need to. Be sure to continue to scan for viruses and spyware, however, and to install a firewall. That said, if you do your banking on your computer and keep personal files and valuable data on it, the idea of having someone return and rifle through it again is rather distressing. If it were me, I'd wipe and start clean just for peace of mind.

Steps You Can Take Immediately After Being Hacked

If you think a hacker has been on your system and you want to take some instant security measures, here are steps you can take to reduce the risk of further visits.

Disconnect While You Assess

The first measure you can take that's instantly effective against a hacker is to disconnect the computer from the Internet. If you have a high-speed Internet connection, locate your modem, usually a box connected to your phone line or cable wire, and turn it off.

Install a Firewall

You have three options when it comes to firewalls:

- Turn on the Windows Firewall

- Install a third-party firewall

- Install a home network router that has built-in firewall capabilities

I detail how to do this at the end of this chapter. On **p. 101**, you'll see how to turn on the Windows Firewall or how to install a third-party software firewall. On **p. 109**, I detail how to install a hardware firewall, which is built into a home network router.

Assess the Damage

Scan your system with your anti-spyware and antivirus programs to see if anything strange has been installed on your computer. Be sure to update your virus and spyware signatures first. You'll have to turn your Internet connection back on (briefly) to update these.

Also look for any new data that has been added or changed. To search for changes, use the Windows search function, following these steps:

- Click Start, Search, and choose All Files and Folders on the left. Leave the All or Part of the File Name and A Word or Phrase in the File fields blank. In the Look In: field, choose My Computer.

- Then click When Was It Modified? and select Specify Dates. From the drop-down box you can choose Modified Date to see files that have been changed. To see files that have been opened and examined, choose Accessed Dates and use Created Date to see new files. Set the From and To dates to the period you are interested in; typically just look at the previous 24 hours.

- Then click Search. A list of the files you've requested begin to show up in the right pane.

This search process might freak you out, especially if you choose Accessed Date, because you'll see many files listed that have been accessed in a 24-hour period.

Remember that Windows accesses many files by itself, even when your computer is idle. So this is not indicative of hacker activity. However, Created Date and Modified Date settings might be useful in determining what files have be created or changed.

Wipe the System and Start Fresh

Remember that wiping your system and restoring it is the best way to start fresh and give yourself piece of mind. It's not a simple task, so steel yourself for a bit of hard work.

You need either a Windows installation CD from a store or the installation CD provided by your computer maker. It might have provided a full copy of Windows or a restore disk that wipes your computer and sets it back to the way it was the day you bought it, including all the preloaded software.

I detail the step-by-step procedure for wiping and restoring your system in Chapter 9, starting on **p. 249**.

If you own a Mac, which uses the Mac OS X operating system, be sure to make a backup of all your personal data to CD or DVD first and then follow these steps:

1. Insert the Mac OS X Install Disc 1 CD and double-click the Install Mac OS X icon.

2. Follow the onscreen instructions. In the panel where you select the destination disk, select your current Mac OS X disk (in most cases, it is the only one available).

3. Click Options. If you want to save your existing files, users, and network settings, select Archive and Install, and then select Preserve Users and Network Settings. If you want to erase everything on your computer—and this is recommended to ensure you are completely starting fresh—select Erase and Install. Note that you can't recover erased data.

4. Click Continue. Then click Install to perform a basic installation.

5. After installation, be sure to re-install any programs you might have wiped out from their original installation CDs.

6. Update the operating system with any updates provided by Apple.

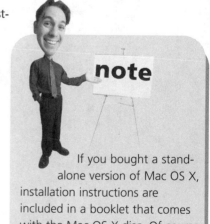

If you bought a standalone version of Mac OS X, installation instructions are included in a booklet that comes with the Mac OS X disc. Of course, if you need additional help with Mac OS X, I highly recommend picking up a copy of Que's *Easy Mac OS X, v10.4 Tiger*.

After scrubbing your Mac, check the Mac OS for any updates since you originally installed it. Here's how:

1. Open System Preferences and click Software Update.

2. Select Check for Updates.

3. From the pop-up menu, choose Daily, Weekly, or Monthly.

4. If you want your Mac to download important updates automatically, select Download Important Updates in the Background. When the update finishes downloading, you are notified that it is ready to be installed.

5. When the installation is finished, Software Update looks for updates one more time. This is because some updates require the presence of previous updates before they can install.

Batten down the Hatches—10-Minute Tactics

The simplest way to defend your computer quickly against hackers is to use a firewall. So let's look at your two fastest options. Either can be done in 10 minutes.

Turn on Windows Firewall

If you have Windows XP's Service Pack 2 installed, your Windows Firewall is probably already turned on. Here's how to check:

1. Click Start and then click Control Panel.

2. In the Control Panel, click Windows Security Center.

3. Click Windows Firewall (see Figure 3.7).

4. Click the button next to On (Recommended) and click OK. The firewall is turned on.

tip

If you run Windows 95, 98, or Me, there is no built-in firewall, but you can install a free third-party firewall such as ZoneAlarm or SyGate.

If you haven't already installed SP2, you need to do that soon. In the meantime, the original version of XP does include Windows Firewall. Though it's inferior to the SP2 edition, it's better than nothing until you can get SP2 installed. Here's how to activate it:

1. Click Start, Control Panel, Network and Internet Connections, and then click Network Connections.

2. If you don't see Network and Internet Connections, click Switch to Category View (on the left side of the Control Panel window).

3. Highlight the connection you want to protect by clicking on it once. Then click Change Settings of This Connection from the list on the left. If you use a high-speed Internet connection, such as a cable modem or digital subscriber line (DSL) service (high speed Internet from your phone company), look for Local Area Connection.

4. Click the Advanced tab and then click the Protect My Computer and Network by Limiting or Preventing Access to This Computer from the Internet check box.

FIGURE 3.7

You find access to Windows Firewall in the Security Center applet in Control Panel, if Windows XP Service Pack 2 is installed.

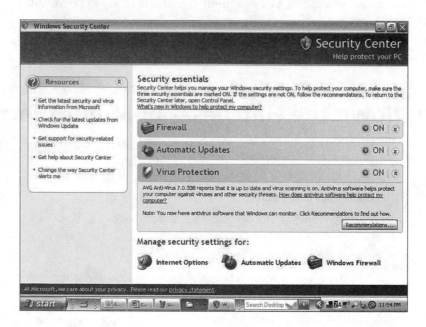

Activate the Firewall on a Mac OS X System

The latest operating system from Apple, called Mac OS X, comes with a software firewall that's turned off. You can switch it on by going to System Preferences, Sharing, Firewall, and clicking on the Start button.

WHEN THE WINDOWS FIREWALL IS OPTIONAL

If your computer connects through a wire to your high-speed modem, which in turn connects to the Internet, I highly recommend that you use a firewall to protect your computer. However, there are other circumstances where the Windows Firewall is optional:

■ **Wireless connection**—If you use a wireless connection to connect to the Internet, you are going through a box called a home Internet router. This has a built-in firewall, so turning on the Windows Firewall is unnecessary because you are already protected. Turning on the Windows Firewall as an additional measure won't hurt, however.

- **Dial-up connection**—If you use a dial-up connection to get on the Internet (meaning your computer's modem uses a phone line to dial your Internet service), when it is not connected a hacker cannot get on the computer.

  The other quirk about this is that your computer changes its Internet Protocol (IP) address each time it dials up the Net. That's the numerical address that other computers on the Internet use to send you data. It would be difficult for a hacker to find you repeatedly because your IP address changes when you use a dial-up service. Conventional wisdom says that a Windows Firewall is unnecessary on a dial-up connection.

  However, turning on the Windows Firewall as an additional measure won't hurt and it could double as a measure against Internet worms, but your antivirus program should be sufficient to catch those.

- **Third-party firewall**—If you already have a software firewall installed, such as ZoneAlarm, SyGate, or Norton Firewall, it's not necessary to also use Windows Firewall.

Wall off the World—Install a Better Firewall in an Afternoon

More advanced firewalls can be time-consuming to install, but they are not difficult to use. Take the time to fortify your defenses. It is really worthwhile.

Install a Two-way Software Firewall

Installing a third-party firewall gives you two-way protection. It stops hackers and worms from coming into your computer from the Internet. And if your computer becomes infected, it stops worms, spyware, and viruses from communicating out to the Internet.

I recommend two free third-party firewalls: SyGate from www.sygate.com and ZoneAlarm from www.zonealarm.com.

Here's how to install the free version of ZoneAlarm, my favorite:

tip

If you already have Norton Firewall or McAfee Firewall, these programs are as good as the pro versions of the free firewalls recommended in this chapter.

1. Use Internet Explorer or Firefox to visit www.zonealarm.com.

2. Choose Home/Office Products from the left menu (see Figure 3.8) and then choose ZoneAlarm from the list of products.

FIGURE 3.8

ZoneLabs makes a free version of ZoneAlarm available for personal use and to charities.

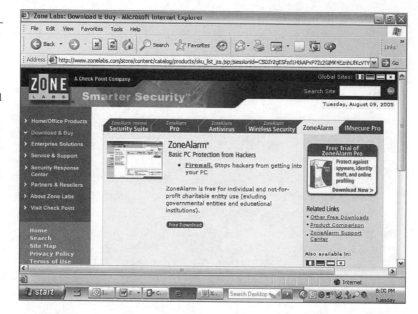

3. On the ZoneAlarm page click the Free Download button and choose the link that says Download Free ZoneAlarm.

4. You are presented with a pop-up window (if you are using Internet Explorer) that says Run or Save. Choose Run.

5. You might get a security warning box. Click Run. The program begins to install (see Figure 3.9).

FIGURE 3.9

When ZoneAlarm downloads you might get a security warning. It's OK to click Run and let the download proceed.

6. Choose a folder to install ZoneAlarm in. The suggested folder is fine (see Figure 3.10). Click Next.

7. Type in your name, company (optional), and email address. In Chapter 5, "Spam: Unwanted Email from Hell," which is about spam, I always recommend you use a secondary email address for things like this. I'll leave the decision up to you.

FIGURE 3.10

The first thing
you see when
ZoneAlarm starts
to install is the
option to change
the folder where
it will install.
The default
folder is fine.

8. ZoneLabs promises not to misuse your email
   address (but I trust no one). Choose not to
   receive news and updates (and an excuse to
   market to you), but do choose to register so
   you can download updates.

9. Choose Next and read the license agreement. Note that it offers the free version to
   individuals for personal use and not for
   profit charities. Accept the terms by checking the box and click Install.

10. The program installs itself and before start-
    ing it asks you some optional survey ques-
    tions. Afterwards, choose to start
    ZoneAlarm by clicking Yes on the box that
    pops up.

11. If your Windows Firewall is turned on, you are asked if Windows Firewall
    should keep blocking ZoneAlarm (see Figure 3.11). Ironic, don't you think?
    Choose unblock. After ZoneAlarm is installed, be sure Windows Firewall
    is off.

note

Steve Gibson, of
GRC.com, coined the term
spyware when a program on his
computer started to communicate
out to the Internet as he was testing an early version of ZoneAlarm.

FIGURE 3.11

Windows
Firewall tries to
block the
ZoneAlarm
installation.
Click Unblock to
let it proceed.

12. Next the install asks if you want to use the free version of ZoneAlarm or the 15-day trial version of ZoneAlarm Pro. Choose ZoneAlarm unless you think the extra features are worthwhile. Personally, I think the pro version is great if you're willing to pay for it. But for these purposes, choose Select ZoneAlarm and click Next, and then click Finish to configure the program.

13. At the Welcome screen, click Next and choose Yes (Recommended) to configure ZoneAlarm with your Internet connection. Click Next and then Done.

14. You are asked to reboot your computer, so close all your running programs and click the OK button to restart.

15. When the system reboots, ZoneAlarm runs and you see a little icon in your System Tray (bottom right) that shows whether it is dormant or active (see Figure 3.12). When it's dormant, it shows as a red Z and yellow A. When data is flowing in and out of the computer, it changes to look like a moving audio meter.

FIGURE 3.12

ZoneAlarm shows up as an item in the Windows System Tray in the bottom-right corner of the screen.

ZoneAlarm is running

16. When a program tries to access the Internet from your computer you see a pop-up alarm (see Figure 3.13). If this program is known to you, choose Yes and choose Remember This Setting so you're not bugged again next time you run that program. It is normal for some programs to use the Internet to check for updates (especially antivirus programs and anti-spyware software), but you'll be surprised how many programs will try to communicate with the Internet.

FIGURE 3.13

ZoneAlarm asks you for input when a program on your computer that is not recognized tries to access the Internet.

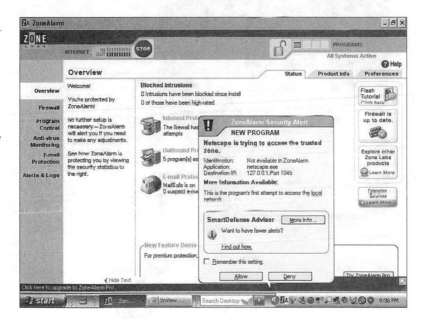

17. Of course, if something weird tries to communicate with the Internet and ZoneAlarm alerts you, choose No and block it. ZoneAlarm should give you a sense of what it is, so record that information and then do either a virus and/or spyware scan or research the program on the Internet to try to figure out what it is. It might be a background Windows process and could be legitimate, but it's worth finding out.

18. You'll have to suffer these for a few days until all the programs that access the Internet are caught by ZoneAlarm and approved by you. Then you shouldn't be bugged much after that until you install new programs or there's a legitimate infection that is caught by the firewall. You'll also start receiving security alerts if you change ZoneAlarm's security settings. For instance, if you change the security level from medium to high, ZoneAlarm starts pestering you again about programs accessing the Internet. It's annoying, but a necessary evil.

19. You might see inbound attacks, too. Most of these could be hackers scanning for opportunities or worms trying to access your computer. Because you've

seen the alert, you are protected (see Figure 3.14) and don't need to take any further action. There is an option for more info, however, if you are interested.

FIGURE 3.14

Incoming attempts to access your computer are shown in a pop-up alert by ZoneAlarm. This inbound contact is coming from a computer on the same home network.

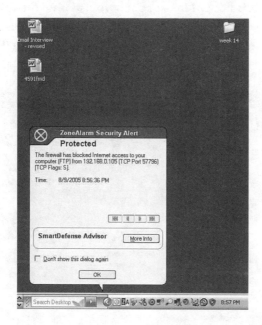

20. If the alerts become too annoying, turn them off by opening ZoneAlarm, clicking Alerts & Logs (on the left side), and choosing Off (see Figure 3.15), although I think the button should say Shut Up, You Are Driving Me Crazy.

FIGURE 3.15

Thankfully, you can turn the inbound alerts off in ZoneAlarm because they will eventually drive you bonkers.

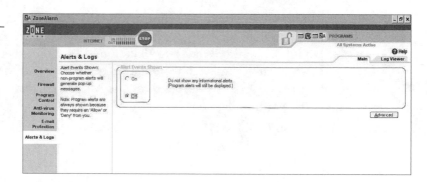

DOUBLE YOUR DEFENSE WITH A DOUBLE FIREWALL

If you have a home network router, your computer and other computers on the network (such as your spouse's laptop and your children's computer) are protected from the outside world.

However, you are not protected from the computers inside the router. So you might want to leave on the Windows Firewall or a two-way firewall such as ZoneAlarm on your computer. Here's why:

- Maybe your children or roommates have their own computers and they regularly infect it with spyware or viruses.

- A friend or family member sometimes comes over with an infected laptop and connects it to your home network.

- You leave your wireless network unsecured and a wireless network snoop connects and exposes your computers on the network to viruses, spyware, or their own curiosity (Learn more about wireless network snoops in Chapter 6, "Wireless Network Snoops: Lock Down Your Wi-Fi Network," on **p. 151**.)

Install a Hardware Firewall

For sheer firewall simplicity, I recommend installing a home network router with built-in network address translation (NAT) firewall capabilities (discussed earlier in this chapter on **p. 95**.

Some things to keep in mind when it comes to a NAT firewall are

- It does not use any memory on your computer, so the firewall is invisible.

- It works silently to defend your network. You'll never see pop-ups, alerts, or other annoyances.

- It stops inbound threats but won't stop outbound nasties that might be on your computer.

To take advantage of a NAT firewall, you need to buy an Internet-sharing device called a home network router from any one of several well-known vendors, including

- **D-Link**—www.dlink.com

- **Netgear**—www.netgear.com

- **Linksys**—www.linksys.com

- **Belkin**—www.belkin.com

> **tip**
>
> If you would like to check your firewall's defenses, check out Steve Gibson's free firewall test called ShieldsUP! It's an excellent and well-documented online test available at www.grc.com that runs tests against your computer or home network and explains in careful detail where you are vulnerable.

- **SMC**—www.smc.com
- **Apple**—www.apple.com

These routers will cost you about $60 or less (unless you choose Apple's Airport Extreme and then you're in for $200). A router connects to your high-speed Internet modem from either your cable TV or telephone company and shares that connection with several computers in your home. Your computer(s) in turn connect to the router via network cables or using a wireless connection (also known as Wi-Fi).

The router configuration is fairly straightforward. When you set the device up, there is a walk-through wizard that configures your computers and the router so they work together. Both Macs and PCs can co-exist on a router together and even share files with each other.

When you install the network, you need settings from your Internet provider to input into the router during setup. Be sure to check Chapter 6, starting on **p. 151**, to learn about wireless network snoops and how to configure your router to be secure. After the router is set up and running and you can connect to the Internet with your computer(s), there's nothing further to do. That NAT firewall runs automatically.

tip

If you choose a wireless connection, most new laptops have built-in capabilities for this. You can, however, buy wireless adapter cards for both a PC and laptop without built-in wireless.

tip

If the idea of setting up a router scares the ham out of your sandwich, you should check out Mark Edward Soper's excellent book called *Absolute Beginner's Guide to Home Networking*.

THE ABSOLUTE MINIMUM

- Among geeks, the word *hacker* has many definitions, including a good programmer, a bad programmer, or a person that modifies technology hardware. In the mass media, it's a person that accesses a computer they don't own without permission.

- A cracker is what computer break-in artists called themselves, but we call them hackers.

- Crackers' motivations are varied. They hack to steal, to protest, to make money, to terrorize to prove a point, or—as George Mallory said about Mount Everest and a very nice donut earlier that day—"because it's there."

- Personal computers are usually hacked so they can be turned into zombies and be remote controlled to attack other computers, used as a storage for illicit information, or used to send spam. Sometimes they are hacked by identity thieves who steal personal financial information.

- Windows XP has a built-in firewall. When installed, Service Pack 2 turns it on for you.

- A third-party firewall is a program that acts as an electronic wall on a computer to stop inbound traffic and, usually, outbound communication that contain viruses, spyware, and other malicious programs.

- A hardware firewall is a device that blocks inbound traffic from the Internet. Network address translation technology in a home router provides a firewall function.

- It's hard to tell if you have been hacked. The only way to have complete peace of mind after you have been hacked is to wipe your computer clean and start fresh.

- You should ensure you have at least one firewall—either hardware or software—turned on, protecting your computer from viruses and worms.

4

IDENTITY THIEVES AND PHISHERS: PROTECT YOUR GOOD NAME AND BANK ACCOUNT

This chapter explains how the Internet is playing a part in one of the largest growing crime trends in the world: identity theft. It also demystifies phishing, an Internet-powered phenomenon used to steal your identity by tricking you into giving up personal information. And there's a warning about pharming, which is phishing with a bigger net. But never phear, the chapter gives you phoolproof tricks to phight back!

What Is Identity Theft?

If you wanted to pretend you were me, what would it take to fool my devastatingly gorgeous girlfriend? Well, you'd need to learn to walk, talk, and look like me. Plus you'd need plastic surgery to web up your toes like mine (my grandmother said I'd never drown!). And you'd have to be a good kisser. It would take some effort.

But if you wanted to convince my bank that you were me, it wouldn't be quite as difficult. You'd need my wallet, my address, a good forged driver's license, and certainly the ability to sign like me. It would be an easier impersonation, but still would take some effort.

But what if you had my online banking user ID and password and an Internet connection? You could log on to the Web as if you were me and then it would be bye-bye savings account and the $637.34 in it.

That's what's called *simple identity theft*. You obtain the electronic keys to my digital piggybank, smash it open, and disappear into the bits and bytes flowing across the Internet. But identity theft can be more complex. It's not always just a smash and grab proposition.

It starts with a thief obtaining your personal information, such as your name, Social Security number, credit card numbers, or other identifying information. They then get financial and identity tools issued to them in your name, including bank accounts, checks, and even government-issued documents. Think of it as creating a clone of a person's paper trail.

A crook can then apply for credit and nurture and protect the accounts, perhaps even making small payments to generate more credit. They might do this over the course of two to three years to generate a decent credit portfolio.

The big pay off comes when they cash out, making a purchase worth $20,000 to $100,000 and then disappear, leaving you on the hook to pay off the debt and deal with a devastated credit history.

Some identity theft basics are discussed next. Later in the chapter, specific technology threats that impact identity theft are covered.

Techniques Thieves Use to Steal Your Identity

Identity thieves use a myriad techniques to steal your identity. To start, all they need is some initial seed information to build on.

Think about the kind of information organizations ask you for when you apply for anything: perhaps a membership, say with your health club; a financial tool such as a credit card or bank account; or even an entry for a contest.

The basics would be your name, address, and phone number. While this information can be publicly available to anyone who cares to look, you become vulnerable when a potential identity thief can pair it with more detailed information about you. Your birth date might be common knowledge among your friends and family but no one else needs to know. Be careful about providing any piece of identification or information that wouldn't be listed publicly.

After a thief has gathered the basics on you and has one critical identity tool, such as a driver's license number or Social Security number, they can then use that to research more information about you and create an identity document. What they do is build a portfolio on you until they have enough information to apply for a credit or financial tool in your name.

After they have that, all they need to do is use the tool and nurture it. They'll make deposits and withdrawals in an account. Or use a credit card to make modest payments and pay off the balance. This can go on for months. Slowly they build up creditworthiness that allows them to apply for more credit.

The endgame is to create such a large credit facility that they can cash out. They'll extract the most money they can out of the credit tools they have nurtured and leave you on the hook. When the credit-offering organization attempts to collect, they will come to you and not the thief because by their records it looks like you are the one who has been using its credit services.

How They Become You: Identity Theft Techniques

According to the U.S. Federal Trade Commission, here's how thieves get their hands on your identity:

- They steal or buy information from insiders at businesses that keep records on you.
- They engage in dumpster diving, where they retrieve information and documents from the garbage.
- They illicitly gain access to credit reports using tools available at their workplace.
- They scoop your credit or debit card information using a special electronic tool when a credit card transaction is processed. This is called *skimming*.
- They snatch purses or steal wallets.
- They steal mail that contains financial or tax information. Sometimes this is achieved by redirecting your mail to a new address.
- During a burglary, information and documents are stolen from your home.
- A scam artist fools you into filling out what seems like a legitimate form or survey that reveals personal information.
- They steal a person's identity after their death by applying for a replacement birth certificate, especially if a person died in a different jurisdiction from where they were born.

Preventative Measures: How to Not Become a Victim

Avoiding identity theft takes just a few slight adjustments in the way you run your life. Here are some tips:

- Avoid providing personal information to anyone you don't know or who doesn't have a pressing need for it.

- Safeguard your identification numbers such as driver's license, Social Security, or passport number. Only provide them when absolutely necessary and to verified employees of organizations that request them.

- Your Social Security number is the key that unlocks all of your personal information. Guard it like it is the last chocolate because it's precious. It's the virtual key to your personal vault of information.

- Destroy with a shredder all unneeded documents that contain personal information, especially old bank account statements, financial records, and discarded or incomplete application forms. Make sure you destroy your junk mail, too, if it has personal address information on it.

- Keep an eye on your credit report. Later in this chapter I list all the credit bureaus in key countries around the world where identity theft is rife. Check with your credit bureau annually at a minimum and better, every quarter, to see what credit activity is being tracked against your name.

- Simplify your financial life. Keep only one or two credit cards on hand so it's easier to track those accounts. Cancel credit and bank accounts you don't need.

- Photocopy the contents of your wallet or purse and keep those documents in a safe place. If your wallet is stolen, you'll have a record of everything that is in there.

- Pay your bills electronically. Minimizing a paper trail reduces the risk that paper documents won't fall into the hands of the wrong people.

- Never give out your credit card number on the phone or in an email. Only deal with people and organizations you trust.

Signs You're a Victim

Victims often don't know they have become victims of identity theft until it's too late. Here are some signs you might already be a victim or might be at risk:

- Strange items on your credit card statements or activity in your financial or other accounts you don't recognize.

- A call from a collection agency demanding payment for a debt you didn't incur.

- New accounts created on your credit record for which you haven't applied.

- A declined credit application, even though you believe your credit is good.

- Strangely missing or stolen identity documents or records.

- A call from law enforcement about a crime that has been committed that they believe you have been involved in or traffic citations for offenses you didn't commit. Someone may be using your ID to represent themselves to authorities.

What to Do If You're an Identity Theft Victim

You're going to be very busy if you discover you have been victimized by an identity thief. Clearing your name is not easy and can take a lot of time. Some key steps you should take to make the process easier are

1. Immediately make contact with the fraud departments of the credit bureaus in your country. There's a list on **p. 131**. The bureaus can place a fraud alert on your accounts and ask creditors to call you before they open new accounts in your name. Ask for credit reports so you can track the abuse.

2. Close or suspend your tainted accounts. Contact your credit card company and bank to report your ATM or credit card stolen. Have your bank stop payment on stolen checks and contact its check verification companies.

3. Call your local police department and file a report with details about the fraud. Provide the police with as much documentation as you can. Credit bureaus might only take action if you can provide them with a copy of your police report.

> **tip**
>
> There are some really good identity theft resources available at www.consumer.gov/idtheft/consumer_helpfullinks.html. They are United States–centric, but even those outside the U.S. will find much of the information useful. Also have a look at www.idtheftcenter.org, especially the detailed Victim Guide at www.idtheftcenter.org/vg17A.shtml.

4. Have all identity documents reissued by government and other issuing organizations.

5. In the United States, file a complaint with the Federal Trade Commission. This can be done online at www.consumer.gov/idtheft/. It maintains a database of ID theft cases for federal investigators. In other countries find out if there is a government body that tracks identity theft and file a complaint with it, if possible.

What Is Phishing?

Phishing is a technique used by identity thieves to steal your personal information, usually so they can gain access to financial accounts.

To understand phishing, let's consider what fishing is. A fisherman casts a line out in the water repeatedly with a lure attached. The lure is a deceiving piece of gear that looks like a tasty smaller fish, but it's actually a nasty hook. Eventually, the lure catches the attention of a fish, which then bites it. The fooled fish is then reeled in on a hook and meets its demise in a frying pan with a sprig of dill.

Phishing is kind of the same, but without the dill. The phisher uses email (or sometimes a pop-up message on the Web) as his lure. He casts out zillions of emails that are designed to trick the recipients into giving up personal information such as user IDs and passwords used to access their bank accounts.

Phishers use a variety of emails to fool their unsuspecting victims. One of the most common is the email that claims to be from a business or organization you deal with: perhaps your Internet service provider, an online payment service, or a government agency. Very often phishers pretend to be your bank.

According to the website www.antiphishing.org, the term *phishing* was coined circa 1996 by hackers who were stealing America Online accounts from AOL members. The buzzword was first used on the alt.2600 hacker newsgroup in January 1996, says the site, adding that it might have been used earlier in the printed edition of the hacker newsletter *2600*.

The email includes realistic company branding and logos and reads like typical communication from the real institution (see Figure 4.1). This sometimes includes, ironically, warnings about protecting yourself from fraud.

Notice that this email, purportedly from a legitimate banking institution, asks the recipient to enter sensitive, personal information—something reputable banks do not request via email. The email asks for validation of personal information including account numbers, user IDs, and passwords. It asks you to click on an included link that takes you to the institution's website so you can enter your information. Of course, it also looks exactly like the institution's website, but it, too, is bogus.

Although many phishers pretend to be major global banks, they have been known to use regional credit unions and community banks. Among other favorites are online companies such as eBay or PayPal (see Figure 4.2).

This email appears to be from Washington Mutual. Clicking on the link, however, would lead to a website run by a phisher, who is trying to gather personal banking information.

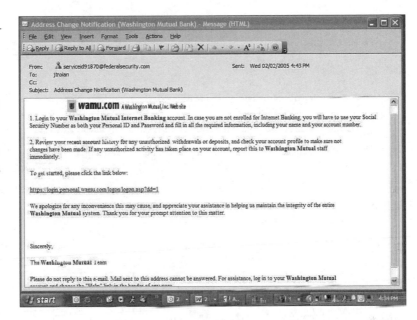

This email looks like it came from eBay, an online auction website. However, it secretly directs the recipient to a website with a Russian web address.

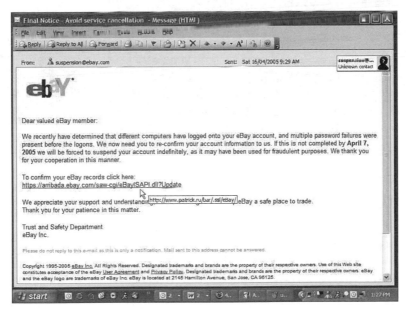

Notice that this email redirects to a suspicious website address in Russia and not eBay. The consequences to not providing the requested information are fairly dire and are a good indicator that this email isn't what it seems.

PHISH FINDER: IDENTIFYING PHISHING EMAILS

Here are some tips you can use to help identify emails from phishers, as suggested by the Anti-Phishing Working Group at www.antiphishing.org:

- Phishers use false statements in the email they send to you, hoping they will upset or excite you, and that you'll react immediately to their request. They might threaten dire consequences if you don't respond, such as terminating an account or instituting a steep fee for reactivation of the account. If the consequences to not replying or acquiescing to their demands seems unnecessarily steep, contact the real organization in question, via phone or email, and ask if this email is theirs.

- They will ask for things such as usernames, passwords, credit card numbers, Social Security numbers, name, address, and other personal data. You will never be asked to provide this kind of information via email.

- Phishing emails are rarely personalized. They rarely address you by name in the text of the email. Valid emails from your bank or e-commerce company generally do.

How Does Phishing Work?

A phisher's email looks like it has been sent from an organization you trust, such as your bank, but of course, it hasn't been. The trickery is achieved using a technique called *spoofing*, which is a techie term that basically means to electronically fool. Phishers use a series of tricks to deceive you and make you think you are corresponding with a legitimate organization. Here's how they do it.

Email Address Spoofing

First off, phishers change the sender's address in an email to make it appear as if your bank and not a tongue-pierced kid in a dumpy apartment in Warsaw sent the correspondence. This is done by simply changing the coding in the header of the email (see Figure 4.3). The header is a set of information roughly equivalent to the address information written on an envelope.

caution

Phishers are starting to use spyware to collect personal and financial information by employing a key logger. That's a program slipped onto your computer via a surreptitious web download or installed by a freebie program that can capture what you type on your computer. This information is grabbed by the bad guy across the Internet. The best defense against this is the use of one or more good anti-spyware programs. Learn more in Chapter 2, "Spyware: Overrun by Advertisers, Hijackers, and Opportunists."

Spoofed return address

FIGURE 4.3

This email header was taken from a phishing email that purported to be from eBay. The phisher has changed the From: field to make it look like it came from the email address suspension@ ebay.com.

Imagine if you sent your best friend a letter by mail but instead of putting your own return address on it, you put the return address of his angry ex-wife's lawyer. On receiving it he might freak out because he'd think that she might be trying to make a claim on his new golf clubs. All you've done is spoofed the return address.

Link Spoofing

The links you are urged to click on in some phishing emails are also spoofed. In the case of web address spoofing, the link looks like a legitimate address, but through some very simple technology redirects to another link.

The phishing email is created with a programming language used to create web pages. In fact, when you receive an email with pictures, fancy fonts, and a nice layout, it is what's called an HTML email. It looks exactly like a web page because it is made with HTML—the same programming language used to create web pages. HTML is short for HyperText Markup Language.

> **tip**
>
> Some email programs give you the ability to see the destination website of a link in an email before you click it. For example, in Outlook 2003, if you hover your mouse over a link inside an email, the destination address appears in a floating yellow box. In Outlook Express, this address appears in the status bar across the bottom of the window.

To create a clickable link in HTML, you use programming code like this:

```
<a href="http://www.realsafebank.com">www.reallysafebank.com</a>
```

This results in a web link that looks like this:

www.reallysafebank.com

Note that the web address inside the angle brackets between the quotes and after the `<a href=` is the web address where you are taken if you click on the link (see Figure 4.4).

Phishers use this programming trick to make it appear as if you are going to one site, but really they put the address of a bogus page in the `href` tag, like this:

```
<a href="http://www.bogusbank.com">www.
reallysafebank.com</a>
```

So you think you're about to go to www.reallysafebank.com but you're actually taken to www.bogusbank.com, which looks like your legitimate bank's webpage and might actually contain a series of web pages to make it look like an actual banking site.

tip

You can see the source code (and linking information) of an HTML email in Outlook 2003 by opening the email and right-clicking in the body of the message. A View Source option appears. If you click on this option, the HTML source code opens in Notepad.

FIGURE 4.4

These two actual web links look exactly the same but the programming used to create them, which appears below each one, have different destinations on the Web.

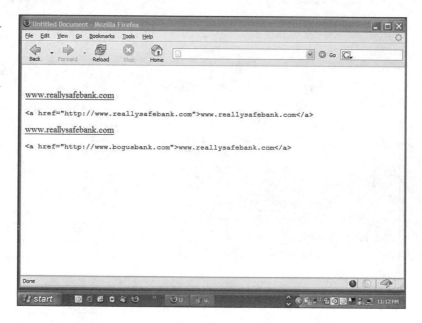

Web Address Spoofing

Phishers have been exploiting a bug (an error) in the programming of Microsoft web browser Internet Explorer so they can display a fake web address in the browser. When you visit a website that exploits this bug, its web address is not displayed in the browser. Instead, another more trustworthy web address is displayed.

So you could be fooled into visiting www. bogusbank.com by a phishing email but your web browser shows you are on www. reallysafebank.com.

The bug affects versions 5.01, 5.5, and 6 of Internet Explorer. However, patches for the vulnerable browser have been issued by Microsoft to fix it. If you run Windows Update and download the latest patches, you will have the patch already installed.

tip

You can tell which version of Microsoft's Internet Explorer you have on your computer by starting the program, clicking the Help menu, and then clicking About Internet Explorer.

To test if you are vulnerable, open Internet Explorer and visit security firm Secunia.com at http://secunia.com/internet_explorer_address_bar_spoofing_ test/. If your web browser is not up-to-date with the latest Microsoft fix, you'll see how the spoofing trick works and a fake address appears in your address bar. If the bug is fixed in your browser, you'll see "This page cannot be displayed."

What Is Pharming?

Even if you think phishing scams are as obvious as angry cats, there's one scary new form of scam that even an expert can be fooled by. It's a technique called *pharming* that, when perpetrated, is invisible to web surfers until it's too late.

caution

Sometimes there is a form to fill out directly inside a phishing email. If filled out, this sends your information directly to a phisher's server. No intermediary fake website is necessary.

In a nutshell, here's what happens: You tell your web browser to open a website. It is secretly directed to a fake website that looks just like the original. And this all happens without any clue that you're being duped.

To understand how pharming works, pretend that surfing the Internet is like visiting the zoo with your niece.

You say to her, "What shall we see first?"

She says, "Let's go see the monkeys!"

So you take her up to the information booth and the nice information officer tells you to follow the banana signs. So you both follow the banana signs until you get to the monkey house.

That's kind of how the Internet works now. When you type a web address into your web browser, your browser makes contact with a domain name service (DNS) server, which is a kind of Internet information booth. The browser gives the DNS machine the destination requested. And in turn the DNS server (like the information booth officer) looks it up in the DNS cache. What comes back is a numerical address called an Internet Protocol (IP) address. The web browser uses the IP address to contact the correct server (a computer that contains a website) you want to visit.

In the case of pharming, the information booth officer has been fooled. He's been given the wrong map by the evil marketing guy at the zoo who wants everyone to go to the gift shop. So when you ask for directions to the monkey house, the information officer looks at his map and sees that the monkey house can be found by following the cabbage signs. That doesn't seem right, but that's what the map says so those are the directions he gives you. (Actually the DNS server isn't smart enough to question the information. It just hands it out.) So you end up at the gift shop. To further the scam, the gift shop might even be decorated like the monkey house with banana wallpaper and stuffed monkeys.

caution

There's not much you can do as an individual to defend against pharming. It's a problem being dealt with by Internet service providers and the telecommunications companies and organizations that own the DNS equipment on the Internet.

Pharmers poison a DNS server by changing its cache so it stores the wrong IP addresses (see Figure 4.5). So when you browse to your bank's web page, the DNS server that translates your bank's dotcom address will hand back the wrong IP address. Your web browser takes you to a fake bank site that looks like your bank but is run by a pharmer.

FIGURE 4.5

Pharmers can poison a DNS server with a bad IP number so when your web browser asks for the correct numerical Internet address of your bank (for example), it gets sent the IP address of a fake bank site.

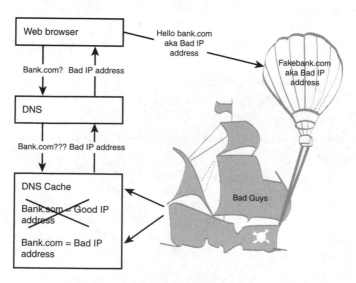

Web browser

Bank.com?   Bad IP address

DNS

Bank.com??? Bad IP address

DNS Cache

Bank.com = Good IP address

Bank.com = Bad IP address

Hello bank.com aka Bad IP address

Fakebank.com aka Bad IP address

Bad Guys

What's alarming about pharming (besides that awful rhyme) is that it can cause a large group of innocent people to be herded off to bogus websites and scammed. Even scarier, during this process your browser displays that you are visiting a correct site even though it's bogus.

LOOK OUT FOR 419 SCAMS!

One of the most common email scams is what's called a Nigerian 419 scam or advanced fee fraud. It's named after a part of the Nigerian penal code (section 419) that relates to fraudulent schemes.

Here how it works: An email (although in the past mailed letters or faxes have been sent) arrives from someone outside your country, often claiming to be from Nigeria (see Figure 4.6) or some other African nation, and sometimes from other countries. The person sometimes portrays himself or herself as a family member of a deposed Nigerian powerbroker, a Nigerian oil executive, or some other person who has access to oodles of trapped cash.

The author admits that they don't know you, but explains there is a substantial amount of money squirreled away that needs to be moved. If you help, you can keep a big chunk of it, usually millions.

If you bite and open a correspondence with the scam artist, you're led by your email address down a path that results in a request for money. It could be for bribes, taxes, or other fees that the scammer needs to help lubricate the system so the money can be freed. After the first payment the correspondence abruptly stops or you're told complications have set in and a further request for funds is made. This continues until you're tapped out or you get wise. There are also stories (although I couldn't verify them) of victims traveling to Nigeria to help further the transaction and the trip ends with kidnapping, theft, and even murder.

To see a collection of Nigerian 419 letters, check out http://axiusnews.com/scampost/.

FIGURE 4.6

This example of a Nigerian 419 scam uses the guise of an English barrister representing a Nigerian national.

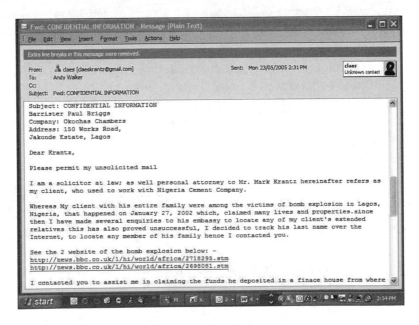

What Damage Can Be Done By Phishing?

Phishing and identity theft are scary threats because they can result in some severe consequences:

- **Financial loss**—The most likely result of phishing is being ripped off and losing the cash in your bank or financial account.

- **Bad credit**—If a wily phisher gets his hands on a credit vehicle such as a credit card or line of credit, he can put you into debt and leave you on the hook to pay the bill.

- **More severe identity theft**—Although phishing victims typically suffer a one-time hit, in which their bank account is drained, the acquisition of personal information could lead to more severe identity theft. People whose identities have been stolen can spend years trying to clean up the mess made of their good name and credit profile. It can lead to a huge disruption in lifestyle, financial loss, and even being wrongly accused of crimes they haven't committed.

Who Is at Risk? Everyone!

Anyone who has an email address or that uses the Internet is a potential victim of phishing scams. Victims of identity theft cross age and gender boundaries almost equally. Even children and teenagers have been targeted. Mac and PC users alike are at risk.

You don't even have to be alive to be a victim of identity theft. One particular insipid technique is what police call *tombstone shopping*. A crook searches for the death of a child, perhaps by researching deaths at a public library or even visiting a graveyard. The criminal looks for someone who was born in one jurisdiction and died in another. Then she applies for a birth certificate at the dead child's place of birth. After they have that document, a whole new individual can be resurrected on paper and applications for government identity documents can be made.

Don't Get Phished: 10-Minute Tactics to Stay Off the Hook

Phishing is an Internet threat that can be easily avoided with a little common sense and some simple technical know-how. Here are several anti-phishing techniques you can implement in about 10 minutes each.

They Won't Ask, You Don't Tell

Banks and other financial institutions are tuned into phishing scams, so they never ask you to verify your user ID, password, or other personal information via email. If you are in any doubt, call the bank or institution and ask. The best course of action is to communicate with the company directly by phone or in person and delete the email. Never reply to it.

Use Caution and Cut and Paste

If you ever receive an email that asks you to click an included link, the safest thing to do is to cut and paste that link directly into your web browser's address field. This is the best way to avoid being fooled by phishing emails.

Follow these steps to cut and paste a link:

1. Place your mouse to the left of the link, hold the left mouse button down, and drag to the right so the whole link is highlighted.

2. Go up to the Edit menu in your email program and choose Copy (using the shortcut key Ctrl+C also works).

3. Open your web browser. Click in the address field, click the Edit menu, and choose Paste (Ctrl+V also pastes the address).

4. Click Go to the right of the address field to load the link.

Communicate Securely

You will often have occasion to fill out a form on the web. When you do, be sure that the form is on a secure web page. These web pages use encrypted (scrambled) data. Anybody watching this data as it flows across the Internet sees a stream of nonsense information.

Here's how to check to see if you're on a secure web page:

- The web address of a secure page includes the prefix https://. Note the *s* in https://. Insecure sites begin with http://.

- When on a secure web page, your web browser displays a closed gold lock in the bottom-right corner of the browser window (see Figure 4.7). I hate to scare you but there is a minor problem with the lock icon. Phishers have been known to create clever emails that disguise the parts of the web browser with an overlay (a digital version of a sticker). They have

caution

Phishers are getting more sophisticated so it won't be long before they implement secure web pages themselves to extend the illusion, but a web page that asks for personal information with an unlocked symbol at the bottom of the browser is a very good indicator that a site is a phake.

done this before with the overlay of the address bar that shows a bank's real address masking the fake address underneath. This technique is easy to do over the lock icon, too. The way around it: Move the browser window. The overlay stays in place but the browser window moves.

FIGURE 4.7

A closed gold lock in the bottom-right hand side of Internet Explorer shows that the web page is secure and data sent from it is encrypted. It's inadvisable to make purchases from any website that isn't encrypted.

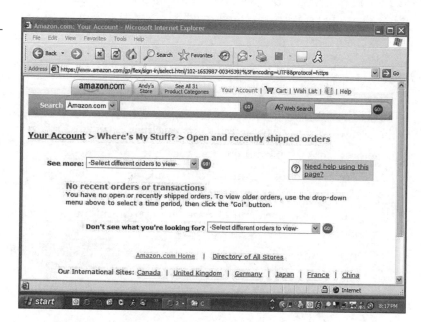

Install an Anti-spam Filter

Spam is unsolicited commercial email. It's the Internet equivalent of those letters addressed to Occupant that show up at your door offering furnace cleaning and raccoon removal.

I deal with anti-spam techniques in depth in Chapter 5, "Spam: Unwanted Email from Hell," but it is worth a mention here because spam filters can identify and filter phishing emails.

Of particular note is Cloudmark Desktop, a plug-in program that works with Microsoft Outlook and Microsoft Outlook Express. More than one million SafetyBar users flag email they consider spam with the program. That information is shared on a common server at Cloudmark. SafetyBar works by comparing each email that arrives in your inbox with the Cloudmark database (see Figure 4.8). If an email looks like spam, it's moved to a separate Spam folder in your email program or it's deleted (your choice).

The system also has an anti-fraud button with which SafetyBar users can mark phishing emails. These are filtered like spam by the program. And it comes with a plug-in for Internet Explorer. It warns you about unsafe websites as you surf.

The software (available at www.cloudmark. com) is not free, but is definitely worth the $39.95 annual fee.

Block Phishing Sites with NetCraft

A really good freebie program called NetCraft rates the website you are browsing and tells you how trustworthy it is (see Figure 4.9). It also blocks websites that it has identified as phishing sites. I highly recommend you install this program. It can be turned off when you don't need it, and turned on when you encounter a site of which you are unsure. The program comes in versions for both Firefox and Internet Explorer and is available from www.netcraft.com.

> **tip**
>
> To improve your browser security, I recommend that you install and use the Firefox web browser as much as possible. Although it has had some security problems (that were promptly fixed) in the past, it's much more secure than Microsoft's Internet Explorer web browser. Firefox can be downloaded free from www.mozilla.org and is available for the Mac, PC, and other computer platforms.

FIGURE 4.8

Cloudmark Desktop filters email in Outlook by cross-referencing inbound messages against a database of known spam and phishing emails.

Cloudmark Desktop

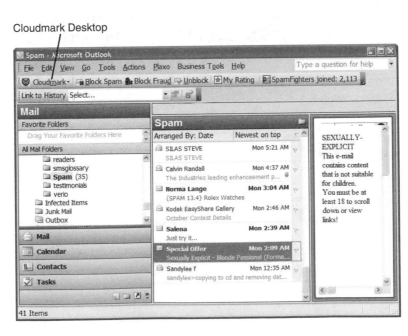

FIGURE 4.9

The NetCraft toolbar blocks a faked SouthTrust banking website, identifying it as a phishing site.

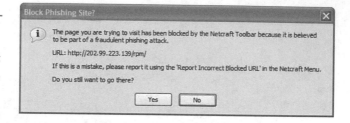

Carry a Big Spoofstick

You can install a free program called Spoofstick as an add-in (often called a plug-in) for your web browser that helps you identify if you're on a bogus website. The program displays the web address you're at in big text at the top of the web browser.

Some Internet crooks use slightly modified web addresses on their bogus sites. So if they faked my website Cyberwalker.com, they might set up a website called Cyberwaalker.com or Cyerwalker.com, two slightly misspelled addresses you might not notice. Spoofstick makes it easier to spot a spoofed website by jacking up the size of the text of the web address (see Figure 4.10).

FIGURE 4.10

On this faked SouthTrust website, the IP address (displayed in large font by the Spoofstick program) is a good indication that the site is a fake.

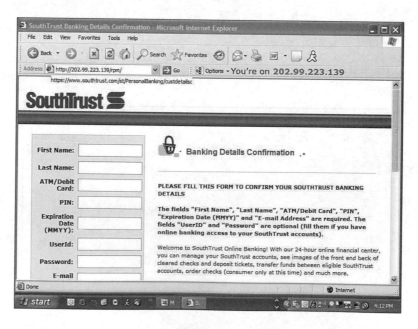

A common phishing practice is to send a user to a website using its IP address. A clue to a spoofed site would be the presence of the IP address in the address field of your browser instead of the dotcom name. Spoofstick makes this more obvious, too.

Spoofstick is free and available for both Internet Explorer and Firefox from www.corestreet.com/spoofstick/.

Keep Your Antivirus and Anti-Spyware Programs Up-to-Date

Many antivirus programs can detect malicious attachments that arrive via email. This includes Trojan horses and key loggers, two types of malicious software that install programs on your computer that can record your personal data and make it available to crooks via the Internet. So be sure to update your virus signatures by using the program's updater.

Anti-spyware programs, mentioned in Chapter 2, can also spot and block Trojan horses and key loggers.

Keep Your Computer Software Up-to-Date

Ensure that you keep your computer software up-to-date with the latest bug fixes. Both Microsoft and Apple issue regular security fixes via the Internet.

Microsoft issues its security fixes through the website http://windowsupdate. microsoft.com. This is also accessible by clicking the Windows Update icon on your Start menu.

Also check with the maker of your email program to ensure it is up-to-date with the latest security patches.

If you have Windows XP with Service Pack 2 (SP2), updates for your computer are downloaded automatically and you are alerted when they are read to be installed.

Ensure You Are You: Take an Afternoon to Protect Your Identity

Defending yourself against phishing is not hard to learn. What really is at stake, however, is your identity. Here's how to protect yourself against identity theft.

Check Your Credit Reports

The easiest way to keep an eye on your identity and prevent thieves from using it is to check your credit report frequently with the credit bureaus in your country. Credit bureaus are for-profit organizations that keep track of the credit ratings of individuals and corporations.

Each time a financial institution does a sizeable financial transaction with someone, they post the experience with the credit bureaus. This allows the bureau to build a credit profile of every borrower, so that in future when a lender wants to determine a credit worthiness of a borrower, he has a credit history he can check against.

It's worth checking your credit record quarterly because you can see which lenders have posted activity on your profile. If there's been an application for credit that you don't remember making, it is likely that you might be a victim in the making.

Some credit bureaus send you a free credit report once a year if you write to them, as mandated by law. If you check your credit online or more frequently, there's usually a nominal fee.

United States

Here's a list of the three credit bureaus in the USA.

- **Equifax**—1-800-685-1111; www.equifax.com
- **Experian**—1-888-EXPERIA (397-3742); www.experian.com
- **TransUnion**—1-800-888-4213; www.transunion.com

In the United States, you can order your free annual credit report at www.annualcreditreport.com or by calling 877-322-8228. You can also request it by mail. More info is at www.ftc.gov/bcp/conline/edcams/credit/ycr_free_reports.htm.

Canada

In Canada, the two credit bureaus are

- **Equifax**—1-800-465-7166 or 514-493-2314; www.equifax.ca
- **TransUnion**—1-866-525-0262 or 905-525-0262; In Quebec, 1-877-713-3393 or 514-335-0374; www.tuc.ca

One free annual credit report is available for each person from each credit bureau by sending a request by mail.

United Kingdom

In the U.K., credit reports are available from three credit reference agencies:

- **Experian**—0870 241 6212; www.experian.co.uk
- **Callcredit**—0113 244 1555; www.callcredit.co.uk
- **Equifax**—www.equifax.co.uk

More information on identity theft in the United Kingdom is available from the Home Office Identity Fraud Steering Committee at www.identity-theft.org.uk.

Australia

In Australia, the three credit reporting agencies are

- **Baycorp Advantage**—(02) 9464 6000; www.baycorpadvantage.com
- **Dun and Bradstreet (Australia) Pty Ltd**—13 23 33; www.dnb.com.au
- **Tasmanian Collection Service for Tasmanian residents**—(03) 6213 5599; www.tascol.com.au

More information on identity theft in Australia is available from the Australian Government Attorney General's Department at www.ag.gov.au.

If Your Country Is Not Listed

If you live in a country other than the ones previously listed, you can very easily find information about identity theft and the credit bureaus that service your area by contacting your bank, financial advisor, or government information line.

Shred It Before You Chuck It

Be careful what you throw out. Even though the Internet can be a happy hunting ground for identity thieves, they also prowl the real world as well. If you chuck out mail, documents, and other paper records, be sure to shred them before they go in the bin. Your garbage is ripe for the picking in more ways than one.

Read Your Statements

It's not great literature, but it's worth reading every credit and bank statement you receive as it comes in. A vast majority of identity theft victims don't discover the problem until months have gone by. Early warning signs show up as weird or unexpected line items on bills or statements.

tip

Ideally, you want to destroy your documents into tiny pieces, so they can't be reassembled easily. Straight-cut shredders slice paper into strips and are less secure than cross-cut shredders that cut across two axes so the document becomes confetti. Cross-cut shredders are slower and require more maintenance.

THE ABSOLUTE MINIMUM

- Identity theft is the use of your personal and financial information to apply for credit in your name without your permission or knowledge. It is also the illegal use of your existing credit.
- Guard your personal information, especially identifying documents. Do not fill out unnecessary applications or provide information to unfamiliar people or organizations you don't trust. Simplify your accounts and credit cards and destroy paper documents with a shredder. Keep an eye on your credit reports annually. Look at them quarterly if possible.
- Thieves steal your identity by acquiring personal information about you and building up enough data to apply for an identity document. They then use this to apply for credit in your name.

continues

- You know you're a victim when credit reports show accounts you did not authorize. Strange transactions appear on financial or credit card statements. Credit you apply for is declined. You are pursued by a collections agency to pay a debt you haven't incurred. You are accused of a crime or traffic offense you did not commit.

- If you have been victimized, file a police report, close tainted accounts, and place a fraud watch with the credit bureaus. Document the process. File an identity theft report with the FTC in the United States or the appropriate government body in other countries.

- Phishing is an electronic method of fooling you into providing personal and financial information to a crook on the Web. It's most commonly perpetrated by email, but information can also be solicited using a pop-up window on the Web.

- Pharming is an attack on special network computers called DNS servers that direct traffic on the Internet. These data traffic cops are poisoned with incorrect information so when a web surfer asks to be directed to a specific website, they are unknowingly sent to a crook's site.

- Avoid any too-good-to-be-true offers of quick money and skip any communication with strange Nigerians that need dubious help. It's a scam to get money out of you. These schemes are called advanced fee fraud. Nigeria is commonly used as a cover story, but they are perpetrated from all over the world.

- Your bank or other financial institutions will never request verification of user IDs, passwords, or other personal information through email. If in doubt, contact the institution.

- If you do send personal information via a financial website, be sure to first type in the company's web address into your browser manually. And check to see if the site is secure—indicated by a closed lock symbol at the bottom on your web browser and https:// in the web address bar.

- Be alert to misuse of your identity by regularly checking your credit reports with the national credit bureau in your country.

- Keep your antivirus and anti-spyware programs up-to-date and scan your system regularly. This protects you from key loggers and Trojan horses that can capture your personal information and send it to crooks on the Internet.

- Keep your computer's operating system up-to-date. And ensure that any fixes issued for your email program and web browser are installed.

- Guard your offline information as well. Read your financial and banking statements and shred mail and documents before putting them in the trash.

5

SPAM: UNWANTED EMAIL FROM HELL

This chapter explains why you get all those emails about cheap Viagra, amazing fat-fighting plant extracts, and attractive pillow-fighting college students. Yes, it's a chapter about spam—the email kind, not the canned meat kind. In these pages I'll tell you what it is, where it comes from, and what to do about it. It's the amazing, natural, and safe chapter about fighting spam! No dangerous stimulants or damaging side effects!

What Is Spam?

Despite its namesake, spam is not a favorite Hawaiian breakfast ingredient, a pig byproduct, or my dad's favorite lunchmeat. That's SPAM, the compressed ham in a can made by the Hormel Foods Corporation.

No, spam is something completely different. And it's so important that it merits its own chapter in a computer security book. Lower-case *spam* is unsolicited commercial email or electronic junk mail.

It's those emails you receive in your inbox from people you don't know that advertise everything from religious T-shirts (see Figure 5.1) to adult websites (see Figure 5.2). Sometimes these ads are offensive. Other times they're stupid. Usually they are just plain annoying, especially because they arrive in huge volumes and rarely do they advertise anything you need. Don't you think spam would be less annoying if it offered to sell you a freshly baked pecan pie or a tasty piece of haddock? Spam never advertises anything good.

> **caution**
>
> Many reputable companies use email for legitimate marketing purposes. If you agree to receive email from an organization (that is to say you opt-in), the email it sends you is not spam. If you find yourself in this situation, go back to the company's website and find out how to opt-out (unsubscribe). Most reputable companies have a mechanism that allows you to unsubscribe from their emails. Often, you'll find directions for unsubscribing at the bottom of the email in question.

FIGURE 5.1

The site this spam links to offers a free "Wherever I go God is with me" T-shirt. It's odd, however, that the spammer has put 666 in the URL. Not a great marketing tactic when it comes to Christians.

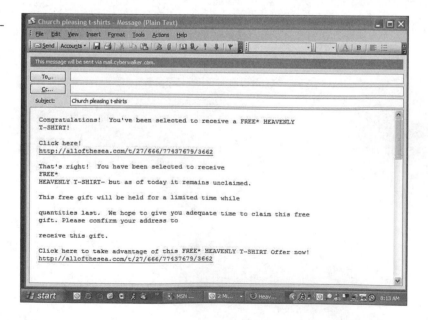

FIGURE 5.2

This spam email features Alyssa, who has dark brown hair (isn't that blonde hair in the picture?) and black eyes (a little odd, too). Don't think she's interested in meeting you. The email clicks through to an adult website.

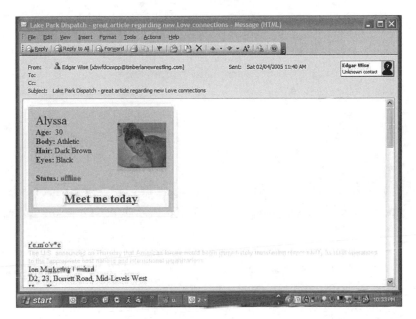

Why Does Spam Keep Coming?

Spam makes spammers money. It's hard to believe, but there are people out there that receive spam email, click the offer, and buy the advertised product. Now, you might think, why would anyone do that? Who knows, but they do because the spam keeps coming.

Personally, I think spam is perpetrated by people like that slightly evil kid in chess club. You know, the one that smelled vaguely sour and hiked his shorts too high in gym class. In reality, spammers are just business people—okay, slimy business people—bottom feeding on yet another Internet opportunity.

Nevertheless, you don't need much more than Grade 9 math to figure out that if you send a lot of emails, a small percentage of the recipients read the email and an even smaller percentage buy the advertised product. Small as it is, it's income with a scaleable formula. If you can send millions of messages for the price of an Internet connection and a computer, you've got an almost free distribution system. And if it costs almost nothing to send and produces an income of any kind, it's profitable. So the spam keeps coming.

LOVELY SPAM, WONDERFUL SPAAAAAAM!
The origin of the term *spam* comes from a sketch by the British comedy troupe Monty Python. They did a bit on a restaurant that only featured dishes made with SPAM (note the uppercase), which is a canned ham product from Hormel. When the waitress describes items on the menu, a group of Vikings sing a song that goes something like "SPAM, SPAM, SPAM, SPAM. Lovely SPAM, lovely SPAM…" So spam was thus named because, like the song, it is an endless repetition of worthless text.

Why Doesn't Someone Stop the Spammers?

Spammers are difficult to stop, partly because email as a technology is easy to use and hard to block.

Each computer connected to the Internet has a unique numerical address called an Internet Protocol (IP) address. It's sort of like a telephone number. To send or receive information to or from a computer on the Internet, you have to know its IP address.

If a computer sends too much information—maybe too many spam emails—its IP address can be blocked by the recipient. This is what Internet Service Providers (ISPs) often do to curtail spam from a particular source.

But if the owner of the sending computer changes the IP address, the ISP has to reblock the new address.

Because of this, spammers can evade being blocked by changing their IP address on a regular basis. They also move their operations overseas to countries that don't care or are more interested in making money than stopping spam.

Anti-spam laws have been enacted around the world in recent years by various countries, including the United States, to regulate commercial bulk email. Some high-profile spammers have been convicted but the laws have had little effect on reducing the total volume of spam. It keeps growing. However, spammers are being driven offshore to countries such as China and Russia, where they are out of the grasp of anti-spam legislation.

According to a report by MessageLabs, an email security company, the Australian Spam Act is one piece of legislation that has resulted in a "significant decrease in spam activity," driving known spammers to shut down activities or go offshore. Still, the volume of spam continues to climb (see Figure 5.3).

FIGURE 5.3

Email security
company
MessageLabs
reported that
spam constituted
between 53%
and 94.5% of
email sent
worldwide
in 2004.

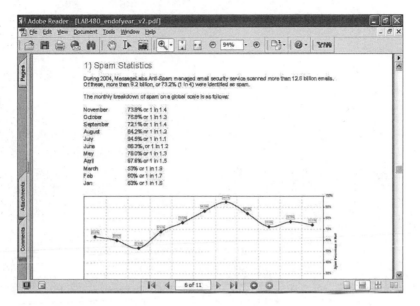

How Do Spammers Get My Email Address?

Spammers are a crafty bunch. They source email addresses wherever they can get
their hands on them.

Website Harvesting

Programs are available that scan public address books on web-based email sites.

Spammers also have software that looks for email addresses embedded in websites.
If you have a personal web page, an email address you post is almost guaranteed to
be found by spammers. In fact, the people who receive the most spam tend to be
webmasters.

After emails are harvested they are compiled into lists and sold on the Internet.

Dictionary Spamming

There are also programs that combine random words and common names and pop
them together in an effort to come up with valid email addresses.

With so many people using email, all the common names for email addresses such
as Bob Smith are long gone at the big ISPs. So people make up their email addresses
from common words.

So let's say your ISP is called reallybigisp.com and your email address is
topdog@reallybigisp.com.

Spammers might find you by running their dictionary program and combining
the words *top* and *dog* together. They'll try sending an email to

topdog@reallybigisp.com. They try this address combination against all the other major ISPs as well, so all the top dogs at aol.com, msn.com, and beyond get spam.

And don't think that becoming topdog1967@reallybigisp.com will help because after the spammers run through the most obvious words, they start combining them with numbers.

They'll even send email to aaaaaaa@reallybigisp.com, then aaaaaab@reallybigisp.com, then aaaaaac@reallybigisp.com, and so on.

Because computers do all this work they can try billions of combinations in hours. Then they spam to all these potential addresses. If they don't receive a bounced email from the address, they log it as valid and put it on their active list.

Commercial Email Lists

Millions of email addresses are available for sale via Internet download or on CD-ROM. Out of curiosity, I bought a list of 10 million Canadian email addresses for $49. The company claimed they were all opt-in email addresses, meaning that the owners of the addresses had agreed to be put on the list. I found one of my addresses that is used for inbound mail only, however. It was never used to opt into anything (see Figure 5.4).

FIGURE 5.4

A list of so-called opt-in emails shows email addresses whose owners never authorized their inclusion, including one owned by me (highlighted). Emails are blurred intentionally.

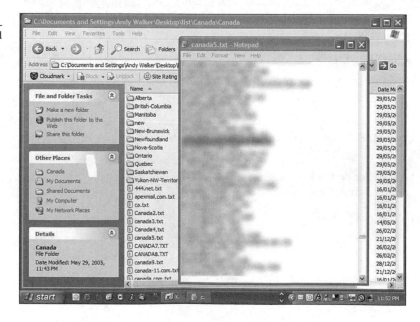

Newsgroups, Discussion Forums, and Interactive Websites

When you post your email address to the Web to receive a newsletter or to sign up for a discussion forum, for example, you expose yourself to spammers.

Email addresses can also be easily harvested from Internet-based discussion groups called newsgroups (see Figure 5.5) and the Web at large. Some companies sell these lists of verified email addresses. Before making this information available, you might want to look for a privacy statement on the website to see what they are going to do with any personal information you give them. Credible websites stick to their privacy policies closely.

FIGURE 5.5

Atomic Newsgroup Explorer is a program that can extract thousands of email addresses and user names from Internet newsgroups in mere seconds. Here it has scanned the newsgroups at msnnews.msn.com.

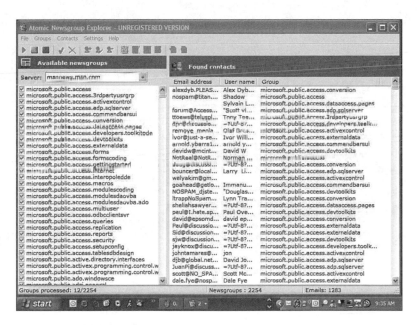

Contests and Other Free Offerings

You can sign up to receive spam legitimately by entering contests or engaging in offers that appear to give you something for nothing. Oftentimes, these deals are email harvesting schemes. Sometimes they even explicitly tell you in the fine print that you will receive bulk commercial email and you actually agree to this.

Email Forwarding

If you forward an email to dozens of people, make sure you send it to yourself in the To: field and put everyone else in the Bcc: field. *Bcc* means blind carbon copy. It's used to send a copy of the email to someone without revealing her email address (see Figure 5.6). If Bcc is not used, you expose everyone's email address to dozens of other people. It's been suggested that your email can be exposed to spammers that way. I know a few public relations people who have scooped my email for press release lists when another person has failed to hide my address in the Bcc: field.

FIGURE 5.6

The Bcc: field is used when you want to send a copy of an email to someone, but hide her email address from others copied on the email.

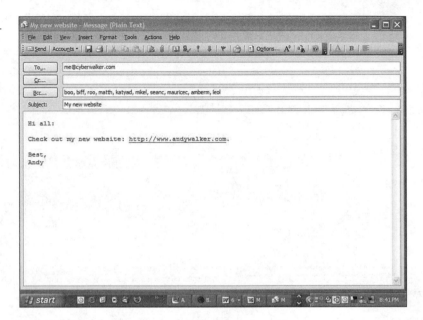

The Damage Spam Can Do

Spam might be free to send, but it is very costly to its recipients and the Internet community in the following ways:

- **It costs you money**—Spam costs millions of dollars a year in Internet resources. It clogs Internet plumbing, forcing ISPs to buy bigger electronic pipes to carry all the information on the Internet. This drives up the cost of operations, which is passed on to you, the ISP's customer.

- **Wasted productivity**—If you're a business owner, spam wastes workers' time and productivity and increases expenses because it consumes helpdesk and IT resources to deal with it.

- **It wastes your time**—Spam wastes your time. Wading through spam to find the legitimate email takes time, especially if you get a lot of spam. If it takes you one second to delete a spam email and you get 900 spam emails each day (for a time I was getting more than 1,000) that wastes 15 minutes of your time.

- **It disconnects you**—If the flow of spam becomes too great, you have to abandon your email address is favor of a new one. This disconnects you from people who lose track of you because they don't update their email address lists.

- **It's annoying and offensive**—Spam is advertising you're not interested in, and that's just plain annoying. And often it comes with content that's offensive or at the very least distasteful.

- **It endangers children**—It exposes children to topics and images that they shouldn't have to worry about, including adult content.

- **It's a spyware and virus carrier**—Some spam carries email attachments that if downloaded can infect your computer with spyware that gathers information on you and distributes it to third parties. (Learn more about spyware in Chapter 2, "Spyware: Overrun by Advertisers, Hijackers, and Opportunists.") Adware that displays advertising to you by installing pop-up ads on your computer can also be distributed this way. Viruses also use mass-mailing strategies to distribute themselves. (Learn more about viruses in Chapter 1, "Viruses: Attack of the Malicious Programs.")

> **caution**
>
> Be sure to run an up-to-date antivirus program on your computer to ensure your computer is not infected with a computer virus that has turned it into a spam distribution machine. Some viruses are engineered to install spam sending software on a victim's computer.

- **It can get you kicked off the Net**—Some viruses can infect your computer so it turns into a spam-sending machine. And if your computer is identified as a source of spam, you can have your Internet account terminated by your Internet provider. Spammers use viruses to hijack other people's computers into sending spam because they create a massive network of spam-sending machines without worrying about having their own computers being identified as a spam sender. The spam also comes from thousands of computers and not just one, making it harder to stop.

Reduce the Flow—10-Minute Tactics to Reduce Spam

You can do a few simple things to immediately reduce the flow of spam to your email address.

Don't Respond

First of all, never respond to spam. That means don't open spam, don't send angry responses to the spam sender, and definitely don't buy anything in a spam offer. If spam failed to work as an advertising medium, there would be little value in sending it. When you buy or respond to spam, you reinforce the notion that spam works as a marketing tool. And when you respond in any manner, you confirm that your email address is an active address. As a consequence, you'll receive more spam.

Don't Post Your Email Address on the Web

Don't give your main email address to anyone on the Web. That's hard to do because many websites insist on your email address when signing up for their services. It's a good idea to maintain an alternate email address with Hotmail.com, Yahoo.com, Gmail.com, or any of the other free email services on the web. Check the secondary address occasionally to check for valid email, such as subscription confirmations, and if the volume of spam to that address gets to be too much, simply abandon it and get a new secondary address.

Webmasters Shouldn't Use mailto

If you run a website, don't post your primary email address to it using the HTML code called mailto.

A mailto link allows you to insert a link in a webpage that, when clicked, triggers the web surfer's email program and inserts the email address in the To field. A link that uses this technique looks like this:

```
Sent me an email at <a href="mailto: me@mymailaddress.com">me@mymailaddress.com</a>
```

Email harvester programs hunt for this code. Using a mailto is like wearing salmon-flavored socks at a cattery. You'll get bombarded with a lot of unwanted attention.

Instead, use the following Javascript code, which achieves the same result but masks the email address. Be sure to customize the parts that say *me*, *example.com*, and *Link text* to your own needs.

```
<a href="email.html" onmouseover="this.href='mai' + 'lto:' + 'me' +
➥'@' + 'example.com'">Link text</a>
```

Learn more about this at www.december14.net/ways/js/nospam.shtml.

Turn Off Image Display in Email Programs

Both Outlook and Outlook Express have a feature that turns off images in HTML email. (HTML is a web programming language that is used to create web pages.) HTML email can include pictures, fancy fonts, and layout like a magazine. If you see a picture displayed in the body of an email, it was mostly likely created with HTML.

The ability to put images in email can cause an increase in spam. That's because spammers put an invisible pixel (an image of a transparent dot) in HTML emails.

When an email is opened or previewed, the invisible pixel is fetched from the spammer's server. That tells the server that the email address affiliated with that image is a good one and is ripe for further spam.

Outlook 2003 and Outlook Express 6 have the ability to block these images from displaying (see Figure 5.7). Here's how to turn the features on in both programs.

FIGURE 5.7

Outlook Express 6 can block images from displaying in HTML emails when they are opened or in preview mode.

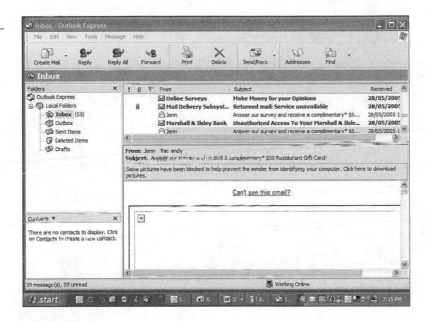

Outlook 2003

1. Click the Tools menu and choose Options.

2. Click the Security tab.

3. Under the Download Pictures heading, click Change Automatic Download Settings button.

4. Put a tick mark in the box marked Don't Download Pictures or Other Content Automatically in HTML Email.

Outlook Express 6

1. Click the Tools menu and choose Options.

2. Click the Security tab.

3. Under the Download Images heading, put a tick mark in the box marked Block Images and Other External Content in HTML Email (see Figure 5.8).

FIGURE 5.8

Outlook Express
has an image-
blocking function
to stop the
display of
embarrassing
images and
invisible tracking
images.

Turn On Junk Mail Filtering

If you use Outlook 98, 2000, or 2003, turn on the
Junk filter. It is not a foolproof method, but it stops
much of the spam headed for your inbox.

Outlook 98, 2000, and 2002

To turn on the Junk filter, follow these steps:

1. In Outlook 98, click the Tools menu, and
   then click Organize.

2. Next, click Junk Email.

3. In the Automatically <action> Junk
   Messages list, select Move as the action,
   and then click to select the destination
   folder from the list. Click Turn On.

4. In the Automatically <action> Adult messages list, select Move as the action and
   then click to select the destination folder
   from the list. Click Turn On.

note

This feature only works
in Outlook Express if you
have Windows XP and have
installed Service Pack 2 (SP2), a
major security add-on released by
Microsoft in August 2004. You can
install it by running Windows
Update. Learn more about SP2 on
p. 238.

Outlook 2003

Outlook 2003 offers new junk email tools that improve greatly on previous versions.
Here's how to turn the new features on:

1. Click the Tools menu and choose Options.

2. On the Preferences tab under Email, click Junk Email.

3. Select the level of protection you want (see Figure 5.9). If you receive a small volume of spam, choose Low. Note that High protection does a better job, but you will have to check your Junk email folder periodically to ensure that no legitimate emails have been mistakenly marked as spam.

FIGURE 5.9

Outlook 2003 offers vastly improved anti-spam tools over previous versions of the program, including conservative and aggressive sensitivity settings.

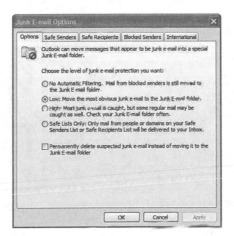

Kill More Spam—In an Afternoon

When you have a few hours to spare, here are a few more tactics to stop even more spam.

Install an Anti-spam Program

Lots of anti-spam programs are available. All the big name software security companies, including Symantec and McAfee, have their own. Choose one and install it; it will drastically reduce the flow of spam to your inbox.

I have had great success with Cloudmark Desktop (see Chapter 4, "Identity Thieves and Phishers: Protect Your Good Name and Bank Account," for more on Cloudmark Desktop). It's a plug-in for Outlook (see Figure 5.10) and Outlook Express that looks at each email as it comes in and electronically compares it to a database of spam email at Cloudmark. If a match is found, the email is marked as spam and is dumped into a spam folder or it can be automatically deleted; it's your choice.

tip

The image-blocking function in Outlook 2003 and Outlook Express has a nice side benefit. When porn-related spam arrives with graphic images of naked people doing surprisingly agile things, the images won't automatically display, saving you some shock and perhaps a little embarrassment if your grandma is nearby.

FIGURE 5.10
Cloudmark
Desktop is a
spam filter for
Outlook and
Outlook Express.
It shows up as a
toolbar near the
top of the
Outlook window.

The flaw in most anti-spam programs is that no matter how clever it is, it will almost always misidentify some legitimate email as spam or let some spam through.

Cloudmark Desktop catches about 80%–90% of spam because humans look at each message. But fear not, there's no team of spam spotters on the Cloudmark staff looking at all your email. The program relies on its users. When email comes in, you can mark it as spam using the program. This reports the message back as spam to the company's servers. If enough of us report the spam, a spam signature is generated and everyone that gets that spam in future has it filtered automatically by the software.

The community approach results in no false positives, which is lingo for a misidentification of a legitimate email as spam.

So if I get an email from my aunt who talks about the cocks crowing on her farm and the nice tits singing in the trees outside her window, the Cloudmark software is not going to treat her email as spam, while others might because of misread keywords in her message.

Cloudmark Desktop costs $39.95 per year, but it does have a free 30-day trial. It's available from www.cloudmark.com.

tip

If you use a web-based email service such as the ones offered by Hotmail.com or Yahoo.com, it's worth investigating their built-in anti-spam features to set spam filtering sensitivity.

If you don't want to use Cloudmark Desktop, you might consider using Norton AntiSpam or McAfee SpamKiller.

For the Mac, check out SpamSieve from http://c-command.com/spamsieve/.

A series of free anti-spam programs for Windows PCs are available for download at www.snapfiles.com/Freeware/comm/fwspam.html.

Fight Back!

If you are angry enough to fight back against spammers, here's how. Forward a message with your spam complaint to the ISP that hosts the spammer's email account. For example, if you received spam from bobby1234@llamasarenice.com, go to the website www.llamasarenice.com and look for a Contact Us page. Often ISPs have an email account called Abuse for such purposes. In this example, you'd send a copy of the spam to abuse@llamasarenice.com. You could also try postmaster@llamasarenice.com or hostmaster@llamasarenice.com. Try to verify what the correct address is first so you don't waste anyone's time.

tip

I've found that turning on Microsoft Outlook's built-in Junk Filter and installing Cloudmark Desktop helps blocks 99% of the spam that arrives in my inbox.

The big problem with this solution is that ISPs are deluged by spam and to investigate every source of spam is not possible. Still, the option is available to you and it will at least make you feel better.

You can also use SpamCop.net (see Figure 5.11), a spam reporting service. It analyzes an email's content and header information (where it came from and how it got there). Then if it is deemed to be spam, it sends a warning to the ISP that provides the spammer with Internet service. ISPs tend to not like spammers on their network, so they often revoke service from them if they receive valid complaints. SpamCop.net has free and paid versions of its service.

FIGURE 5.11

SpamCop.net analyzes your spam and reports it to the ISP that connects the spammer to the Internet.

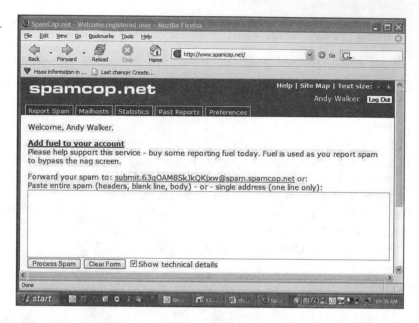

THE ABSOLUTE MINIMUM

- Spam is unsolicited commercial email or electronic junk mail.

- Spammers send massive volumes of email because they make money at it. Someone, somewhere, buys the products they advertise.

- A spammer's computer can be blocked but it's easy for him to evade this by changing his computer's IP address, the numerical address used to identify his computer on the Internet.

- Spam is free to send but costs recipients time, productivity, money, and aggravation.

- Never respond to spam.

- Never post your main email address to the Web. Instead, use an alternate email for web forums, subscriptions, and the like.

- Use the junk mail filters in Outlook and Outlook Express.

- Install an anti-spam program. I recommend Cloudmark Desktop.

- Fight back by reporting spam to the spammer's ISP.

IN THIS CHAPTER

- What Is a Wireless Home Network?
- Why Wi-Fi Scares Security Experts
- The Snoopers: Bandwidth Bandits, Wireless Hackers, and Wardrivers
- Damage a Snooper Can Do
- Secure Your Wi-Fi with WEP and WPA
- Stop the Scottish (and Everyone Else) with MAC Address Filtering
- Emergency Lock-down—Dealing with an Attack
- Router Security Tweaks that Take 10 Minutes
- How to Turn off File Sharing

6

WIRELESS NETWORK SNOOPS: LOCK DOWN YOUR Wi-Fi NETWORK

Wireless networks are everywhere. You might even have one in your home. If you do, did you know you've just left an electronic door into your home wide open to anyone who walks by? In this chapter you learn the risks posed by a wireless network and how to lock it down so no one pulls up to the curb outside your house and tiptoes through your personal data. Plus, you get to learn about exciting encryption technologies such as WEP and WPA and how to scramble data so well as it flies through the ether that people can't read your bank statements or your grandma's top secret cookie recipe.

What Is a Wireless Home Network?

Better go look out your window. There could be someone lurking in her car outside your home connecting to your wireless network right now.

I am not kidding. It happens every day. In fact, it could have been me. I've been at curbside in my car numerous times waiting for someone and checked my email on my laptop by connecting to someone's open wireless network. I didn't do anything bad. But I could figure out what brand of wireless router they had, what settings it had, and what computers were on the network. It would have even been possible to print a note on their printer—"Andy was here. Thanks for the toner."

I didn't, but I could have.

To understand how strangers can access your computer just by parking outside your house, it's important to understand what a wireless home network is.

Let's first look at the basics. A *home network* is a way to connect computers and other devices together so they can share stuff such as files, access to the Internet, and printers.

Businesses have been networking for a long time, but the technology has recently become available so you can do this at home very cheaply.

This is achieved by attaching wires from each computer—called CAT-5 cables—to a little box called a *home network router* (see Figure 6.1) or connecting them wirelessly across radio waves. The router, in turn, is connected to a high-speed Internet modem, which connects to the Internet.

> **tip**
>
> Wi-Fi is usually used with a laptop, but if you have a desktop computer, you can add Wi-Fi to it by buying a Wireless adapter card. The adapter card, which contains an antenna and Wi-Fi circuitry, fits into an open slot (called a PCI slot) in the rear of the PC. This is useful if the computer is located in a different room from the Wi-Fi router because it saves running a cable.

> **tip**
>
> If you have a Wi-Fi router in your home, you probably already know it. But if you're not sure, here's how to check. Locate the modem that connects to your high-speed service. If it connects directly to your computer with a cable, you don't have Wi-Fi network. If the modem connects to a small box with one or two pencil-sized antennas, that small box is likely a Wi-Fi router.

A printer can also be attached to this set-up so any computer on the network can print to it. And computers on this network can send or get files from each other.

To make wireless work, you need a router that has Wi-Fi or Wireless Fidelity capability and a computer with a wireless network adapter.

Most home network routers these days come with Wi-Fi built in. Since Wi-Fi is turned on by default in these routers, any computer that has a Wi-Fi adapter can connect wirelessly to the router within a range of about 300 feet.

This is useful at home because it means you can sit by the pool with your laptop and order urgent groceries, such as margarita mix, using the Web.

The bad part is you can also get email wirelessly from your egomaniacal boss who can chastise you about your expense report that includes a receipt for margarita mix.

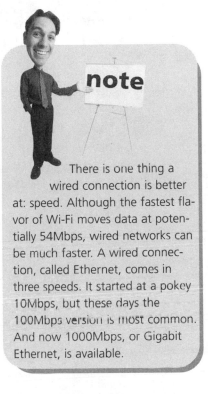

note

There is one thing a wired connection is better at: speed. Although the fastest flavor of Wi-Fi moves data at potentially 54Mbps, wired networks can be much faster. A wired connection, called Ethernet, comes in three speeds. It started at a pokey 10Mbps, but these days the 100Mbps version is most common. And now 1000Mbps, or Gigabit Ethernet, is available.

FIGURE 6.1

At the heart of a home network is a router. It's a junction box that connects computers together so they can share files. It also gives them access to the Internet and resources such as a printer.

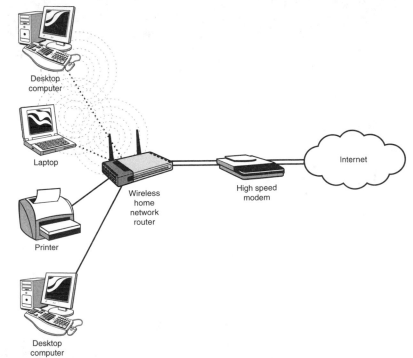

WHAT'S WITH THE WI-FI ALPHABET?

If you listen to Wi-Fi geeks chat, you'll sometimes hear some weird terms when they refer to different types of Wi-Fi technology: "Oh yeah, my Wi-Fi network uses eight-oh-two-dot-eleven-gee!"

If you want to play along with this wiener, here's the magic decoder ring for that conversation.

There are three types of Wi-Fi: 802.11b, 802.11a, and 802.11g, plus one new one on the way:

- **802.11b**—This is the slowest version of Wi-Fi with a maximum speed of 11Mbps (and a real-world speed of 2–4Mbps). It's the oldest Wi-Fi technology around. It works in the 2.4GHz radio spectrum—the same part of the radio dial that your cordless phone, baby monitor, garage door opener, and microwave work in. It has a range of up to 300 feet.

- **802.11a**—This is the fastest version of Wi-Fi with a maximum speed of 54Mbps (with an actual speed of 20–30Mbps or so). It's the second oldest. It works in the 5GHz part of the radio spectrum where some new cordless phones work. It tends to have a reduced range of 150 feet, instead of 300 feet.

- **802.11g**—This is the latest version of Wi-Fi. It's 802.11b on growth hormones. It works at a theoretical 54Mbps (or real world 20–30Mbps), but it also works in the 2.4GHz radio spectrum. And it works with old 802.11b gear. It also has a range of up to 300 feet.

- **802.11n**—This is super-fast and super-new Wi-Fi that's supposed to work at more than 100Mbps. It's also supposed to have super-far range. The smart people thinking about it are still arguing about what rules it should follow, but by the time you read this, they might have kissed and made up and be on their way to agreeing to what kind of snacks to stock the break room with.

What Damage Can a Wireless Network Snoop Dish Out?

Wireless network snoops tend to be curious and not malicious. In fact, most people who access your Wi-Fi network are just looking to borrow an Internet connection, perhaps to check their email (see Figure 6.2).

That said, there are still real dangers to leaving your Wi-Fi network unprotected because a network snoop can also do the following:

- Use your Internet connection to anonymously download illicit material from adult content sites, including child pornography.

- Use the connection to hack someone else's computer and perhaps steal data.

■ Use your network to send spam. This is handy for snoops because you'll get the blame for the spam, not the sender.

■ Install viruses or spyware onto your computer or network. This can also happen unintentionally. If the snoop's computer is infected, some malware looks for opportunities on nearby networked computers to infect them.

■ Steal credit card data, other banking access information, or personal information from you to use for criminal purposes.

■ Gain access to your company network via your home computer.

FIGURE 6.2

You can be sitting at home surfing HotorNot.com and a stranger in a car outside can be accessing your network with his wireless laptop.

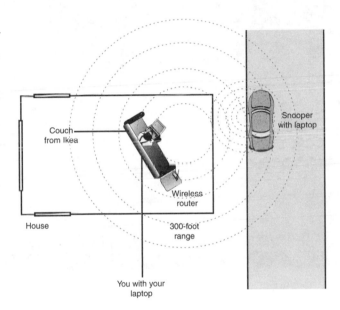

Couch from Ikea

Snooper with laptop

Wireless router

House

300-foot range

You with your laptop

Who Are the Snoopers?

If it's easy to access a wireless network, who's snooping? Well, there are a few types of interlopers. Generically, I call them wireless network snoops, but they come in three basic varieties.

Wardrivers

Wi-Fi is such a huge phenomenon that all you have to do is drive down a city street with a Wi-Fi enabled laptop to pick up dozens of open Wi-Fi networks. Approximately 40%–60% of all wireless routers are unprotected by security measures.

These wireless networks make geeks curious. They can't resist probing them, poking them, and sampling them a bit. These geeks are kind of like kids around a bowl of cake icing. Most just sneakily sample a little bit of the wireless offering and move on. The problem is that more nefarious geeks take it too far. These are the people that when they were kids would steal the icing bowl, lick it clean, and wear it as a hat. They are the ones you should be concerned about.

The practice of probing wireless networks is called *wardriving*. All wardrivers need is a car, a Wi-Fi laptop, a snooping program downloaded from the Internet (see Figure 6.3), and optionally an upgrade antenna. Sometimes these are made out of cylindrical potato chip cans.

FIGURE 6.3

Network Stumbler is a free program that can be used to electronically sniff out Wi-Fi networks.

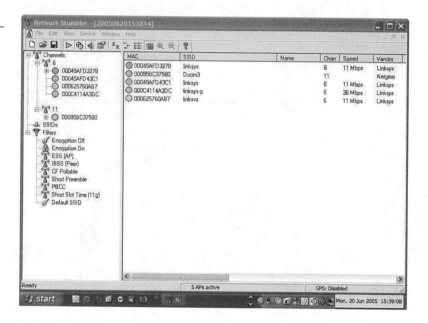

Wardrivers also sometimes use Global Positioning System (GPS) receivers to register the exact geographical location of an open Wi-Fi network. These coordinates are cataloged and sometimes published to the Web so others can locate the open networks when they need to connect to the Internet.

How Wardrivers Operate

Want to see what wardrivers see? If you live in a well-populated urban area, there are probably at least half a dozen Wi-Fi networks detectable right where you sit. If you live in an apartment building, there might be dozens. I once opened my laptop in an apartment in one of those clusters of high-rise apartments and detected 23 Wi-Fi networks.

Now, I am not advocating that you engage in wardriving practices. Trespassing on networks you do not own is illegal in Canada and the United States and likely other jurisdictions. However, I want you to know how easy it is to do it. Here's the fail safe: If you don't actually connect to the wireless network, you're not doing anything wrong.

That said, here's how to peek at the networks near you:

1. First you need a Wi-Fi–enabled computer. Most laptops are Wi-Fi–enabled today, so if yours is fairly new, you probably already have the capability.

2. You might need to turn Wi-Fi on with a switch. Some laptops have a slider that needs to be switched on to turn on the wireless capability.

3. Look for a little icon (a tiny picture) that looks like a screen with radio waves emitting from the right side of it. You'll find this in your System Tray on the bottom right of your Windows XP screen. Windows 95, 98, and Me need an add-on Wi-Fi program to do this.

4. Double-click on the icon and the Wireless Network Connection Status box appears. Click on the View Wireless Networks button (see Figure 6.4).

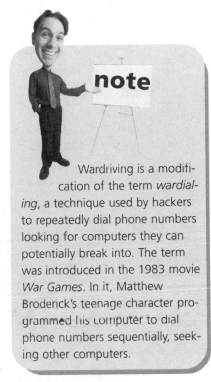

note

Wardriving is a modification of the term *wardialing*, a technique used by hackers to repeatedly dial phone numbers looking for computers they can potentially break into. The term was introduced in the 1983 movie *War Games*. In it, Matthew Broderick's teenage character programmed his computer to dial phone numbers sequentially, seeking other computers.

FIGURE 6.4

In the Wireless Network Connection Status box, click View Wireless Networks to see what Wi-Fi networks are available to connect to.

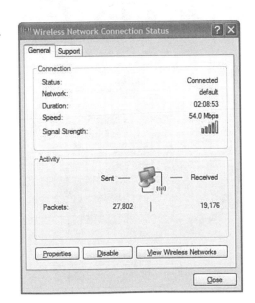

5. The Wireless Network Connection box appears, listing all the wireless networks that can be detected by your wireless computer (see Figure 6.5). Next to the name of each network is the signal strength.

6. If the network has security measures, a little lock icon appears next to it and its security status appears below its name (see Figure 6.6).

tip

Warchalking is the practice of tagging pavement near an open Wi-Fi network to alert others that wireless access is available at that location.

FIGURE 6.5

The Wireless Network Connection box contains a list of the Wi-Fi networks detected by your computer that you might be able to access.

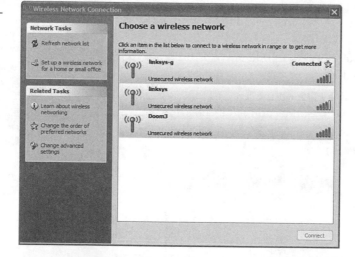

FIGURE 6.6

A lock next to the Wi-Fi entry means the router has wireless security measures turned on.

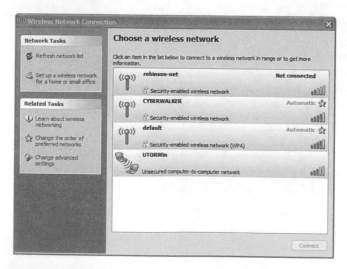

Bandwidth Bandits

The most likely damage you can expect to your wireless home network is not really damage, but more of an inconvenience: People will steal your bandwidth.

caution

In many jurisdictions around the world— including the United States and Canada— accessing a network without its owner's permission is illegal.

Bandwidth is your Internet connection's capacity to carry data. In plumbing terms, bandwidth would be the diameter of the pipe that carries water through your house. This is not to be confused with bumwidth, which is the mathematical capacity for a plumber's pants to ride down based on the girth of his belly.

If you notice a slowdown on your Internet connection, it could be because a bandwidth bandit is accessing your network and sharing your bandwidth.

Because wireless connections are possible up to 300 feet from the Wi-Fi router, it's easy for someone outside your home to log on to your Wi-Fi connection, access the Internet, and get her email or surf the Web without your permission. By doing this, she is stealing your bandwidth.

If you live above or very close to a coffee joint, bus station, or any place where people with laptops might gather, I can guarantee that the local bandwidth bandits love you and are happily using your open Wi-Fi Internet connection.

Long ago, before I wrote fun books like this, I commuted to work on a train into Toronto. (I also put pants on before noon and shaved daily.) When the train stopped at a station on the way, I'd pick up a local Wi-Fi signal for a minute or so. This was long enough to download my email. Many of the people around me did the same with their laptops. If the person who owned the connection was trying to surf the Internet when the train pulled in, he'd see his Internet service slow drastically until all us bandwidth bandits disappeared out of range as the train pulled out of the station again.

caution

In the contract you have with your Internet provider, there is likely a clause that sets a ceiling on the amount of bandwidth you can use before being billed extra. This is probably more than you would ever use yourself. But if hordes of bandwidth bandits use your wireless connection, you could find yourself going over the limit and being surcharged or having your service cancelled.

DON'T GET WI-PHISHED

A new phenomenon called Wi-Phishing is hooking bandwidth bandits.

Bad guys are setting up wide open Wi-Fi routers to lure bandwidth bandits to connect. When they do, all the data the victim sends and receives over the rogue wireless connection is captured.

If it's credit card, banking, or personal information, the Wi-Phisher steals it and rips the bandwidth bandit off.

This practice is rare and perpetrated by small time crooks, but if it pays off, it could become a bigger threat.

A tip here: If you borrow someone's connection, do not send sensitive data with it. Someone could be watching.

To learn more about phishing in general, see Chapter 4, "Identity Thieves and Phishers: Protect Your Good Name and Bank Account."

Wireless Hackers

Perhaps the most insidious wireless network snoops—besides pantless book writers—are criminally minded people who are out to hack onto your network and steal your banking access information, identity, or other valuable data on your home network. Although these people are rare, they are also the most dangerous type of wireless network snoop.

If you work for a big corporation, these people might also be able to get onto your wireless network and access a computer that has security access to your company's network. If you have access to a virtual private network (VPN)—a secure connection which you use to access your company's servers from home—you are at risk.

A VPN uses the public Internet to tunnel like an electronic gopher across the public Internet into the company's network. The data that runs through this digital tunnel is protected from snoops because the data is scrambled. However, a wireless snoop can make his way onto your computer, access the open end of this electronic tunnel, and march down it into your company's network.

Your Wi-Fi Network Is Full of Holes!

Is your Wi-Fi network secure? The answer to that question is the same as the answer to this question: Is your cold beer safe on a hot day with sweaty men around? Nope.

If you bought your Wi-Fi router and set it up without changing any of the factory settings on the device, you are a prime target for a wireless network snoop. That's because Wi-Fi routers ship with all the security protections turned off.

Why? Because if they were all turned on, they would be difficult to configure. It would be like buying a minivan with the child locks on, the hazard lights flashing and the parking brake engaged. It would take you a while to get the vehicle unencumbered so you could fishtail off the lot and speed home into the arms of your fashion model spouse.

In the next few pages I am going to show you some critical steps you need to take to make your network more secure. Many tips require that you electronically crawl inside the router using your web browser. This in itself can be a challenge, so before we get any further into these deliciously fun procedures, let me show you how to access a router's settings.

How to Access Your Router Set-up

To get into your router, you'll need to determine what internal IP address has been assigned to it. Each device attached to your home network has one of these numerical addresses.

You can get this information by using a hidden Windows function and using the following steps:

1. Click the Start menu, and select Run.

2. If you have Windows XP, type **cmd** (see Figure 6.7).

   If you have Windows 95, 98, or Me, type **command** instead.

> **tip**
>
> A little lingo alert here. When I say *default*, I mean the way the settings were configured when they came from the factory. You might hear this word a lot in the context of computers and technology. It just means the way things are originally set by the manufacturer or programmer.

> **caution**
>
> Accessing your router's settings is a critical step in securing your home network, so make sure you don't skip this section. I'll refer to it often and without warning. Uh-oh. I sound like your ninth-grade history teacher, don't I?

FIGURE 6.7

Type **cmd** into the Run box.

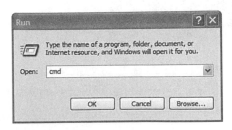

3. Click OK and a DOS emulation window opens.

4. You'll see a command prompt (flashing cursor) where you can type instructions (see Figure 6.8).

5. At the flashing cursor, type `ipconfig`.

6. Press Enter.

7. Information about your network appears below the line where you typed `ipconfig`. Look for the line that says Default Gateway. This displays the IP address of your network router. Make a note of it. It will probably look like one of the following IP addresses:

   - 192.168.0.1
   - 192.168.1.1
   - 192.168.2.1
   - 192.168.x.1—Where x is any number from 0 to 255. Normally this shows that the person who installed the router has customized it from its default settings set by the factory.
   - 10.0.0.1—Common in the Apple world.

note

In the early days of personal computers before Windows, computers used a command-line operating system called MS-DOS or Microsoft Disk Operating System. The DOS emulation window is faked DOS. It's not real; however, it still has functions that look and work like DOS.

This DOS window is useful because you can ask for very specific information about your network connection here.

FIGURE 6.8

Type `ipconfig` at the DOS prompt to display your network's settings.

```
C:\WINDOWS\system32\cmd.exe

C:\>ipconfig

Windows IP Configuration

Ethernet adapter Wireless Network Connection:

        Connection-specific DNS Suffix  . :
        IP Address. . . . . . . . . . . . : 192.168.0.100
        Subnet Mask . . . . . . . . . . . : 255.255.255.0
        Default Gateway . . . . . . . . . : 192.168.0.1

Ethernet adapter Local Area Connection:

        Media State . . . . . . . . . . . : Media disconnected

C:\>
```

To get inside the router and look at its settings, follow these steps:

1. Open your web browser and type the router's IP address you just retrieved (see Figure 6.9), like this, for example:

   `http://192.168.0.1.`

2. Press Enter or click Go on the web browser.

FIGURE 6.9

Type your
router's IP
address into your
web browser to
access the
device's settings
information.

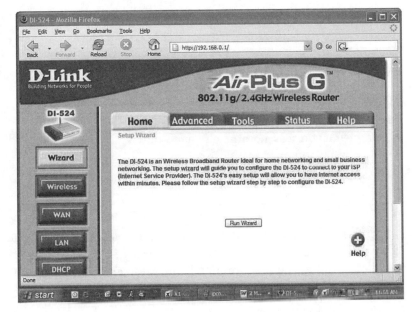

3. Next, the router asks for a user ID and
   password. If the router has never been
   customized, this information can be
   obtained by checking the manual for the
   router or accessing the support area of
   the website of the router's manufacturer.
   If the site has a search engine, use these
   search terms: *router user ID password.*

4. Type in the user ID and password into
   the router and you'll be given access to
   the router's settings page.

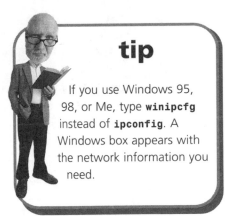

tip

If you use Windows 95,
98, or Me, type `winipcfg`
instead of `ipconfig`. A
Windows box appears with
the network information you
need.

Table 6.1 shows some common user ID and passwords for various brands of popular
routers. If it says (blank) next to your brand of router, don't type `(blank)`—that
means enter nothing in that field when you access your router.

Table 6.1   Common Default Router User IDs and Passwords

Router Brand	User ID	Password
D-Link	admin	(blank)
Netgear	admin	password (Note: on older routers it's 1234)
Linksys	(blank)	admin
Belkin	admin	(blank)
SMC	admin	smcadmin

First Line of Defense: Secure Your Wi-Fi Network

Three key technologies are available to lock out wireless network snoops: WEP, WPA, and MAC address filtering. This is your first line of defense. This is the most useful bit of information in the chapter. If you read nothing else, read this! Here's an explanation of each technology and how to activate them.

> **caution**
>
> Manufacturers ship consumer Wi-Fi routers with all their security settings turned off. This minimizes the complexity of setting them up.

Turn On WEP

One of the most common security features on wireless routers (especially older routers) is a feature called Wired Equivalent Privacy (WEP). WEP is a way of scrambling information as it flies through the air between a computer and a router.

It's about as fun to set up as shaving with a piece of cheddar, but with a little patience you can get it going.

First you'll need to set up a *key*. That's a special code that's input to both the router and the computer that connects wirelessly to the router. The key is used to scramble all the data moving between the computer and the router. At either end the key is also used to descramble the information. You can think of it just like a key that locks and unlocks a door.

Wireless network snoops are shut out if WEP is engaged because they don't have the key to communicate with the router. Well, that's the theory. The problem with WEP is that it's not very tough as security measures go. WEP is like a paper door. It looks like a big thick door that blocks bad people from entering. But you can put your fist through it and walk through the hole.

> **caution**
>
> The shaving with cheese analogy is an attempt at humor. Do not attempt, especially if lactose intolerant.

WEP is a good bandwidth bandit repellent, but a wireless hacker can break the code using a piece of software called a sniffer if they have a little patience. All they have to do is use the sniffer to watch the data flow back and forth between a router and a computer and look for patterns, and eventually this can be used to figure out the key.

Here's how to turn it on. First, you blow in its ear. Wait, that's the *Absolute Beginner's Guide to Seduction*. Let me rephrase. Here's how to activate WEP.

I am going to use a D-Link router in all the examples in this chapter (see Figure 6.10).

FIGURE 6.10

The D-Link DI-524 router is an easy-to-use wireless home network router with a well-designed inter-face that can be used to configure the device with a web browser.

If you use another brand, your steps are different, but the settings are similar:

1. Access your router's settings by typing in its IP address in your web browser (as explained earlier in this chapter).

2. Locate the wireless settings. In a D-Link router, click the Wireless button to the left of the Home tab.

3. On the Security setting, click on the WEP radio button.

4. In Authentication, choose Open System.

5. In WEP Encryption, choose 64 bit, 128 bit, or 256 bit (if available). A bigger number of bits means more characters in your key (see Figure 6.11). The bigger the bit count, the longer it takes crack.

6. Under Key Type, choose either HEX or ASCII. HEX means your key has to be written in hexadecimal format, which means it contains characters that include letters A through F and numbers 0 to 9. ASCII means plain text. ASCII comprises characters that are letters A through Z, numbers 0 to 9, and common punctuation marks, including a white space character. There's no way to make HEX and ASCII pretty. Read it again and when you understand it, reward yourself with a tasty cold beverage.

tip

You might be thinking: If WEP is so weak, why bother? Good point. If you have a router security feature called WPA, you'll want to use that instead.

FIGURE 6.11

The WEP settings on a D-Link router can be found in the Wireless control panel.

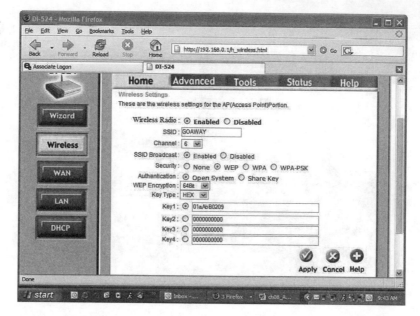

7. Now select Key1 and type in a sequence of letters called a key. Note there are four slots for keys, but only one is active. If you chose 64-bit HEX, this has to be a hexadecimal number which consists of characters like this: A4B1C0DDE2. If you chose 128 bit, this has to be 26-character hexadecimal number.

8. If you chose 64-bit ASCII, this is five ASCII characters, such as snack. If you chose 128-bit ASCII, it is 13 ASCII characters such as mmmmmmmsnacks. If you choose a 256-bit key, you have to a write a short sentence about snacks (29 characters).

9. When you click Apply, your router restarts and you are disconnected from it.

10. To reconnect, double-click on the wireless icon on the bottom right of your Windows XP screen and choose View Wireless Networks. Now your router's name has a lock under it. Double-click on it to connect and input the key you set in your router twice (see Figure 6.12).

11. When you are successfully connected to the WEP-enabled router, the window shows your new secure status (see Figure 6.13).

FIGURE 6.12

Double-click on your WEP-enabled wireless network and type in your WEP key twice when prompted.

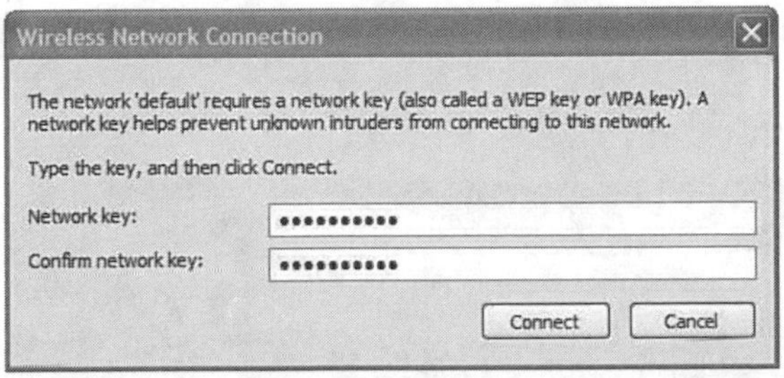

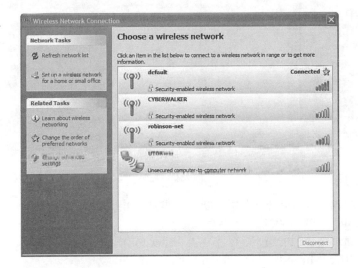

FIGURE 6.13

When you have successfully set a WEP key, Windows XP shows that you are connected to your secure router.

Turn On WPA

Wi-Fi Protected Access (WPA) is probably your best choice for wireless security. This security measure is a lot stronger than namby pamby WEP. In fact WPA came along because businesses needed a tougher measure to keep network snoops out.

Experts say WPA is hackable, too, but you need a big honking computer and a lot of determination. If you have missile launch codes on your home network in your house, worry about this. If not, your prom photos are safe.

Similarly to WEP, WPA uses a code at each end of the wireless connection; however, it's in the form of a phrase (see Figure 6.14). When you set up WPA, it asks you for a *passphrase*, an easy-to-understand sentence or series of words such as "Andy's cat is called Roo," which is not only a good passphrase because it's hard to guess, but it's also true.

Here's how to turn on WPA. First, you hold its hand and tell it that it's beautiful. (Oops, recycled joke.)

FIGURE 6.14

To enable WPA on your router, choose WPA-PSK and enter a passphrase you can remember. Try to make it funny because there's not enough humor in home computer security.

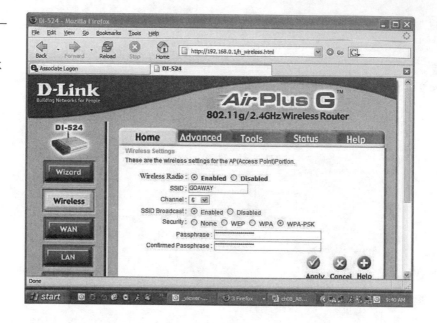

Here are the step-by step instructions:

1. Access your router's settings by typing in its IP address in your web browser. (I told you I'd refer to this a lot.)

2. Once again I'm using a D-Link router for this example. If your router is a different brand, follow along because the steps are similar. From the Home tab, click the Wireless button on the left.

3. Next to Security choose the WPA-PSK radio button.

4. Two passphrase boxes appear. Type in a passphrase you can remember, such as "Sausages are delicious" or "pet goats mow lawns." Have fun here; just be sure to remember what you typed in.

5. Click Apply. The router restarts.

6. After your router is restarted, you'll need to reconnect. Double-click on the wireless icon on the bottom right of your Windows XP screen and choose View Wireless Networks. Now you'll see your router's name with a lock under it. Double-click on it to connect, and input the WPA passphrase you set in your router. You'll need to type it in twice.

tip

If a friend comes over with her laptop and wants to connect to your WPA-protected wireless network, you can simply give her the passphrase. All she needs to do is try to connect to the router and enter it when prompted by her computer.

7. When you are successfully connected to the WPA-enabled router, the window shows your new secure status (see Figure 6.15).

FIGURE 6.15

The Windows XP connection screen shows the computer is connected to a WPA protected Wi-Fi router.

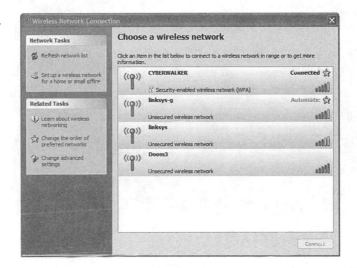

MAC Address Filtering: Keep Out the Scottish

The third option to secure your Wi-Fi network is to use *MAC address filtering*. When it is engaged, it means that no Scottish people can access your wireless network. Of course, they are not the only ones shut out. Everyone else is, too, whether they wear kilts or not.

Here's how it works. Every networked device is assigned a MAC address by its manufacturer when it is made (see Figure 6.16). The MAC address is a unique identifier that is a series of codes separated by dashes. It looks something like 00-90-96-96-5C-3E.

No two MAC addresses are ever the same, which is useful because the MAC address can be used like an identity card to control access to your network.

This is called MAC address filtering. You can set your router to only allow certain MAC addresses to connect to it wirelessly. Two major steps are involved in this process. First you have to gather up all the MAC addresses on the computers you want to allow to connect. Then you'll have to enter these into your router.

> **note**
>
> You might sometimes hear WPA referred to as WPA2 or 802.11i. This is the second generation of WPA. The specification was created by the nice geeks at the Institute of Electrical and Electronics Engineers (IEEE).

FIGURE 6.16

Devices such as routers and network adapters that connect computers to a network each have their own unique MAC address. The MAC address for a piece of gear is usually found on a sticker on the bottom of the device, like it is on this Belkin router.

How to Locate Your MAC Address

First off, your computer does not have a MAC address. It's your network card that does.

Some computers have two network cards: one that's for wired connections and one that uses Wi-Fi. So a computer will have a different MAC address depending on which network card it uses to connect to the network.

The MAC address can be found written directly on the network card, but since that is sometimes concealed inside a computer, it's impractical to use this method to find your MAC address.

The best way to determine a computer's MAC address is to access it on the computer. Here's how to do it on various operating systems.

note

The same passphrase is used for all wireless computers (and other wireless devices) that connect to your Wi-Fi router, so remember you might have to configure the other computers in your home if they use wireless.

Windows XP

1. Click the Start menu, and then choose Run.

2. Type **cmd** and click OK. A black box appears.

3. At the C:\> prompt, type **ipconfig /all** (see Figure 6.17). You'll see the network information listed for each network adapter on the computer and this includes the MAC address, which is identified as Physical Address in the listing. If the computer can connect via a wireless and wired connection, it has two network adapters and each has its own MAC address.

FIGURE 6.17

The MAC address for your computer's network adapters can be found using the ipconfig /all command in a DOS box in Windows XP. The MAC address is shown on the Physical Address line.

```
C:\WINDOWS\system32\cmd.exe

Microsoft Windows XP [Version 5.1.2600]
(C) Copyright 1985-2001 Microsoft Corp.

C:\Documents and Settings\Andy Walker>ipconfig /all

Windows IP Configuration

        Host Name . . . . . . . . . . . . : andylaptop
        Primary Dns Suffix  . . . . . . . :
        Node Type . . . . . . . . . . . . : Broadcast
        IP Routing Enabled. . . . . . . . : No
        WINS Proxy Enabled. . . . . . . . : No

Ethernet adapter Wireless Network Connection:

        Connection-specific DNS Suffix  . :
        Description . . . . . . . . . . . : Atheros AR5001X+ Wireless Network Ad
apter
        Physical Address. . . . . . . . . : 00-90-96-96-5C-3E
        Dhcp Enabled. . . . . . . . . . . : Yes
        Autoconfiguration Enabled . . . . : Yes
        IP Address. . . . . . . . . . . . : 192.168.0.100
        Subnet Mask . . . . . . . . . . . : 255.255.255.0
        Default Gateway . . . . . . . . . : 192.168.0.1
        DHCP Server . . . . . . . . . . . : 192.168.0.1
        DNS Servers . . . . . . . . . . . : 192.168.0.1
        Lease Obtained. . . . . . . . . . : June 22, 2005 12:57:29 PM
        Lease Expires . . . . . . . . . . : June 29, 2005 12:57:29 PM

Ethernet adapter Local Area Connection:

        Media State . . . . . . . . . . . : Media disconnected
        Description . . . . . . . . . . . : Realtek RTL8139/810x Family Fast Eth
ernet NIC
        Physical Address. . . . . . . . . : 00-02-3F-D3-AD-4A

C:\Documents and Settings\Andy Walker>
```

Windows 95, 98, and Me

1. Click the Start menu and choose Run.
2. Type **winipcfg**. A grey box appears with all network settings, including the MAC address.

Mac OS X

1. Open the Applications folder on your hard drive.
2. In the Applications folder, double-click on the Network Utility.
3. Under Info, choose the network card from the drop-down menu that you want to allow access to your network. Below this you'll see an entry for Hardware Address. This is the network card's MAC address (see Figure 6.18).

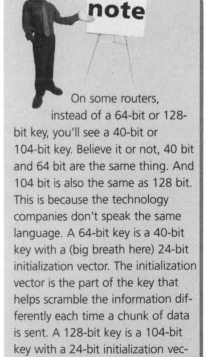

note

On some routers, instead of a 64-bit or 128-bit key, you'll see a 40-bit or 104-bit key. Believe it or not, 40 bit and 64 bit are the same thing. And 104 bit is also the same as 128 bit. This is because the technology companies don't speak the same language. A 64-bit key is a 40-bit key with a (big breath here) 24-bit initialization vector. The initialization vector is the part of the key that helps scramble the information differently each time a chunk of data is sent. A 128-bit key is a 104-bit key with a 24-bit initialization vector. It's okay to go take a nap now.

FIGURE 6.18
The MAC address on your Mac can be found using the Network Utility program.

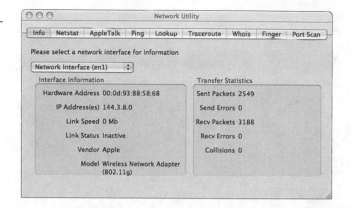

How to Filter by MAC Address

After you have collected the MAC addresses you want to allow on your network (wired computers should be included in your list), follow these steps to engage filtering:

1. Open your router's settings page using your web browser and look for MAC address filtering, which will likely be in the Advanced area of the menus.

2. In a D-Link router, click the Advanced tab and then the Filters button on the left.

3. Under the Filter area, click on the MAC Filters radio button to select it.

4. MAC Filters settings appear. Choose Only Allow Computers with MAC Addresses Listed Below to Access the Network (see Figure 6.19).

tip

A MAC address has nothing to do with Macintosh computer from Apple. It's a unique registration code that every network-enabled device is given when it is manufactured. For the intrepid among you, MAC stands for Media Access Control.

caution

MAC addresses can be spoofed, meaning a computer can fake its MAC address when representing it to the network. The problem is the spoofer has to know allowable MAC addresses first.

FIGURE 6.19

MAC address filtering is a common setting on most routers. It's found under the Advanced tab on this D-Link router.

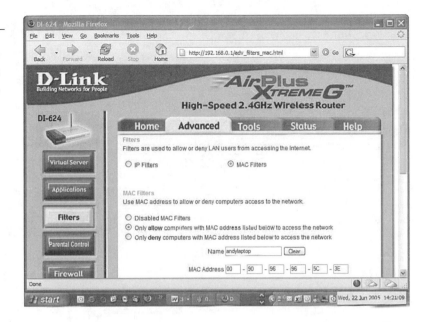

Detecting a Visit from a Wireless Snoop

Most routers have a function that logs information about each computer that has connected to it.

What you are looking for is the DHCP log. DHCP is short for Dynamic Host Configuration Protocol. It sounds complicated, but it's not really. You can think of DHCP like a restaurant hostess. She guides you to a table where you will eat a meal. That table has a number and the wait-staff use that number to identify your table and to keep track of what dishes ordered from the kitchen belong to what tables. It's a temporary assignment. When you leave, someone else gets that table.

tip

If you ever use an external adapter to connect your TV or printer to your network, an easy way to find its MAC address is by flipping the device upside down. It's usually written on the bottom.

DHCP does something similar. When a computer joins a network, it needs an Internet address called an Internet Protocol (IP) address so information it asks for (such as email or a web page) gets sent to the right place. This IP address is called an internal IP address because the address is only used inside the home network.

To the Internet, a home router looks like one computer because it has one public IP; however, it can be the keeper of several computers and it manages all their needs using these internal IP addresses assigned by DHCP.

Inside your router is a log of DHCP clients. This is a list of people who have visited the network and used an internal IP address. To see who's been visiting, all you need to do is locate the log and read through it.

On a D-Link router's Home screen, click the Status tab, and then click Log on the left menu. The log shows a computer's visit to the network and lists its name, the time of the first access, and the IP address assigned by your router (see Figure 6.20).

caution

A savvy visitor to a wireless network can easily hide his tracks by logging on to your router (if the manufacturer's initial settings have not been changed) and clearing the log.

FIGURE 6.20

This is a log of visitors to a D-Link wireless router. It's my router, so you can see visits by my computer, noted as andylaptop. Notice the visitor called Lappy, who is an uninvited guest—probably one of the guys who lives downstairs from me.

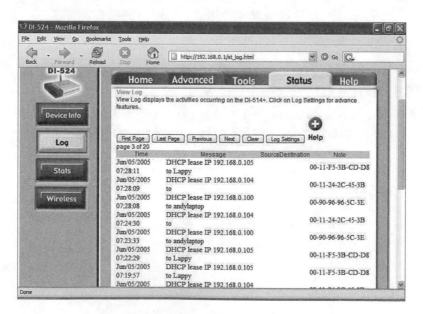

You'll see that it also lists the visiting computer's MAC address. No two MAC addresses are the same, so this is a unique way to know if a computer has been on your network. Of course, to verify this you'd need to get your hands on the computer's network card to compare its MAC address to the one in your router's log.

I'm Under Attack! What to Do If You Discover a Wireless Network Snoop

So you've discovered that someone is accessing your wireless network. Don't panic! Chances are the snoop is just a harmless bandwidth bandit. However, you need to decide what to do about this and other snoops.

Turn Off Wireless Access

The simplest way to stop someone from accessing your wireless router immediately is to turn wireless off.

That might be impractical in the long term; however, if you find someone on your wireless network and you want to instantly protect yourself, this is the quickest way to do so.

In your router configuration there is a setting to turn wireless access off. I'm going to show you how to do this on a D-Link router; however, the settings on your router are similar:

caution

If nobody uses the wireless function on the router in your home, you should turn this feature off.

1. Start on the Home screen (see Figure 6.21) and click the Wireless button on the left side. You'll see the router's wireless settings.

2. Here you'll see a setting that says Wireless Radio and an option to turn it on or off.

FIGURE 6.21

To turn off wireless access to your router, look for an on/off switch in your router's control panel.

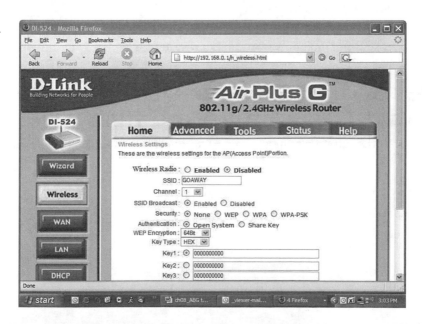

Of course, if someone in your home has a wireless laptop, this can cause a problem because he won't be able to wirelessly access the Internet anymore.

Activate Security Measures

With your wireless settings turned off, you have denied access to the snoop. The next step is to engage one of the security measures I talked about earlier in the chapter. Choose WEP, WPA, or employ MAC address filtering. Then turn wireless back on.

Assess the Damage

Look at your router log to see if the snoop has been on your network before. This is not an absolutely reliable way of determining if a particular snoop is a threat, but it might give you some evidence to see if she is a regular visitor to your network.

There is no way to tell for sure if the snoop is a bandwidth bandit, wardriver, or wireless hacker. If in doubt, you might want to change any passwords or sensitive accounts you might keep stored on your computer. The only way to be sure that nothing has been left behind by the hacker is to scrub your hard drive and start fresh. See **p. 310** to learn how to do this.

However, not every snoop is out to steal your identity or wrong you in some malicious way. How you proceed is up to you.

If you feel that your personal data has been compromised, go change your passwords, alert your bank, and keep an eye on your bank accounts. You might also want to change account numbers, account passwords, and identity documents the snooper might have accessed.

It's important to also do a scan of your computer with your antivirus program and anti-spyware programs to ensure your system is clean of any threats.

Wireless Security Workup: Quick Tactics and Some That Take a Little More Time

Even though it takes more than 10 minutes, you should definitely turn on WEP, WPA, or enable MAC address filtering as a first line of defense, as outlined on **p. 164** earlier in this chapter.

There are also some quickie steps that minimize the threat posed by a wireless network snoop. The following procedures shouldn't take you more than 10 minutes each to implement.

10-Minute Tactic: Change the Router's User ID and Password

When you first set up your wireless router, it has a default password to access its settings. This is set up by the manufacturer. I talk about this earlier in the chapter. See **p. 161** for a list.

It's important that you change this because it's easy for a snoop to determine which brand of router you have and then log in to its settings. The default user IDs and passwords for each manufacturer are commonly known.

Savvy snoops can log in to the router's settings to cover their tracks. They'll locate the router's log and clear it. Malicious snoops might commandeer it by changing the password, locking you out.

To change the router's log-in info

1. Access your router's settings page with your web browser.

2. Seek out the password update screen. You might find it in the Options or Administration area of your router's settings. In D-Link routers it can be found by clicking the Tools tab and then the Admin button to the left of that screen (see Figure 6.22).

3. Enter a new password that will be hard for anyone to guess. A good password should be longer than six characters and include a combination of lower- and upper-case letters and a couple of numbers thrown in for good measure.

FIGURE 6.22

The router password can be updated in a D-Link router in the Admin area under the Tools tab.

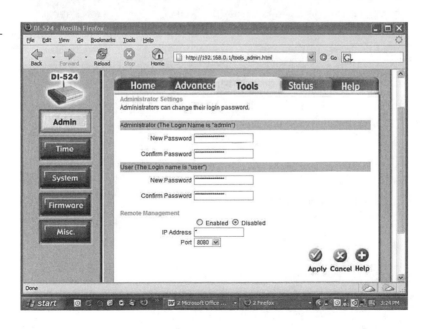

10-Minute Tactic: Change Your Default SSID

When you connect to your wireless network with a wireless computer, you look for a router identifier that it broadcasts called an SSID. That's short for Service Set Identifier. That's the name of the Wi-Fi network. Table 6.2 lists the factory-set SSIDs in various brands of routers. It's a sampling and not exhaustive because every now and then companies decide to change it on some models. I guess that's how some engineering geeks get their jollies.

Table 6.2   Factory Set SSIDs

Router brand	Default SSID
Linksys	linksys
D-Link	default
Netgear	NETGEAR
3Com	comcomcom
Belkin	WLAN or Belkin54g
SMC	WLAN or wireless

> **tip**
>
> If you cannot access your router's settings page because you have forgotten either your WEP or WPA settings or the router's user ID and password, you can reset it. To do this, locate the Reset pinhole feature on the back or underside of the router. Push a pin or paper clip into it and hold it in for 10 seconds. This resets the router to the factory settings, wiping out any customizations you have made and turns off any security features.

It's a good idea to change the default SSID because it demonstrates to anyone who's looking that the owner of the network has taken measures to customize the router settings beyond the factory settings. The subtext is "I know what I am doing on this router, don't mess with me."

Leaving the SSID as the factory default (see Figure 6.23) is like putting a dog cookie in your lap. You'll attract sudden and voracious interest in a place where you don't really want it.

The SSID can be reset as follows:

1. Log into your router's settings using your web browser.

2. Locate the wireless settings. In a D-link router, click the Home tab and then click Wireless on the right. The SSID can be changed on this page (see Figure 6.24).

3. Type in a new and unique SSID, but don't reveal any personal information such as your address or name. You can mix in numbers and letters. Try to

> **tip**
>
> My brother Simon uses the scary sounding VIRUSVAULT as his customized SSID. Of course, this could work either way: Although it might scare bandwidth bandits off, it could also make wireless hackers curious.

use as many of the 32 allowable characters as possible. Think like a hacker. LUV AND KISSES is probably going to attract a lot less interest than MY FAT WALLET.

FIGURE 6.23

The D-Link router detected here is still named with the factory set SSID: default.

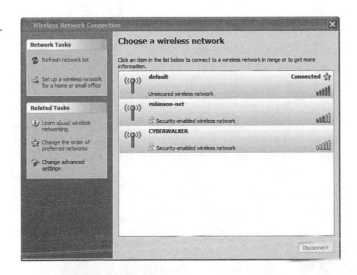

FIGURE 6.24

It's a good idea to change the SSID (the router's name) when you first set it up. In a D-Link router, change it on the Home tab under the Wireless section.

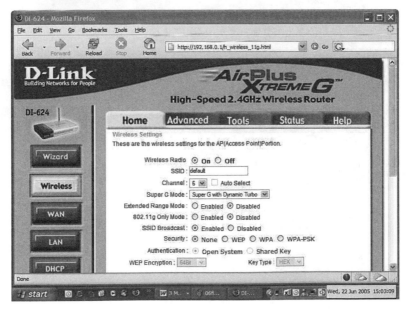

10-Minute Tactic: Turn On the Windows Firewall

One of the best ways to defend your computer against unwanted wireless intruders inside your network is to turn on the built-in Windows XP firewall. This is an electronic fence that sits between your computer and your network and ultimately the outside world. A firewall watches what computers attempt to connect to the computer it defends and stops rogue computers that have no business making contact. Think of it like a really big kid that protects you from having your ice cream stolen.

> **tip**
>
> You can tell if you have Windows XP's Service Pack 2 installed by clicking Start, Control Panel, Performance and Maintenance, and then System. (If XP's Control Panel is set to Classic View, you'll see System in the list on the Control Panel.) If SP2 is installed, it is listed in the System window on the General tab under the heading System.

If your Windows XP computer has Service Pack 2 (SP2) installed, Windows firewall is turned on automatically. Here's how to check and turn it on if it's not already:

1. Click the Start button, choose Control Panel, and then choose Security Center.
2. Click the Windows Firewall link at the bottom of the window.
3. Click the On (recommended) button and click OK (see Figure 6.25).

FIGURE 6.25

Turn on your Windows Firewall for an added level of protection inside your network.

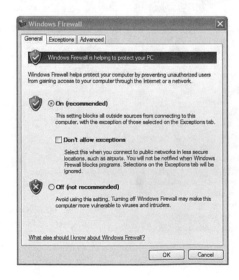

If you don't have Service Pack 2 installed on Windows XP, you can turn on the firewall by doing the following:

1. Click Start, click Run, type `control.exe netconnections`, and then click OK. (You can get at the Network Connections through the Network and Internet Connections link in Control Panel, too.)

2. Right-click the connection on which you would like to enable the Windows Firewall, and then click Properties.

3. On the Advanced tab, click the box to select the option to Protect My Computer or Network.

> **caution**
>
> If you already use a software firewall on your computer, there's no need to turn on Windows Firewall as it's redundant and might slow things down. That would be like putting two security checkpoints on the UFO hanger at Area 51.

If you have already installed Service Pack 2 (SP2) for Windows XP (through a CD or via the Windows Update service on your PC), the firewall has been turned on automatically.

10-Minute Tactic: Turn Off UPnP

A common feature on most home network routers is something called *UPnP*, or *Universal Plug and Play*. It's a powerful yet insecure technology that allows a computer to open inbound ports through the NAT router to which it is attached. This means that your computer can open an electronic door in the router's firewall so that computers on the outside can get in.

The feature was designed to make it easy to use peer-to-peer file sharing, instant messaging, and other interactive computer-to-computer connections. The problem is that while this feature is supposed to make your life easier—saving you the headache of messing with router ports—it also opens up a huge security hole.

Why? Because any program on your computer—including malware—can use UPnP to open an inbound hole in your firewall without your knowledge. A virus, for example, could use the technique to import more malware, or give someone out on the Internet remote access to your computer.

So what to do? Unless you really need to enable peer-to-peer programs or instant messenger programs, simply disable the router's UPnP option.

Here's how to turn of UPnP on a D-Link router:

1. Access your router's control panel using the technique explained earlier in this chapter.

2. Click the Tools tab, and then click the Misc button on the left.

3. Look for the UPNP Settings option and choose Disable.

4. At the bottom, click Apply. The router will restart.

10-Minute Tactic: Turn Off Your Router When Not in Use

If you don't use the wireless feature on your router, turn it off. There is usually a switch in your router's settings that enables you to do this. On D-Link routers, for example, it can be found in the router settings by clicking the Home tab and then clicking the Wireless button on the left (see Figure 6.26).

If you want to be extra cautious—like a stiletto-wearing supermodel in a busy dog park—you should power down your router when you're away or asleep. If you choose this conservative approach, remember that any network-reliant computer or device will not be able to access the Internet. For example, your antivirus signatures will not be able to update automatically.

FIGURE 6.26

Turn wireless access on your router off if all of the computers on your network are connected using wires to the router. The setting shown is on a D-Link router.

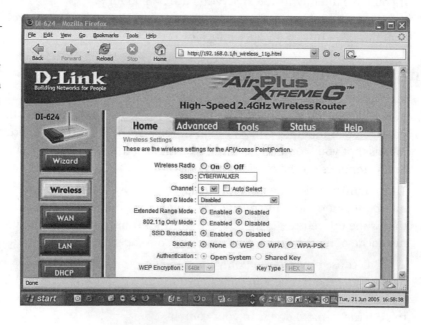

Time Intensive Tactic: Be Careful with File Sharing

When you're on a network you have the ability to share folders and files with other computers on the network.

This allows you to play your ABBA music collection stored on the computer upstairs on your laptop in the kitchen.

Here's how you share a folder. Right-click on the folder, choose Properties, and click the Sharing tab. You'll need to name the shared folder something unique. This is called a *share name* (see Figure 6.27).

FIGURE 6.27

To share a folder
on Windows XP,
right-click on the
folder, choose
Properties, and
then the Sharing
tab, and enter a
share name.

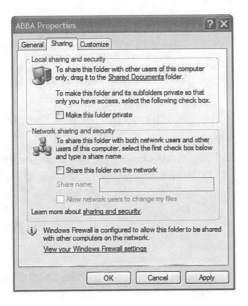

Anyone connected to the network can access your shared folders across the network
by browsing the Network Neighborhood and locating your computer or by clicking
Start, Run, and typing in your computer's private IP address and the share name
like this:

`\\192.168.0.100\ABBA`

Although this is a great way to share data, it
can also pose a big privacy and security problem. If a wireless network snooper connects to
your network, he has access to your shared
folders. And if the folder contains a file that
lists your banking passwords, you're probably
not going to Aruba on holiday this year.

At the risk of sounding like a man whose den-
tures have fallen out of reach, the best way to
stop a bad person from accessing your shared
files is to stop them from accessing the network.
Turn on WEP, WPA, or use MAC address filtering
to stop them. See **p. 164** to learn more about
these procedures.

> **tip**
>
> To figure out which version
> of Windows you have, click
> Start (and then Settings on
> some versions of Windows),
> Control Panel, and double-
> click the System icon. The
> General tab displays which
> version of Windows you are using.

You'll know a folder is being shared because its icon (the little picture that represents
the file) has a hand cradling it.

If you want to turn file sharing off, follow the steps for your computer.

Windows 98/Me

File sharing can be turned off in the Windows Control Panel using the Network applet. Follow these steps:

1. Click on the Start button, and click Settings, Control Panel. Double-click on the Network icon.

2. When the Network box appears, click on the File and Print Sharing button on the Configuration tab.

3. If file sharing is on, check marks are in the check boxes next to I Want to Give Others Access to My Files and I Want to Be Able to Allow Others to Print to My Printer. To turn file sharing off, click on those boxes to uncheck them. Click OK.

Windows XP Home

In Windows XP Home Edition, a function called Simple File Sharing is turned on by default. This is useful because if a file is purposely shared, anyone on the network can access it. If that's your spouse, this is probably a good thing. If that's the 15-year-old kid with the Kill All Humans T-shirt from down the street, it's probably not so good.

To protect yourself, you need to set a password for the Guest account on your computer, following these steps:

1. Click the Start button, and then Run, and then type `cmd`. (In older versions of Windows, type `command` instead.) Click OK.

2. A black box appears. Now figure out a password—maybe *angryrabbits*.

3. At the C:\> prompt, type `net user guest angryrabbits`

4. If you don't want your password to be angryrabbits, type something else instead. The password happyrabbits is just as good.

5. Hit your Enter key. The system responds with The Command Completed Successfully (see Figure 6.28).

6. The password for the Guest is now set. Close the window. Now if anyone tries to access a shared folder, they are asked for a password.

> **tip**
>
> If you need to keep simple file sharing turned on but you only want to share folders with specific people (such as your spouse), here's a trick. When you right-click on a folder to share it, you'll need to assign it a share name. This is the name that appears on the network when it is browsed. To hide the shared folder, add a dollar sign to the end of the share name, `bagelrecipe$`, for instance. This way, only people who know the share name are able to access it. It does not appear when someone browses the Network Neighborhood.

FIGURE 6.28

Change the
Guest user's
password in the
DOS emulator in
Windows.

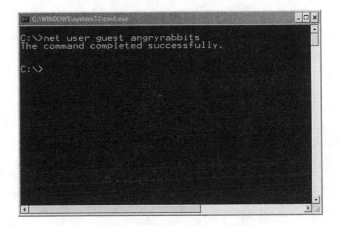

Windows XP Professional

If you have a Windows XP Professional system and you choose not to protect your
wireless network with WEP, WPA, or MAC address filtering, you'll want to turn
Simple File Sharing off, using these steps:

1. Click Start, Control Panel, Appearance and Themes, and choose Folder
   Options.

2. Click on the View tab, scroll down to the bottom, and uncheck the option
   that says Use Simple File Sharing (Recommended) (see Figure 6.29).

FIGURE 6.29

Turn off simple
file sharing in
Windows XP
Professional if
you are not
going to use it
(uncheck the last
box).

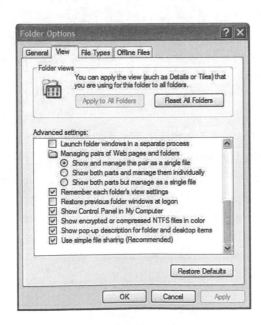

3. When you right-click on a folder to share it, choose the Sharing and Security option. Then choose the Sharing tab to configure sharing options.

4. By choosing the Security tab you can also manually edit read/write permissions for individual users who have access to your computers. Just be forewarned: It's easy to get confused by these permissions and misconfigure them, so tread lightly and chew a big stick of gum. Don't mess with this stuff too much if you're new to it. A misstep with permissions can lock you out of a file or folder. If that's your late grandma's secret fabulous cookie recipe, you'll have to rely on the Keebler elves for your cookie needs.

THE ABSOLUTE MINIMUM

- A home router is an appliance that connects home computers together by creating a network and sharing an Internet connection among them.

- Most routers are wirelessly enabled. This technology is called Wi-Fi.

- Straight out of the box, Wi-Fi has no security features turned on.

- Anyone can connect to a Wi-Fi network if it's not configured to be secure.

- Wireless network snoops come in three types: bandwidth bandits, wardrivers, and wireless hackers.

- Bandwidth bandits are people who just want a free Internet connection.

- Wardrivers catalog open wireless networks and share them with bandwidth bandits.

- You have to worry about wireless hackers who are malicious network snoops, but fortunately, these types of snoops are rare.

- Three ways to lock out wireless network snoops are WEP, WPA, and MAC address filtering.

- WPA is the easiest and most convenient wireless security mechanism.

- Turn off the UPnP feature in your router.

- Changing the factory settings of your router makes you look like less of a target.

- Turning off file sharing and turning on the Windows Firewall adds additional layers of security.

IN THIS CHAPTER

- Why Your Computer Privacy Is Important

- What Data Trail Do You Leave on Your Computer?

- Who's Snooping and Why?

- Consequences of Being Snooped

- Obscure Your Trail—In About 10 Minutes

- Cover Your Tracks—In an Afternoon

7

PRIVACY SNOOPS: COVER YOUR TRACKS AND YOUR REPUTATION

What you do on the computer is your own business, but when it's accessible by the whole household (or office), your privacy might not be as sacred as you'd like. This chapter shows you what kind of trail you leave behind on the computer, and how to cover your digital tracks. Whether you're researching birthday presents, perusing naughty websites, or budgeting for a surprise family holiday, if you don't want your computer activities discovered, this chapter will help you keep your secrets secret and your computer evidence-free.

Why Your Privacy Is Important

Do you lay awake at night and worry about the safety of your Oreos? Do you wear tin foil hats to protect yourself from government mind rays? Do you see angry messages in your cereal?

Yes? Then this book is not for you because you're probably crazy. But, if you worry about people snooping on your computer, I can help.

Let's pretend—even for a little while—that you are a little paranoid about your teenagers looking at your electronic bank statements, your spouse snooping on your web habits, and your co-workers reading your email.

Guess what? You have reason to fear. A computer is a great big data recorder. Almost everything you do with it leaves a trace and anyone curious and skilled enough can easily discover what you have been up to.

Knowing what information is recorded and where this audit trail is kept is important because then you'll know what kind of information can be revealed by someone who's savvy enough to look.

Perhaps you have little to hide. After all, most people's day-to-day computer activities are not that exciting. However, here's why revealing personal activities on a computer might be a problem for you:

- The first thing that comes to mind is surfing adult content on the web. While this is a completely legitimate activity for an adult (I'm not saying it's moral; I'm just saying that it's legit), exposing children to such material is not something you want to do. If a computer is shared by a family, you'll have to ensure any such content is removed or hidden on the computer. Some people won't want a spouse to encounter it, either.

- You want to keep financial records, bank accounts, and access to financial accounts away from unauthorized eyes. That might be your children, your family, or co-workers if this information is kept on a computer owned by your employer.

- You want to safeguard activities such as planning birthday celebrations, wedding anniversaries, and surprise parties; or purchasing a gift. If you use your computer to plan or execute these activities, you'll want to ensure no one with access to the computer can discover your plans.

- Communications sometimes need to be secret, too. And if there's one thing a computer is good at, it's helping you communicate—that includes chat conversations, email, and letters written in a word processor.

What You Leave Behind on Your Computer

You'd be surprised at what kind of a usage pattern you can leave behind when using your computer. Every time you touch the keyboard or mouse, you create an electronic trail. Following are the key areas you should be concerned about.

Web Browser

Your web browser is the biggest liability to your privacy. Everything you do and see on the Web is tracked and stored, including the following:

- Websites you visit
- Web images and other web page content you see
- Movies and audio you play
- User IDs and passwords for restricted websites you might visit
- Files you download
- Search terms you enter

All this information is captured and saved unless you instruct the browser to discard it.

Documents

Many programs keep a list of documents you have opened under a list of files in the program called Most Recently Used (MRU) documents.

Windows separately keeps track of these files in its registry. Also, search programs can find content of files as well as file names and types.

Movies and Audio Players

As a convenience, any movie, video clip, or audio file you play can be tracked in most common multimedia players, including Windows Media Player. This feature allows you to easily access what you've seen or heard again. Unfortunately, anyone else can also access this information just by looking it up in the right place in the program.

Email

Email programs are great places for snoops to go. Not only can they see email you have received, but they can also see email you have sent. And they can see the time and date your emails were sent and received, and the frequency with which the communication has been made.

Chat Programs

Real time chat programs that are used to communicate via typing text with someone live have logging functions. These logs can be read later.

Who Are the Privacy Snoops?

So who is snooping on you? Many people might be interested in what you are doing on your computer:

- **Your family**—A clever teenager, a wily spouse, or a nosy relative might be interested in your electronic activities.

- **Your co-workers**—If you use equipment owned by your employer, anyone with access to your computer can easily track what you have been doing with it.

- **Your boss**—Your employer has a right to know what you have been doing with company-owned equipment and your privacy when using its equipment is limited.

- **The authorities**—Under certain circumstances, your computer can be seized and possibly used as evidence in criminal proceedings if there's suspicion of illegal activity.

The Consequences of Being Caught

The consequences of having your computer habits exposed vary from mild embarrassment to criminal conviction if you're doing something illegal with the system. Here's what you might be subject to should someone discover your computer usage patterns:

- **Embarrassment**—You computer habits could divulge your interest in adult content or even perhaps private details about your life, such as your health, financial well being, or lifestyle preferences.

- **Marital discord**—Illicit computer use can cause discord with your spouse if he or she finds out what you are doing.

- **Ruined plans**—If you're doing something secret to surprise a family member or friend, discovery of your plans could ruin the surprise.

- **Employment termination**—Using a company computer for unauthorized purposes can lead to backlash from your superiors and perhaps even termination. Imagine if you posted a rèsumè to job websites and that was discovered!

- **Theft**—Financial or banking access information could be stolen that might lead to theft of assets.

■ **Blackmail or extortion**—Discovery of secrets you have on your computer could expose embarrassing or compromising behavior that someone could use against you.

■ **Criminal or civil action**—In extreme cases, your actions on a computer could lead to criminal or civil litigation if revealed to authorities.

Emergency Tactics—I Am Being Snooped On!

If you suspect someone is snooping on your computer activities, there's not much you can do if he has already seen the evidence. However, you can limit further snooping.

You need to set up an account on the computer and password-protect it. This step seems simple, but there are some tricks to it that you need to know. Let me whisper in your ear.

First, you need to understand a little bit about how user accounts work on XP. Many people can share one Windows XP computer, and each has his own unique desktop, files, and even programs.

What follows applies to both Windows XP Home and Windows Professional; however, XP Pro has the ability to create custom types of users with special privileges.

note

Before I go any further, I think it's really important to tell you that neither I nor my publisher are suggesting that you use the information presented here to break the law. If you are, know that there are sophisticated tools available to the authorities that can forensically expose your actions anyway, but the advice in this chapter will guard you against your run-of-the-mill snooper. I'm merely pointing out where your privacy could be breached. It is important to know what information is easily accessible to a third party. It's up to you to determine the morality, ethicality, or legality of your actions with your computer.

By default, XP allows three types of users:

■ **Administrator**—This user can access and change anything on the computer, including information in limited accounts.

■ **Limited user**—This user can only access information in her account and she can't install certain programs or make system changes.

■ **Guest**—This account is used by computers on the same network accessing files on another computer. It can also be used for visitors who want to use the computer.

Administrator

In order to preserve your privacy on a computer, you want to ensure you have a password-protected administrator account and ensure you are the only administrator on the system. (If another account is designated an administrator, this account holder can get at your data.)

The administrator is an all-powerful system deity that has certain superpowers. He can do the following:

- Make system-wide changes
- Install and remove programs
- Create and destroy user accounts and edit their passwords
- Access all files that haven't explicitly been marked private

Limited Users

The second type of account on a computer is called a *limited user*. This type of account does not have administrator privileges. Limited users get their own desktop and password-protected log in ID; however, they have no privacy, can't install programs, and can't make changes to the system. Limited user accounts are perfect for children, roommates, and even spouses who need access to the computer, but who don't necessarily need administrator rights. They might also have trouble running some programs, including games.

Limited users get frustrated very quickly when they can't do certain things with their accounts, especially if they are children and they like to play games.

You can get around this by running the program with administrator permissions, using the Run As option. Here's how:

1. Log in as the limited user.

2. Right-click on the program you want to run and choose Run As (see Figure 7.1).

3. Click the radio button next to The Following User option (see Figure 7.2), choose the administrator's account from the drop-down User Name: box, and then type the account's password.

4. Click OK. The program runs under administrator privileges.

5. Be sure not to give the child the password, as she can then gain access to your account.

caution

If you don't plan on using the guest account, it's wise to disable it. Click Start, Control Panel, Users, and click the guest account. Then choose Turn off the Guest Account.

FIGURE 7.1

Right-click on the program the limited user wants to run and choose Run As to run the program with administrator privileges.

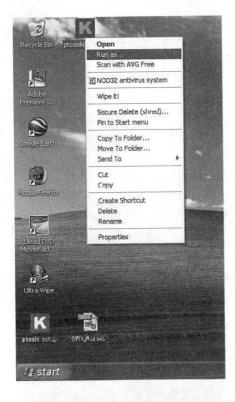

FIGURE 7.2

Select The Following User option, choose an administrator account, and type the administrator's password to run the program as an administrator.

Guest Accounts

Guest accounts are the least privileged accounts of all. A guest user can access programs that are on the computer. So, for example, she can surf the Web, use Photoshop, and create a spreadsheet, but she has no ability to change anything on the system, including changing the account type to administrator or a limited user. The account is ideal for people like your Great Uncle Frank who comes to visit and wants to order you a new book on whales with which he is so taken. Note, too, that a guest user cannot access anyone else's files.

XP PRO'S HIDDEN USER GROUPS

Under XP Pro are some advanced user features that lie deep inside Windows. These custom users are typically assigned by IT administrators at businesses. If you are ambitious, you can use these, too, by following these steps:

1. Click Start, Control Panel.
2. Click Administrative Tools and then Computer Management.
3. On the left of the window, you see Local Users and Groups.
4. Click the plus sign (+) to reveal Users and Groups.
5. Click Groups and a list of custom users appears on the right. Note the Power Users group that has more permissions than the Limited Users group (they can install programs, for example), but not enough to be administrators.
6. To assign a user to one of these groups, click Users on the left.
7. Right-click the user you want to modify and choose Properties.
8. Then click the Member Of tab and click the Add button.
9. Under the Enter the Object Names to Select box, type in the custom user group, such as Power Users, and click Check Names, OK.
10. Next time you are in the Users area in the Control Panel, you'll see that the user you have given special permissions to is marked as an unknown user type.

And here's a tip within a tip. A hidden user management tool in Windows XP Pro can be used to manage the hidden user types. To access and use it, follow these steps:

1. Click Start, Run, type `control userpasswords2`, and click OK.
2. To change a limited user to a power user, click the user's name to select it, click Properties, and then the Group Membership tab.
3. You can make the user a power user by clicking Standard User, leave him as a limited user by clicking Restricted User, or set him as one of the other user types by clicking Other and choosing the user type from the drop-down menu.

Note that power users can see and change any file on a computer, so granting someone these powers does not protect anyone's privacy. They cannot, however, change any core system settings or mess with things such as the registry.

How to Create PC Privacy

To create some privacy for yourself on your computer, you'll need to make three key changes to the system.

Administrate Your Fate

First, you need to ensure that you have an administrator account. Then you need to password protect it. This provides you with a personal desktop in which to do your computing and protect it from prying eyes.

You likely already have an administrator account. You can tell by going into the Control Panel, choosing User Accounts (see Figure 7.3), and clicking the Change an Account option to see what accounts are on the system.

Look for the account you use to sign in to the system and see if *Computer administrator* is listed next to it.

FIGURE 7.3

All the users on the system are listed in the user accounts. You can also tell here whether they have limited accounts or are administrators.

To password protect your administrator account, follow these steps:

1. If you're not already in User Accounts, go there by clicking Start, Control Panel, User Accounts.

2. Next click Change Account.

3. Then click the account you want to add a password to.

4. Next, click Create a Password.

5. Now type in your password twice in the boxes provided and enter a reminder phrase so if you forget the password at some point, the system will prompt you to remember it. If your password is halfabagofcookies, your reminder phrase could be "What I ate for breakfast on my birthday" (see Figure 7.4).

tip

When you add a password to an administrator account, the system asks you if you want to make your files and folders private. Say yes to this to stop others from browsing your files.

FIGURE 7.4

Create a password for your account and be sure to include a reminder so if you forget the password, you can get the system to prompt you with a hint.

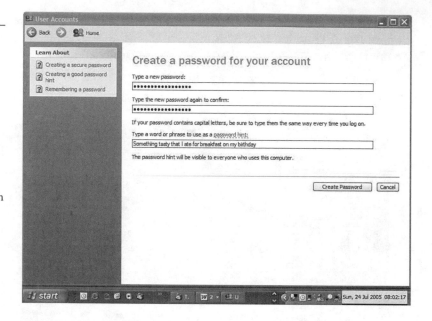

THE GREAT PASSWORD CHALLENGE

It's hard to create a password that is both difficult for others to guess and easy for you to remember. Here are some tips that should help:

- Be sure the password is at least six characters long and preferably longer.
- Use a mix of upper- and lowercase characters and mix it up with letters and numbers.
- Don't use a real word in any language.
- Don't use consecutive letters or numbers such as *abcd* or *1234*.
- Don't use any personal info such birth dates, name, home town, or phone number.

One of the great ways to create a password is to take a phrase and edit it into something obscure that you won't have trouble remembering. The phrase "I am Pamela Anderson's number one fan" can be turned into the password ImPAM&rsonsNo1fan. Feel free to be Brad Pitt's number one fan if you've never seen *BayWatch*.

FIGURE 7.5

A login screen like this one indicates there is only one administrator account on the system and it has a password. If you remove the password, you won't see a login screen at all when Windows starts.

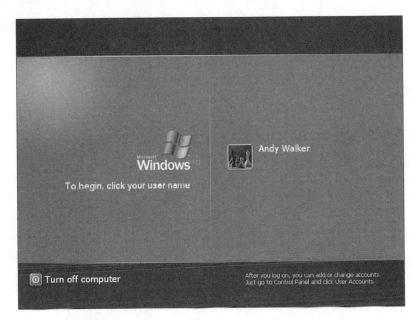

Be Like Fidel: Take Control and Limit Users

To ensure your privacy, you need to become a computer fascist and eliminate all other administrators on the system and turn them into limited users. This is a handy trick if you have children. They probably already think you're a fascist anyway.

Here's how to change your child's administrator account into a limited user account:

1. Click Start, Settings, Control Panel, and then User Accounts.

2. Click the Change an Account option to see which accounts are on the system and what their status is.

3. Click the account marked Administrator and click Change My Account Type, set it to Limited, and click the button marked Change Account Type (see Figure 7.6).

4. Repeat this for all Administrators on the system except for your account.

> **tip**
>
> If you are not prompted to choose a user account when you enter Windows, there is only one account set up on your system. It is an administrator account and it is not password protected (refer to Figure 7.5).

FIGURE 7.6
Change all the users on the system (except yourself) to limited accounts.

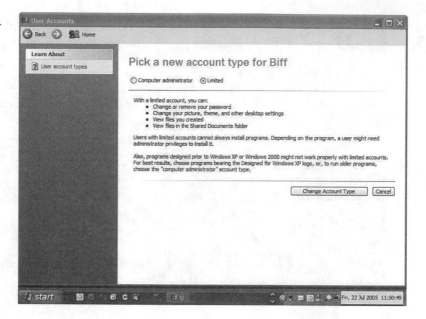

With this step complete, no one can access your desktop or your data in your account.

You might run into resistance from a spouse, co-worker, or other system user with whom you share the system. But most people probably won't know the difference until they try to install software, at that point they'll get a cryptic error message (see Figure 7.7).

Password Protect the Hidden Administrator

When Windows first installs, it creates a hidden administrator account without a password that is not visible to anyone. If you know it's there, you can use it to access the system as an administrator, make changes, and access other people's data.

tip

Of course, it doesn't do any good to have a password-protected administrative account if you leave your computer on all the time, logged into your administrative account. This is sort of like leaving the keys in your shiny new sports car in downtown New York while you sip a mocha in a nearby Starbucks. At the very least, log off your account if you're going to be away from your computer for more than a few minutes. Click Start and then choose Log Off. When you return, click your account on the Windows log-in screen and enter your password to log on again.

FIGURE 7.7

Users with a limited account won't be able to install software. When they try, they'll get a cryptic error message like this one.

Here's how to find and password protect the hidden administrator account:

1. Restart the computer.
2. Press the F8 key repeatedly as the computer starts until you see the Windows Advanced Options Menu that includes the Safe Mode option (see Figure 7.8).

FIGURE 7.8

Press the F8 key repeatedly when the computer starts up and the system displays the Windows Advanced Options Menu that allows you to boot into Windows using a troubleshooting mode called Safe Mode.

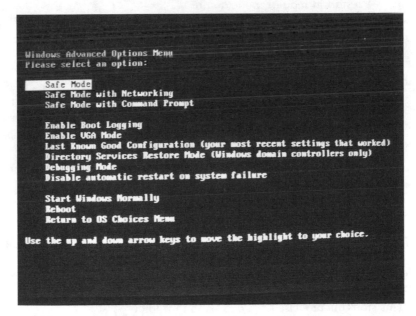

3. Choose Safe Mode by hitting Enter, and then on the next screen, select the Windows installation on your machine. There should only be one and it should be named either Windows XP Home or Windows XP Professional. After choosing this and hitting Enter, you'll see the Windows login screen.
4. Here you see several user accounts, including one that you haven't seen before. This one will be marked Administrator. It is the hidden administrator account.

5. Click this account to enter the hidden administrator account in Windows Safe Mode. By default, the password is blank.

6. You see a warning reminding you that you are entering Windows in Safe Mode. Click Yes to enter Windows.

7. After you're in Windows Safe Mode, the system looks like a Windows desktop but appears slightly more barren. Click Start, Control Panel, and then User Accounts.

8. Choose Change an Account and then click the hidden administrator account. Now choose Create a Password.

9. When you are done, exit Windows and restart in regular mode again.

Privatize Your Files

Finally, take the files you don't want anyone to see and make them private.

If you are the only administrator on the system, this is an unnecessary step. But if you have to share administrator access with someone else on the system—maybe your spouse—create a folder and put personal your-eyes-only files in it. Then make it private as follows:

1. Right-click on the folder and choose Properties.

2. Click the Sharing tab.

3. Check the Make This Folder Private option.

This stops anyone else from accessing that folder from his account—including other administrators. However, if you have left another administrator on the system, you should know that he can change or remove the password on your user account. After he has done this, he can log on as you and access your private files.

> **caution**
>
> Wily teenagers who know about the hidden administrator account can use it to make themselves administrators again. So it's important that you password protect this account.

> **tip**
>
> If someone has already password protected the hidden administrator account, enter Safe Mode with your usual administrator account and change the hidden administrator password to one you'll remember.

> **caution**
>
> The hidden administrator account is an emergency account. It's not advisable to delete it. It should be password protected and left as a backup.

FIGURE 7.9

Make your files private so no one else can access them.

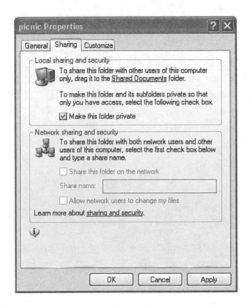

Obscure Your Trail—In About 10 Minutes

If someone gains access to your account or if you can't be bothered to set up your system as previously suggested, anyone wanting to check your computer habits will likely check your web browser first.

Here's how to wipe those web tracks away in about 10 minutes. If you have more time on your hands, jump ahead to the section called "Cover Your Tracks—In an Afternoon" on **p. 207**.

Microsoft Internet Explorer

Microsoft Internet Explorer 6 is notoriously disorganized. Cleaning your tracks requires kangaroo-like agility. You'll have to hop around a bunch of menus to wipe it all away. It helps at this point to mime a kangaroo to get in the right frame of mind. So go ahead and hop around the room, even if your kids think you are weird.

note

Windows Safe Mode is a Windows mode used for troubleshooting. It loads a minimal amount of software and drivers and gives you access to the system in a raw state so you can fix problems.

Clear Your Cache

Okay, let's get to it. The *web cache* is a place that saves web pages and their various components, such as pictures, sounds, and multimedia components. It's designed to speed up the loading of web pages so the next time you visit a site, you don't have to download the same pages again.

To clear your cache in Internet Explorer, follow these steps:

1. Open the browser and click the Tools menu at the top of the window.

2. Click Internet Options and then click the Delete Files button on the General tab in the Temporary Internet Files area.

3. If you want to see what files will be deleted, click the Settings button first and then click the View Files button. You'll see a list of all files in the browser's cache (see Figure 7.10).

tip

The private files feature is a good way to give your children some computer privacy.

FIGURE 7.10

You can use the View Files button to see a list of the files stored in Internet Explorer's cache.

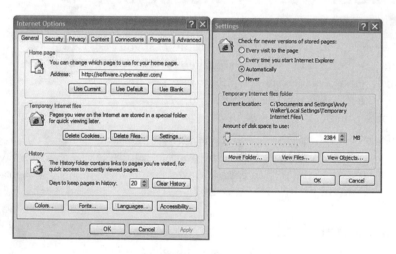

Clear Your History

The IE's history function is a list of all the websites you have visited. It can be viewed by clicking the View menu and choosing Explorer Bar, History. A sidebar opens up on the left side of the browser and reveals all the websites you have visited for the last seven days, as well as those visited in prior weeks.

To clear this, click Tools, Internet Options, click the General tab, and then click the Clear History button under the History section (see Figure 7.11).

FIGURE 7.11

Wipe away traces of websites you have visited in Internet Explorer by using the Clear History button in IE's Internet Properties window.

Clear Your Cookies

Cookies are little text files placed on your computer by a website that contains tracking information. They contain a variety of data including

- Items in your shopping basket on a pay site
- Log-in information so you don't have to remember your user ID and password for membership sites
- Date, time, and other session information that shows the last time you visited a site
- Data used to track or control advertising you have seen

Getting rid of cookies periodically is a good idea—especially if you frequent naughty websites, as the advertisers on these sites place cookies on your computer to customize ads for you and to track the frequency of your visits. These can reveal to someone looking at your computer that you have been visiting adult websites (see Figure 7.12).

Here's how to get rid of cookies:

1. Open Internet Explorer and click the Tools menu.
2. Click Internet Options.
3. In the General tab, click the Delete Cookies button in the Temporary Internet files section (see Figure 7.13).

FIGURE 7.12

Web browser cookies are little text files that can reveal websites you have visited, like this one from a pornography site. Please note that I visited this site for the good of science, just to show you a real live cookie.

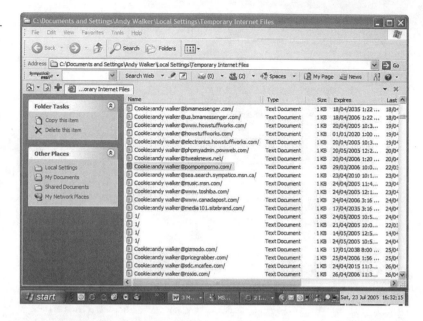

FIGURE 7.13

To get rid of cookies in Internet Explorer, simply click the Delete Cookies button in the browser's Internet Options window.

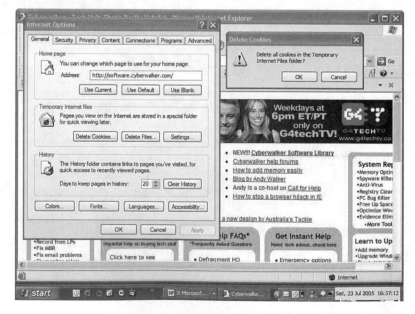

Clear Search Forms

One of the most potentially embarrassing functions of a web browser is what's called AutoComplete. The embarrassing situation occurs when someone borrows your computer and merrily types in a search engine looking to buy hardware. When they begin to type *nails and hammers*, a drop-down box with *naughty naked people* appears (see Figure 7.14). Oops. Now they know what you were searching for on your day off.

FIGURE 7.14

If embarrassing keywords pop up when you are search Google, you want to turn off AutoComplete in Internet Explorer.

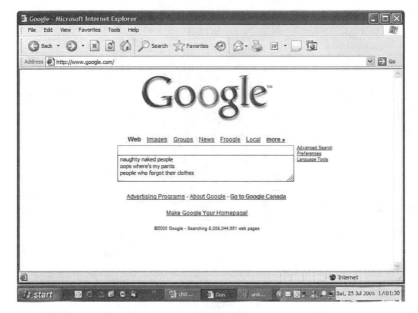

AutoComplete works for forms and web addresses. The forms are boxes you enter information into on a web page like the one you enter search terms into on Google.com. But the web browser also saves web addresses you've been to and suggests those when you start typing in a few letters.

Here's how to turn AutoComplete off:

1. Open Internet Explorer, click the Tools menu, and then Internet Options.

2. Click the Content tab and then the AutoComplete button under the Use AutoComplete For section.

3. Unclick the check boxes for Web Addresses and Forms. If you don't want the browser to save usernames and passwords that you use to sign into membership-based websites, uncheck those options, too. To clear Auto-Complete's cache of saved form data, click Clear Forms (see Figure 7.15). Optionally, click Clear Passwords to wipe away remembered password data in website password fields.

> **tip**
>
> If you are thinking, "Okay, Andy, I understand AutoComplete, but how do I clear my Google searches," then go back to step 3.
> When you clear forms, you clear the Google search box because it is a web form!

4. To clear remembered website addresses from your web browser's address bar (where you type in web addresses), go back to the General tab by clicking OK and then the General tab.

5. Finally, click Clear History in the History section.

FIGURE 7.15

FIGURE 7.15

To clear
AutoComplete's
cache of saved
form data, click
Clear Forms.

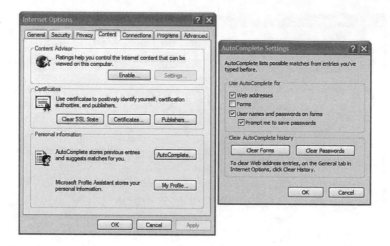

Mozilla Firefox

Mozilla makes it a lot easier to manage web tracking data in its Firefox browser. It's all on one screen. You can clear the following items with one button:

- Website address history
- Saved form information
- Saved passwords
- Download manager history
- Cookies
- Cache

Here's how to clear web tracking data:

1. Open Firefox, and click the Tools menu and then Options.

2. Click the Privacy icon on the left of the Options windows.

3. A list of all the content that affects your privacy is shown (see Figure 7.16).

4. You can delete the items in the list one at a time by clicking the Clear button next to each one. Or for further options, click the plus sign next to each item.

5. To wipe it all away at once, click the Clear All button at the bottom of the Privacy window.

FIGURE 7.16
Firefox keeps its privacy settings all in one place and even has a single Clear All option.

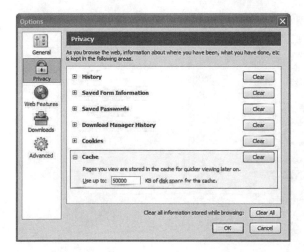

Cover Your Tracks—In an Afternoon

A lot of hidden data on your computer reveals what you have been doing on your computer. So here are some of the dustier corners of your computer that you should occasionally clean out.

Clean Multimedia Players

Multimedia players often keep track of the video and audio files you have played. There are so many programs that there's no space here to list the way to clean them all. But if you look carefully in each program, and search for a preferences or privacy menu or tab, you should be able to find the options yourself.

That said, here's how to turn off and clear the play histories for two of the most common media players for Windows.

Windows Media Player 10

Follow these steps to clear play histories for Windows Media Player:

1. Open Windows Media Player 10.
2. Click the Tools menu and then Options.
3. Click the Privacy tab. Under the History section, click the Clear Cache and Clear History buttons to remove any evidence of previously played media files (see Figure 7.17).
4. Also, uncheck the box next to Save File and URL History in the Player.

FIGURE 7.17

Windows Media Player keeps track of video and audio files you have been watching, but this feature can be disabled.

Real Player 10

Follow these steps to clear play histories for Real Player:

1. Open Real Player 10.

2. Click the Tools menu and then Preferences.

3. Under the General area, click the Clear History button under the History section.

4. Uncheck the box that says Enable a History List in the File menu to turn off the list of most recently played files on the File menu (see Figure 7.18).

FIGURE 7.18

Real Player keeps track of multimedia files that have been played. However, the list can be easily cleared.

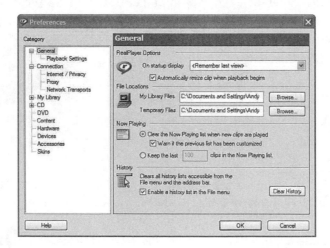

Protect Your Email

Email programs are a great way to snoop on people. You can see communications back and forth and even search by sender, recipient, date, and contents. Getting inside a person's email program is like being given access to her whole life, especially for someone who relies on email as her primary mode of communication. It's often an excellent diary of someone's life. If your email falls into the wrong hands, a snooper can discover a lot about you.

Here are the basic privacy concerns that apply to many email programs:

- Every email you send is saved in the Sent Items folder (or a similar folder), unless that option is turned off in the program.
- All email received remains in your inbox unless it is deleted.
- When deleted, email goes to a deleted items folder sometimes called the Trash Can or Recycle Bin folder. It's held until you empty the folder.
- Sending email is as private as sending a postcard. Anyone who has the know-how can look at its contents as it travels to its destination.
- Email is fetched from your mail server, but can be set to be left on the server for later retrieval (by you or someone else).

Turn Off Saved Sent Items

Here are some email privacy guidelines to help keep your email private in two of the most common email programs, Outlook 2003 and Outlook Express 6.

Each time an email is sent, it is saved by the email program. You can, however, turn off this function by following these steps in Outlook 2003:

1. Open Outlook and click on the Tools menu.
2. Click Options and then click the Preferences tab.
3. Click E-mail Options.
4. Under the Message Handling area, uncheck the box next to Save Copies of Messages in Sent Items Folder.

In Outlook Express 6, follow these steps:

1. Open Outlook Express and click on the Tools menu.
2. Click Options and then the Send tab.
3. Uncheck Save Copy of Sent Messages in the Sent Items Folder (see Figure 7.19).

FIGURE 7.19

FIGURE 7.19

Most email programs save sent emails in the Sent Items or Outbox folder. You can turn this feature off to protect your privacy, as shown in the Send tab of Outlook Express 6.

Empty Deleted Items Folder

Just like in Windows, when you delete an email, it goes into a deleted items folder. This should be emptied periodically. Here's how to actually delete the deleted items in Outlook 2003 and Outlook Express 6:

1. Open Outlook or Outlook Express.

2. Right-click on the Deleted Items folder.

3. Choose Empty Deleted Items Folder.

Another good option for managing the deleted items folder is to have it automatically clear each time you close Outlook. Here's how:

1. In Outlook, select the Tools menu.

2. Click Options, and then click the Other tab.

3. Check the Empty the Deleted Items Folder upon Exiting option.

4. The next time you close Outlook, the Deleted Items folder is emptied.

caution

Of course, you must realize that in disabling the storage of sent items, you will have no record of the emails you send. If your job requires that you maintain a record of conversations or you need to be able to forward items you sent to one person, disabling this feature could be crippling. Sure, it's a double-edged sword, but choosing to not save sent items could be disastrous under the right circumstances.

Don't Leave Email on the Server

When email is sent, it arrives on an email server waiting to be picked up by your computer's email program. Think of this server as a kind of post office. The server can be set to hold a copy of the received email for a period of time before it is deleted. This is useful if you access your email from several computers. However, it also makes your privacy vulnerable. Anyone with your email account's user ID and password can retrieve copies of the email from the server.

Here's how to turn that function off in Outlook 2003 so email is deleted from the server after it is downloaded by your computer:

1. Open Outlook and click on the Tools menu.

2. Choose E-mail Accounts

3. Select View or Change Existing Email Accounts and click Next.

4. In the E-mail Accounts window, click on the name of your email account in the list and click Change.

5. Click More Settings, and then the Advanced tab.

6. Uncheck the box next to Leave a Copy of the Messages on the Server, and click OK.

In Outlook Express 6, have your emails deleted on the server after you've downloaded them by doing the following:

1. Open Outlook Express, click the Tools menu, and then Accounts.

2. On the Mail tab, select your mail account and then click the Properties button.

3. Next click the Advanced tab on the Mail Properties window.

4. In the Delivery area, uncheck the box next to Leave a Copy of Messages on the Server. Click OK and then click Close on the Internet Accounts window (see Figure 7.20).

FIGURE 7.20

Leaving your messages on your mail server can provide a snoop with the perfect opportunity to look through your email. Good thing this feature can be turned off.

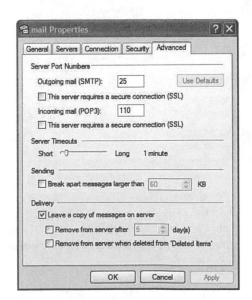

Wash Windows

Windows has some very obvious places that track your computer behavior. Here are the key areas you need to know about. The program CleanCache takes care of the less obvious problems. It's a one-stop program that wipes away all the web content in Internet Explorer and Mozilla Firefox, plus all kinds of Windows data, Download CleanCache 3.0 from the very charming ButtUglySoftware.com. It's free for use on up to two computers. If you're going to use it for more than two computers, the author asks that you donate a few dollars to help support the software.

tip

If you hold the Shift button down when you delete a file, it bypasses the Recycle Bin and is deleted. If you use this trick, make sure you want the file deleted because it's a headache to undo this.

Empty Your Recycle Bin

When you delete files in Windows, they go into a holding area called the Recycle Bin. Be sure to clear the Recycle Bin periodically by right-clicking on it and choosing Empty Recycle Bin. Note that if this option is grayed out, there is nothing in your bin (see Figure 7.21).

FIGURE 7.21

Be sure to empty your Recycle Bin regularly. Even on a computer someone can go through your garbage.

Clear My Recent Documents

Windows keeps track of documents you open in a list on the Start menu called My Recent Documents. This can include movie and audio files. To clear the list and turn the menu off, follow these steps:

1. Right-click on the Start button and choose Properties.

2. Click the Customize button on the Start Menu tab.

3. In the Taskbar and Start Menu Properties window, choose the Advanced tab. Click the Clear List button under the Programs area and uncheck the box next to List My Most Recently Opened Documents (see Figure 7.22).

FIGURE 7.22

The My Recent Documents folder that appears on the Start menu can be turned off.

Turn Off AutoComplete in Windows Search

The Windows Search feature keeps track of what you have searched before using a drop-down menu to show you keywords used in the past. To turn this off, follow these steps:

1. Click Start, Search.

2. On the Search menu on the left side of the Search pane, click Change Preferences.

3. Choose Turn AutoComplete Off (see Figure 7.23).

Erase the Contents of Your Temp Folder

The Temp folder is kind of a Windows scratch pad. All kinds of files are put here when Windows is working on them. The problem is that it is not cleaned after Windows is finished with it. So clear it out periodically by following these steps:

1. Click Start, All Programs, Accessories, and choose Windows Explorer.

2. In the Windows Explorer address bar, type `%temp%` and press Enter (see Figure 7.24).

   This opens the Temp folder.

3. Press Ctrl+A to select all the items in this folder. Press and hold down the Shift key and then press the Delete key. This deletes the files and bypasses the Recycle Bin.

FIGURE 7.23

Turn off previous
search terms in
Windows Search
by choosing
Turn
AutoComplete
Off in Search
preferences.

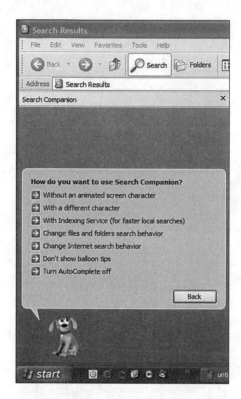

FIGURE 7.24

Your personal
Temp folder can
be accessed by
typing %temp% in
Windows
Explorer.

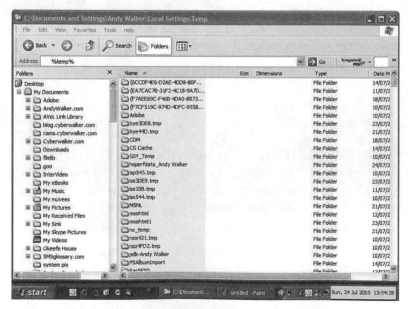

Clear the Clipboard

If you have ever cut or copied and then pasted anything in Windows, you have used the Windows clipboard. This function is used to move a file from one folder to another or move or copy text from one document to another. In fact, almost any type of data can be cut and pasted using the clipboard.

After something is in the Windows clipboard, it remains there even after it has been pasted. If you cut (or copy) and paste something and walk away from the computer, anyone else that comes along to use the computer can also paste the object from the clipboard.

To clean the clipboard, all you need to do is reboot and the clipboard is cleared. If you want to clean it manually, simply do the following on any word processor:

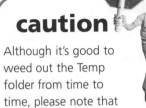

caution

Although it's good to weed out the Temp folder from time to time, please note that deleting these items can be costly the next time you try to recover a document or data that was lost when your application and/or computer crashed. Often, Temp files are the only existing copies of the lost data.

1. Open Notepad, which is found in Start, All Programs, Accessories.
2. In an empty document, press the spacebar to insert one space (or any other random character).
3. Highlight the space by clicking your mouse and dragging it from left to right over the space to highlight it.
4. Press Ctrl+C to copy it into the clipboard. It replaces whatever is there.

Scrub Microsoft Office

Microsoft Office keeps track of the documents opened in the MRU list in the File menu (see Figure 7.25).

Here's how to clear this list in the 2003 versions of Word, Excel, Access, PhotoDraw, and PowerPoint:

1. Click the Tools menu of any of the programs and then click Options.
2. Click the General tab.
3. Uncheck the Recently Used Files check box and click OK (see Figure 7.26).

FIGURE 7.25

The MRU list of documents shows the most recently viewed documents in a program.

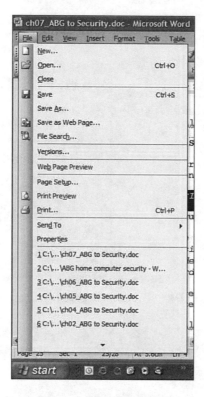

FIGURE 7.26

The MRU list of documents can be turned off easily in most Microsoft Office programs.

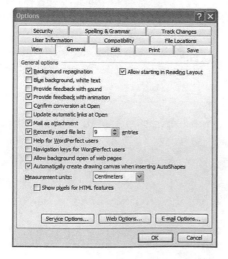

Deleted Files Are Not Gone

Simply deleting a file and clearing the Recycle Bin doesn't wipe away a file permanently. Windows removes references to it on the computer's hard drive and marks the space it occupies as free. However, an unerase program (such as the one found in Symantec's Norton Utilities) can find files that have been deleted and recover them, as long as they have not been overwritten by new data.

This can pose a problem if you are giving away an old computer or want to ensure that a particular file is not recoverable.

There are many free programs that permanently destroy files. Try either of these:

> ### tip
>
> If you want to clear the MRU in the Microsoft programs FrontPage, Publisher, and Photo Editor, you need to edit the Windows registry. Microsoft has instructions on how to do this in its knowledge base website at http://support.microsoft.com/default.aspx?scid=kb;en-us;313454.

- **Simple File Shredder**—This free utility kills files one at a time and overwrites them up to 25 times with garbage data so they can't be recovered. It can also wipe history and cached files saved in Internet Explorer and Firefox. It also wipes clean the contents of the Windows Recycle Bin and the Recent Documents folder. Get it from www.Scar5.com.

- **UltraWipe**—This free program wipes free space on your hard drive as well as files in the Temp folder and Windows Recycle Bin (see Figure 7.27). Get it from www.snapfiles.com/get/ultrawipe.html.

Turn Off Chat Logs

Internet chat programs can be set to record the text that goes back and forth between two people. Reading these logs is a great way to snoop on someone.

MSN Messenger 7

MSN Messenger can auto-log your chat conversation. In order to ensure chat privacy, turn this feature off as follows:

> ### caution
>
> Although programs such as Simple File Shredder and UltraWipe are fairly intuitive and will try to prevent you from shooting yourself in the foot, they are inherently dangerous programs. If you carelessly jack around with any file-erasing utility, there's bound to be trouble. My advice: Read the directions, go slowly, and if you aren't sure, don't click erase. Failure to observe these simple rules could result in the loss of your hard drive or important data that you didn't intend to erase, which will then be immediately followed by much weeping and gnashing of teeth.

1. Open MSN Messenger.

2. Click the Tools menu, and then click Options.

3. On the left, click Messages. On the Messages screen, locate the Message History area, and uncheck the box that says Automatically Keep a History of My Conversations and click OK (see Figure 7.28).

FIGURE 7.27

UltraWipe can scrub empty hard drive space so no files can be undeleted.

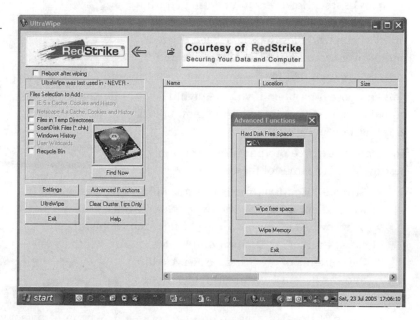

FIGURE 7.28

Make sure your chat conversations are not being saved by turning off the logging feature in MSN Messenger.

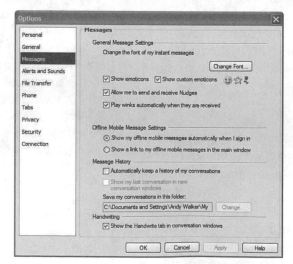

Yahoo! Messenger and AOL Instant Messenger

Yahoo! Messenger does not automatically save chat sessions. You can, however, save a conversation to a file by clicking the Conversation Menu and choosing Save As.

AIM doesn't have a chat logging mechanism built in.

Clean Restore Points

Windows also has a feature called system restore that enables you to roll the computer back to a configuration in the past. These archival snapshots are called *restore points*. If someone did a system restore, he could roll your computer back in time, returning it to how it was in the past.

So these restore points are worth clearing now and then. Here's how to delete them:

1. Click Start, Control Panel, System.

2. Click the System Restore tab.

3. Click to add a check mark beside Turn off System Restore on All Drives, and click Apply.

4. You are warned that all existing restore points will be deleted. Click Yes to continue.

5. All the restore points are deleted. Then uncheck the check box to turn the System Restore feature back on.

> **caution**
>
> Programs called snoopware exist to secretly spy on a person's computer activities and capture what he does for later perusal by the spy. Learn more about these programs on **p. 41**.

Create a new restore point after clearing your computer of any privacy-threatening content (by following the tips in this chapter). When the system is clean, create a new restore point as follows:

1. Click Start, All Programs, Accessories, System Tools, System Restore, and choose the Create a Restore Point.

2. Click Next and name the restore point with a descriptive phrase that includes the date. Finally, click Close.

THE ABSOLUTE MINIMUM

- People who know how to gain access to your computer can learn lot about you and your computer habits.

- Having your web habits exposed can cause all kinds of problems. Anything from embarrassment to criminal charges could be a consequence.

- The most likely privacy snoops are members of your family, but other snoopers could include your employer or the authorities.

- You can protect yourself by becoming an administrator on your computer, assigning a password to your user account, and downgrading system privileges of other users.

- Your web browser is the most likely place a snoop will look because there's a wealth of information about your Internet habits stored inside.

- You can easily clean your web tracks in both the Internet Explorer and Firefox web browsers.

- If someone gains access to your email, he can learn a lot of about your life.

- Multimedia players store lists of played movies and audio files.

- There's a lot of information stored in the nooks and crannies of Windows that can reveal what you have been doing on your computer.

- Deleted files are not permanently gone. They can be unerased. You can permanently delete them with free file-shredding programs.

- Check to see if MSN Messenger is logging your chats. If it is, turn this function off.

- Clear your restore points and create a new one when your system is clean.

PART

Strategies for Safe and Secure Computing

8

LET'S SMASH-PROOF WINDOWS: TWEAK WINDOWS XP NICE AND TIGHT

In its raw virgin state, Windows XP is horribly vulnerable to viruses, spyware, and other ugly pieces of digital misery. Your best bet is to strip it down naked and rebuild it from the beginning. But if the idea of that gives you a throbbing headache, simply clean it and lock it down with these must-do security tips. Consider this a 10-step, do-it-yourself guide to rock-solid security for Windows XP.

If Windows XP Is a Dike, You're a Little Dutch Boy

If Windows XP was a dike, that little Dutch boy would run out of fingers and quickly be treading water. The operating system is rife with security holes and there aren't enough Dutch kids in all of the Netherlands to plug them all. Of course, it's not seawater that's the problem here, its Internet attackers. That means viruses, spyware, hackers, and a whole chowder of other Internet threats that can come pouring in.

This is going to take some patience on your part and a free afternoon. Stock up on snacks, send the kids to grandma's, and stick with me; we'll do this together—and mostly for free.

caution

If your computer is horribly slow for no apparent reason and you have an inkling it's filled with spyware and viruses, you might want to cut your losses and scrub the system clean and start from scratch. If so, go straight to Chapter 9, "Starting from the Beginning: Wiping a Hard Drive and Rebuilding from the Ground Up."

Step 1: Trash Unnecessary Programs

Let's start by getting rid of programs that you never use. Be aggressive, like a kitten chasing a tuna-splattered mouse. Get rid of as much software as you can. This helps in many ways:

tip

If you have an older version of Windows (older than XP), many of the tips and recommended software in this chapter will work on your older systems.

- You might find strange and unwanted programs on the system that might contain spyware and possibly be infected with viruses.

- It makes your computer run faster and better.

- It frees up resources such as your hard drive and memory, and when there are lots of spare resources, your computer crashes less.

- Installing fixes and patches on a cleaned computer reduces potential problems.

Follow these steps to get rid of programs:

1. Click your Start menu, and select the Control Panel (see Figure 8.1).

FIGURE 8.1

A tool in the Control Panel called Add or Remove Programs is used to remove unwanted programs from your computer.

2. Double-click on the Add or Remove Programs icon and a dialog box opens, showing installed programs.

3. If your computer is slow and you have many programs installed, be patient. It can take some time for the list to appear. After the list is visible, click on a program to get you more information about it, including how often you use it (see Figure 8.2).

FIGURE 8.2

The list in Add or Remove Programs tells you how big the program is and how often it is used.

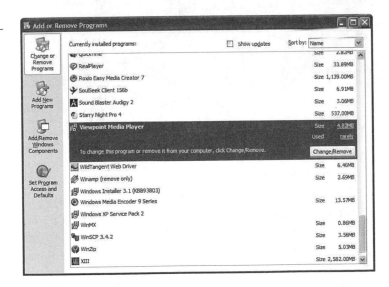

4. Go through the list of programs, noting which ones you use regularly and which ones you never run. Be wary of any items you don't remember installing. However, before you uninstall anything, you'll want to be 100% sure what it does, so you don't uninstall something necessary.

5. To remove a program, click the one you want to purge, and then click on the Change or Remove Programs button on the right side. You might be asked to

restart your computer following the uninstallation of programs. Restart and repeat as many times as necessary.

If you're feeling really proactive, you can also check for programs that load when Windows starts, but which don't appear on the Add or Remove Programs list—in some cases because they're very evil programs that shouldn't be there in the first place.

These programs are like pickled beets. They should be chucked into the road because they're icky. (Author's bias there—apologies if you're a beet farmer or if you really like the little Satan-flavored vegetables.)

To get rid of programs in Windows start up, follow these steps:

1. Click on the Start menu and select the Run option. In the Run box that pops up, type `msconfig` and press Enter (see Figure 8.3).

FIGURE 8.3

When you type msconfig in the Run box, it launches the hidden, but highly useful, utility called Windows Configuration Utility.

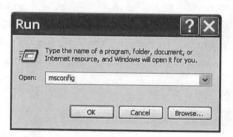

2. The System Configuration Utility appears. Click on the Startup tab (top right of the window) to list all the programs that run during Windows startup.

3. A tiny upright bar between Command and Location can be dragged to the left or right to show more or less of a program's location and actual name of the *executable* (the file that runs).

4. To remove an item from the startup process, click the check box to the left of the item to remove the check mark (see Figure 8.4).

tip

Knowing where a program file is located can give you hints as to whether it is a legitimate program. If you're not sure it's a useful file, a part of Windows itself, or a nasty bit of software secreted on your system, do some detective work. Use Google.com to search for the name of the item and see what you can find. Usually this tells you if the file is a good or bad file.

FIGURE 8.4

Uncheck items in the System Configuration Utility's Startup tab so they don't start the next time you reboot.

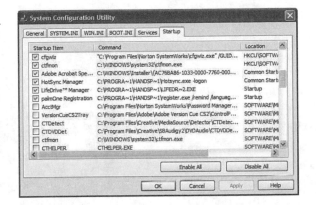

5. Next, go to the Services tab and check off Hide All Microsoft Services (see Figure 8.5). This filters out Windows components that need to run. What are left are programs that are parts of third-party programs that run on your computer in the background. Your antivirus program may be here, as well as printer utilities and even helper programs for video and graphics editors and more. Uncheck the ones you don't recognize or don't need.

6. Click OK. You are told that you need to restart your computer. Go ahead and restart your computer before going any further.

tip

For a really complete list of startup programs, check out the startup file list at www.sysinfo.org/startupinfo.html that my editor, Rick, uses. It tells you what each item is, how it was installed, and whether to keep it or chuck it. Rick says it's the easiest way to track down startup stuff, and I agree!

FIGURE 8.5

Use the Services tab in the System Configuration Utility to turn off unneeded program components. Be sure to hide Microsoft services first by checking that box.

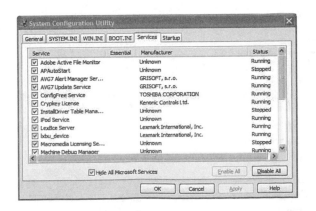

Step 2: Install Firefox

If you're using Internet Explorer to surf the Web, get yourself a better browser by downloading the Firefox web browser from www.mozilla.org (see Figure 8.6). It's much more secure and actually better and easier to use. And, better yet, it's free.

Firefox is more secure because it doesn't use ActiveX, which is a Microsoft technology that allows mini-programs to run in Internet Explorer without your permission. ActiveX controls, as they are called, can autodownload viruses, spyware, and Trojan horses without your knowledge. Follow these steps to install Firefox:

tip

By deselecting items in the System Configuration Utility's Startup and Services tab, you might inadvertently stop some programs that you need from working. Write a list of all of the items you've unchecked and keep it handy. If you run into troubles, run `msconfig` again and check the items you shouldn't have unchecked.

FIGURE 8.6

The Firefox browser (shown displaying the Mozilla.org website) is more secure than Internet Explorer and it's free.

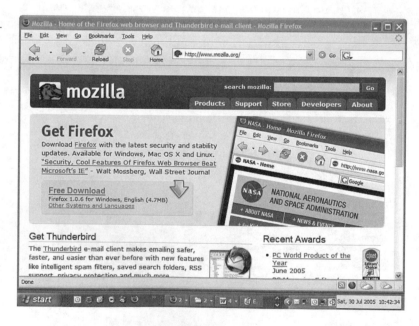

1. To install the browser, download it and double-click on the installer program's icon. When the program launches, click Next.

2. Click the dot beside the I Agree option for the license agreement, and click Next (if you agree to the legalese, of course).

3. Choose the standard installation, and click Next twice. Then click Finish.

4. If the program asks you if you want to import your settings from Internet Explorer, it's safe to say yes. All of your Internet Explorer bookmarks are automatically imported, which is a nice little bonus feature.

5. There are some websites that insist you use Internet Explorer (including Microsoft's own Windows Update) so you have to keep IE around. But after you have Firefox installed, you should rarely need IE.

Step 3: Install Antivirus Software and Scan for Viruses

If you don't already have an up-to-date antivirus program on your system, make sure you get one. For the uninitiated, an antivirus program stops computer viruses from getting on to your computer and in the event that one slips by, it can clean it after the fact.

Many antivirus products are available commercially, but there are also some great free programs that are simply fabulous. So there's no excuse not to install one.

I like Grisoft's AVG Free Edition, available at http://free.grisoft.com.

I explain how to install AVG in Chapter 1, "Viruses: Attack of the Malicious Programs," so if you haven't already, zip on over there starting on **p. 32** and follow the instructions to install it.

> **caution**
>
> Don't install a second antivirus program if you already have one installed. Running two virus programs together causes conflicts.

By the way, I used to think AVG didn't stand for anything, although you could arguably assume it means Andy's Virus Guard. Recently, however, I learned from the good folks at Grisoft that it means Anti Virus Guard. How apropos. I like AVG because it offers a blend of speed with all the features you'd want (see Figure 8.7), including virus scanning for email.

You might also consider using either AntiVir from www.free-av.com or avast! from www.avast.com.

AntiVir is easy on system resources such as memory and hard drive space, which is good, but it does not scan email, which is bad. That's where most of the infections come from these days.

avast! offers all the features of AVG but is a little more burdensome on the system. It's kind of like walking around with a tank as a hat. You'll be extremely well guarded but it slows you down a bit.

FIGURE 8.7
Grisoft gives
away a free
version of AVG,
a very good
antivirus
program.

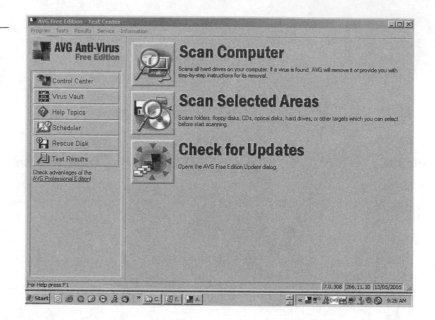

Step 4: Install Anti-Spyware Software and Scan for Spyware

The next major protection you'll want to install is an
anti-spyware program. Spyware is a digital plague. It
finds its way onto your computer and either
snoops on your behavior and reports it back to
someone on the Internet or it displays unwanted
ads to you. It's the largest growing threat on
Windows computers today.

One of the worst parts of it is spyware gets on to
your system and slows it down horribly. Chances
are if you have any kind of infection on your computer, it's spyware.

In fact, I bet you a Boston cream donut (mmm,
my favorite) that there's spyware on your system
right now. Even if I lose that bet with you, I am
going to really get fat on donuts because I'll win
that bet against the vast majority of computer
owners.

The secret to spyware programs is that you can
and should install more than one. Unlike antivirus
programs that like to be the only program
installed on a system, anti-spyware programs co-
exist with each other happily.

note

If you rushed out to the
bookstore to get one of
the first copies of this book, and
you've noticed that I never mention that Microsoft AntiSpyware is
a beta version, you've caught me!
The program was still in beta (a
version of a program that is still
being tested) when I wrote this
book. However, sooner or later it
will be released, possibly by the
time this book is published.

You should install at least two anti-spyware programs, maybe even three. I like these three programs because they are good, free, and co-exist nicely:

- Microsoft AntiSpyware from www.microsoft.com/spyware
- Spybot Search & Destroy from www.safer-networking.net
- Ad-Aware SE from www.lavasoft.de

Microsoft AntiSpyware

Microsoft AntiSpyware is a free anti-spyware program that is one of your key defenses against spyware (see Figure 8.8). It has a good, up-to-date, and comprehensive spyware database and catches a lot of infections.

I show you how to install Microsoft AntiSpyware in Chapter 2, "Spyware: Overrun by Advertisers, Hijackers, and Opportunists," starting on **p. 41**, so if you need help in installing it, flip over to the easy-to-follow instructions I lovingly wrote there, especially for you.

FIGURE 8.8

Microsoft AntiSpyware is an excellent free program that defends your computer against spyware.

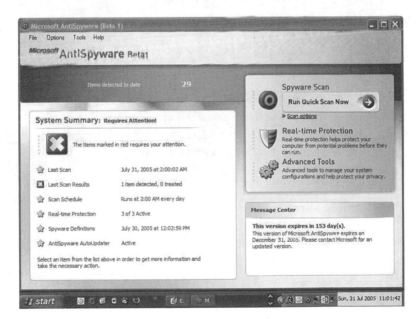

Install a Second Anti-spyware Program

It's important to install a second anti-spyware program because no single program catches all the infections.

My tests have shown that in the realm of freeware, Microsoft Anti-Spyware catches most with Spybot and Ad-Aware filling in the blanks. You might find running three will get all of the infections, but that's a bit of a hassle.

I talk about Spybot in Chapter 2, so let's look at the installation of Ad-Aware SE Personal (SE is the free edition of the software) here.

You can get the latest version of AD-Aware SE Personal at www.lavasoft.de.

Here's how to install it:

1. After downloading Ad-Aware SE Personal, close all unnecessary Windows programs so the installation doesn't trip up on them (see Figure 8.9) and launch the installation program.

FIGURE 8.9

Installing Ad-Aware is very quick. Be sure to close all unnecessary programs during installation.

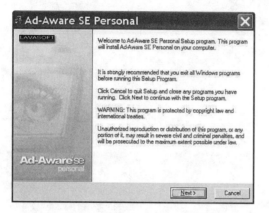

2. When the welcome screen appears, click Next. You see the license agreement. Click the box beside I Accept the License Agreement, and click Next several times until the installation runs. It happens very quickly.

3. At this point, you'll see a screen with three check boxes all checked. It's a good idea to run a scan now and it's definitely critical to update the definition file. (Definitions are digital snapshots of spyware infections.)

4. You can probably deselect the last item which offers to open up a help document. Leave it checked if you want to see it, of course. Finally click Finish (see Figure 8.10).

note

If Microsoft AntiSpyware looks familiar to you, it's probably because it was created by Giant Company Software, but was bought by Microsoft.

FIGURE 8.10

Update defini-
tions and run a
scan for spyware
at the end of the
installation of
Ad-Adware SE.

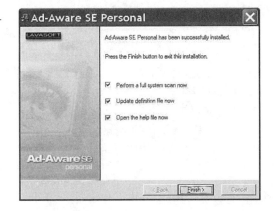

5. At this point, you see a notice that your anti-spyware definitions are out-of-
    date, asking if you want to check for updates. Click OK, and then choose
    Connect to get the new definition files (see Figure 8.11).

FIGURE 8.11

Make sure you
let Ad-Aware
check for new
spyware
definitions.

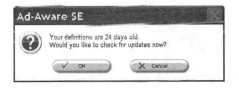

6. If Ad-Aware finds updates, it asks if it can download and install them; click
    OK. After the update is complete, the scan runs. Ad-Aware keeps a tally dur-
    ing the scan of any bad things it finds, and gives you the option to remove
    them at the end of the scan (see Figure 8.12).

FIGURE 8.12

After the scan,
Ad-Aware shows
any questionable
program that it
finds. You can
then choose to
have it removed
if it's something
you don't want
on your system.

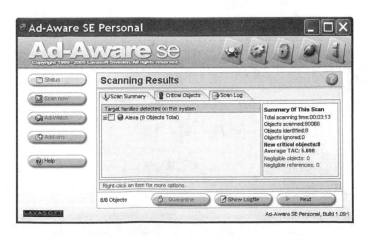

Step 5: Block Out the Bad Guys and Install a Firewall

A *firewall* is an electronic wall between you and the Internet. It keeps out hackers who are interested in accessing your computer and it also blocks network traveling viruses that are called worms. A firewall can be either a hardware device, such as a home network router, or a software program.

Windows XP has a built-in software firewall, though early versions of Windows XP didn't make it obvious or easy to get to. The quickest way to enable the Windows firewall is by installing Service Pack 2, which is available free from Microsoft. SP2 is a great big security fix that repairs dozens of security holes and problems in Windows XP.

caution

When you type in the web address of free programs, especially security programs, be sure you type them correctly. Bad people rig web address that are slightly different from the real thing to entice you into visit their websites or download their products which could get you infected with malware.

When SP2 installs, it turns the firewall on for you. If you don't want to install SP2, you can still enable the Windows firewall manually. Here's how:

1. Open your list of connections to the Internet by clicking Start, selecting Control Panel, and then choosing Network and Internet Connections.

2. At the bottom of the screen, find the icon that says Network Connections, and click on it (see Figure 8.13).

FIGURE 8.13

Before SP2 is installed, the Windows firewall is only accessible several clicks deep inside the Network Connections applet in Control Panel.

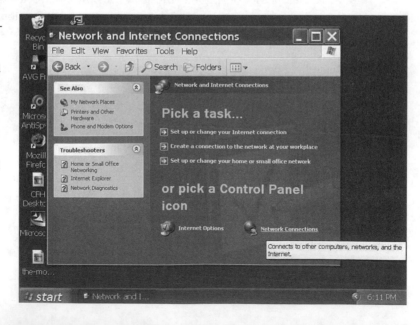

3. Usually, there is only one entry in this list and it is the primary device you use to connect the computer to the Internet (see Figure 8.14). Think of each one of these items as a doorway out to the Internet. Like any home, a computer has many doorways out and in, but you use only one primary one.

FIGURE 8.14

A list of network devices that can be used to connect your computer to the Internet is shown. Choose the one you use.

4. Click once on the connection you use to access the Internet the most to select it. A pane appears on the left side. Click the option that reads Change the Settings of This Connection.

5. This opens a dialog box that looks a little intimidating. Don't sweat it. Click on the Advanced tab at the top. Then, in the Internet Connection Firewall area, click the check box beside the option that reads Protect My Computer and Network by Limiting or Preventing Access to This Computer from the Internet near the top, and then click OK at the bottom (see Figure 8.15).

6. If you use the second network connection in the list, switch on the Windows firewall for that one as well.

tip

You might have several connections in your Network Connections list. One might be marked IEEE-1394 Connection. This is a FireWire port on your computer usually used to connect a camcorder or possibly a digital music player, such as the insanely popular Apple iPod. However, it can be used to make a network connection. You might also see a wireless network adapter in this list if your computer can connect using Wi-Fi (wireless) technology.

FIGURE 8.15

You have to dig into the Advanced tab of your network connection to turn on the firewall that protects that connection to the Internet.

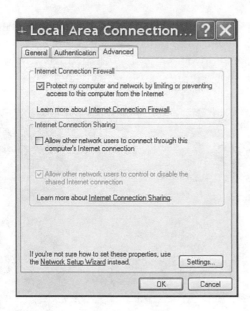

Step 6: Install and Configure Microsoft Updates and Service Pack 2

If you haven't run Windows Update in a long time or at all, it's time to get to it. This is one of the critical ways to defeat security vulnerabilities, and it's free and easy.

Microsoft has a reputation for shoddy workmanship on its software. It tends to release products not quite ready for sale and then fixes problems on the fly, issuing software fixes later. This approach is what got it into trouble with Windows XP in the first place. XP was released with little attention paid to security and so it hit the marketplace with Chunnel-sized holes in it.

Windows Update is a facility in Windows that is used to download and install those fixes from the Microsoft website. It can be accessed by going to http://windowsupdate.microsoft.com. There's also a Windows Update icon on the Start menu you can click to take an express ride to the website. To access Windows Update, follow these steps:

> **tip**
>
> If you'd want a better firewall than the Windows firewall, consider ZoneAlarm. It's a free firewall that gives you more information about what data is coming into your computer and what programs on your computer are trying to send data out. Get the program from http://download.zonelabs.com.
>
> Alternatively, look at SyGate, which is another really good free firewall. It's available at http://smb.sygate.com/products/spf_standard.htm.

1. Click Start, choose All Programs, and then locate the Windows Update icon near the top. It launches Internet Explorer and takes you to the update page (see Figure 8.16).

FIGURE 8.16

Find the icon that says Windows Update at the top of the Programs menu and click it. It launches Internet Explorer and takes you to the updates.

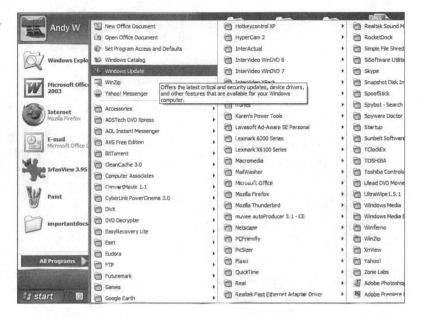

2. Look for the Express Install button and click on it (see Figure 8.17).

FIGURE 8.17

For now, use the Express Install option so you can get all the high priority updates.

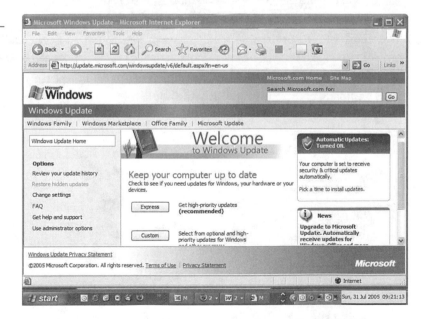

3. Windows Update might have to upgrade some components. If so, click Download and Install Now at the bottom of the page.

4. When you have finished updating, you are asked to restart your computer for the updates to take effect. Click the Restart Now option.

5. After restarting, repeat this Windows Update process until you have all new updates. Scroll down the screen to see which updates will be installed. Accept any license agreements as they pop up during the update process.

If it's not installed already, eventually you get to the Service Pack 2 installation. It's worth pausing here.

Installing SP2: The Big Fix

I'll warn you now that SP2 is not a very friendly update for computers that have seen a lot of combat. By that I mean if you have tweaked, twisted, and customized XP and added loads of software over the years, SP2 can cause problems when it installs.

It can cause strange anomalies where some programs act oddly. It might stop you from connecting to certain devices. In extreme cases, it can cause the computer to stop functioning altogether.

Before you plow on and install SP2, you should do some basic preparation:

- Be sure you safeguard all your data. That means backing it up so it can be replaced if there's a problem. For backup tips, see **p. 259**.

- Make sure you have your Windows XP installation CD on hand with the license key in case everything goes horribly wrong and you have to wipe the system clean and start again.

- Make sure you have installation CDs and license keys for all your programs.

- Ensure you back up your email data files, music files, and everything you would be devastated to lose.

> **tip**
>
> If you have a home net-work that uses a little box called a router to connect your computers and share the Internet, you have a hardware firewall installed already. In that case, you don't need to turn on Windows Firewall or install a third-party software firewall (unless you want to stop outbound traffic, such as would be generated by spyware and viruses already on your computer).

> **tip**
>
> A hardware firewall like the one in a home router is preferable to a software fire-wall because it has no effect on the performance of your computer. It only stops inbound threats from the Internet, however. A third-party software firewall, such as ZoneAlarm or SyGate, checks out-bound traffic as well, which stops spyware and viruses trying to reach the outside world.

- Do a spyware scan with at least two anti-spyware programs and remove anything you find.
- Do a virus scan and remove anything you find.

TO INSTALL OR NOT TO INSTALL SP2—THAT IS THE QUESTION

You hear a lot of warnings and whining about SP2. It has created a lot of problems for people who simply install it without any preparation.

Here's why you absolutely, positively should install it:

- It provides you with an enhanced automatic updates process to keep your system up-to-date on the latest security features and fixes.
- It gives you an easier-to-use security control panel, instead of an intimidating dialog box.
- It adds alerts to protect you against potentially unsafe email attachments.
- It adds an information bar to Internet Explorer to let you know if potentially unsafe content has been blocked.
- It also gives IE a pop-up ad blocker.
- It turns on Windows Firewall by default, and protects the system even during boot-up and shutdown.
- It protects against email address validation by spammers by turning off images in what's called HTML (or web page like) email. Spammers can insert an image that displays when you open or preview an email and this alerts the spammer's server that your address is valid and spam-worthy.
- It adds improved wireless connection tools to help you use Bluetooth and WiFi more easily.

When you are ready to install SP2, pop on over to Chapter 9 where I show you how to install it step-by-step by downloading it from the Internet via Windows Update. Instructions start on **p. 281**. I also show you how to configure it, starting on **p. 284**.

Step 7: Install Netcraft's Anti-Phishing Toolbar

Phishing is a nasty new trend that you'll want to defend against. These are emails you receive from imposters that look like they are from your bank or financial institution and ask you to validate your account information or user ID and password.

caution

Windows Update won't work with the Firefox browser because it doesn't use ActiveX technology (which is a security hazard). So you need to use Microsoft's Internet Explorer browser for this.

They are increasingly hard to spot. The rule of thumb is to never respond to email that requests personal data from your financial institution or visit any website to submit that data. Still, you might want to opt for a little help.

Go to http://toolbar.netcraft.com, and download the toolbar. This helps you protect yourself from phishing emails, on the off-chance that you click a link in a phishing email without realizing it might be a fraud.

When you follow the installation links, it takes you to a page where you have to choose whether you're using Firefox or Internet Explorer (see Figure 8.18).

Here's how to install it on Firefox:

> **caution**
>
> It is absolutely critical that your computer is completely free of spyware before you install SP2. Most of the failed or problematic installs happen because they are done on computers that are infected with spyware.

FIGURE 8.18

The Netcraft toolbar is available for both Internet Explorer and Firefox. Simply choose which one you want on the company's website.

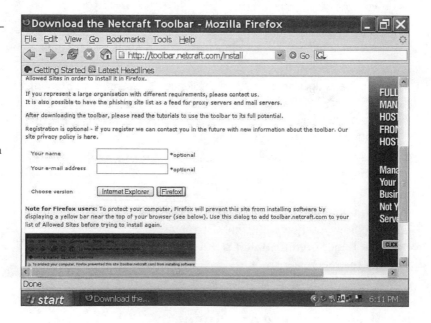

1. Click the Firefox link, and then click OK.
2. You might be blocked from installing the toolbar. In this case, a message appears near the top of the screen telling you that the installation was blocked. Click the Edit Options button on the right-hand side to add the Netcraft URL to the browser's allowed sites, and then try again (see Figure 8.19).
3. When the installation window appears, click Install Now (see Figure 8.20).

FIGURE 8.19
Firefox blocks downloads from websites unless they are explicit added to an allowed sites list. A warning appears across the top of the browser.

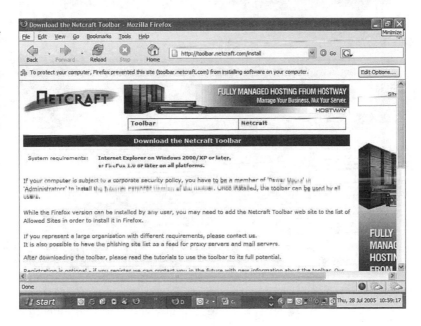

4. To activate the toolbar, close Firefox, and then relaunch the program. The

FIGURE 8.20
When you download the Netcraft toolbar for Firefox, you are prompted to install it.

Netcraft toolbar appears (see Figure 8.21).

Now when you launch a website that is considered dangerous, the risk-rating bar turns red to alert you that it's not safe to divulge any personal data and a pop-up window warns you.

You should also add the Netcraft Toolbar to Internet Explorer. Here's how:

FIGURE 8.21

The Netcraft toolbar loads across the top of your web browser and rates the phishing risk assigned to each website you visit.

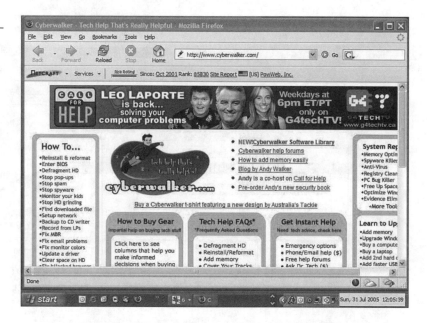

1. Choose the Internet Explorer button on the Netcraft download page.

2. When the Run/Save dialog appears, click Run and the file downloads (see Figure 8.22).

3. When the download is complete, you are asked if you want to run the file,

FIGURE 8.22

Install the Netcraft Toolbar in Internet Explorer by clicking the Run button on the File Download window when it appears.

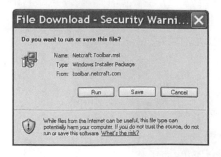

so go ahead and click the Run button.

4. An installer program launches. Click the Next button, deal with the license agreement, and then click Next a few times until you can click Close.

5. If the Netcraft toolbar doesn't appear in Internet Explorer, activate it by selecting View, Toolbars, Netcraft Toolbar (see Figure 8.23).

> **tip**
>
> Even if this toolbar is not for you because you know not to respond to the phishing emails, it a good tool to install on your grandma or grandpa's computer if they're not that computer savvy.

FIGURE 8.23

If the Netcraft Toolbar doesn't display in Internet Explorer after installation, turn it on using the View menu under Toolbars.

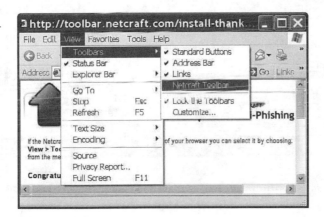

Step 8: Protect Yourself from Spam

One of the best ways to make sure you aren't tricked by a phishing scam is to make sure the phishing emails never arrive in your inbox in the first place. There are a number of anti-spam products designed to filter out spam messages and known phishing scams. McAfee and Norton both offer anti-spam products, but the best product on the market for my money is Cloudmark Desktop (formerly called SafetyBar).

In this book I wanted to provide a way to use free software products that are as good as paid products. In the case of anti-spam, I've not been able to find a freebie anti-spam program that I believe is effective enough and easy to configure

> **tip**
>
> If you use Outlook 2003, don't forget to turn on the program's built-in spam protection feature called Junk Email Filter. On the Tools menu, click Options. On the Preferences tab under the E-mail section, click Junk E-mail and choose the level of protection you want from the list. It works well in concert with Cloudmark Desktop.

for most people. There is, however, one anti-spam product that I swear by and I'm willing to shell out forty clams a year for it.

It's called Cloudmark Desktop. It's a plug-in to both Outlook and Outlook Express. When installed, it appears inside those programs (see Figure 8.24).

FIGURE 8.24

Cloudmark Desktop appears as a toolbar across the top of Outlook (shown) or Outlook Express.

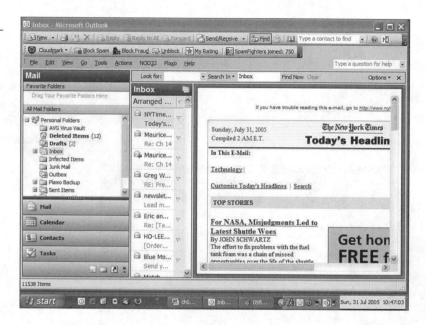

It works like this: A spam message is sent to a list of a million or more people. Someone with a copy of Cloudmark Desktop installed is one of those million recipients. She uses the program to mark the message as spam and it is removed from her inbox and placed in her Spam folder.

The software sends a message to the Cloudmark server on the Internet with a profile of the spam message. After several people who are part of the Cloudmark community mark the message, it is verified on the Cloudmark server as spam.

Then the program filters the spam automatically for all the other users. It's very effective. You still get some spam in your inbox if you're one of the first to receive a particular spam message. Cloudmark claims it catches 98% of what comes in. My experience shows it filters about 90% of my inbound spam. The other bonus is that false positives—that's email that isn't spam, but gets marked as such—are rare. You can download the

caution

Cloudmark Desktop is designed for Outlook 2000, 2002, or 2003, and Outlook Express 5 and 6. It won't work on earlier versions. You can find out which version you are running by starting Outlook and clicking the Help menu and then clicking About Microsoft Office Outlook.

program from www.cloudmark.com on a 30-day trial. Thereafter it costs $39.95 per year.

Cloudmark Desktop is easy to install. Here's how, if you use Outlook:

1. Download and launch the installer program. When you see the Welcome screen, click Next to get started.

2. Read and accept the license screen, click Next, and then click Install. When the installation completes, click Finish.

3. Next time you run Outlook, a First Use dialog box appears to show you how to use the program.

> **caution**
>
> Check your Spam folder now and then to ensure it's not dumping valid email in there. This is called a false positive. It does do this occasionally, as most anti-spam programs do. If you see a false positive, click on it and click the Unblock button on the Cloudmark Desktop toolbar.

To use it, all you do is check your email as normal. The software grabs spam and dumps it in the Spam folder as it comes in.

In the event that a spam message slips through into your inbox, all you do is click on it to select it and click the Block Spam button on the Cloudmark Desktop at the top of the Outlook screen (below the menus).

FIGURE 8.25

Cloudmark Desktop allows you to mark messages as either spam using the Block Spam button or as a message from a scam artist using the Block Fraud button.

Step 9: Managing Your File Sharing Security

Microsoft's Simple File Sharing system allows you to share your files and folders on a home network. Unfortunately, it poses some risks.

First of all, if you must share files or folders, just share specific ones. Don't right-click on a drive in Windows Explorer and share the whole drive. That poses too great a risk.

For loads of fun and stimulating details about this topic, see **p. 151**. That said, here are some quickie fixes.

Windows XP Home Edition

Simple File Sharing in Windows XP Home is turned on by default and cannot be turned off. All connection attempts to your computer are allowed using the computer's built-in Guest account. If someone has logged onto your wireless network in a car outside, however, this poses a problem because he can get at your shared folders.

The best way to protect your computer from unauthorized access is to password protect the Guest account (learn how on **p. 151**) and avoid sharing any files or folders on your computer.

> **tip**
>
> You'll also see a Block Fraud button on the Cloudmark Desktop (see Figure 8.25). This is used to mark phishing and scam emails. Most of those get caught by the program and are tossed into the Spam folder.

Unfortunately, this might also hamper your ability to perform useful tasks, such as streaming music to a music-sharing device or letting your spouse access your ABBA music collection on your PC.

Adding the Security Bar

If you're feeling ambitious, you can also add the Security bar to Windows XP Home edition. Download the Security Configuration Manager from Microsoft from www.microsoft.com/ntserver/nts/downloads/recommended/scm/ and follow these steps:

1. Select the x86 option, and save the file to a location on your computer.

2. When the download is complete, open the folder where you saved the file, and run the file. It extracts more files to that location.

3. Right-click the file setup.ini and choose the Install option. It installs the file, and then asks you to restart your computer.

4. When you restart, the Security tab appears when you right-click on files and choose Sharing and Security, giving you more control over who can access the files (see Figure 8.26).

> **tip**
>
> When you set up a shared folder in Windows XP, add a dollar sign to the end of the share name. For example, if the share name is bankaccount, call it bankaccount$. This way, only people who know the name of the share are able to access it.

Windows XP Professional Edition

If you have a Windows XP Professional system and you want to be more secure, you want to turn Simple File Sharing off by following these steps:

FIGURE 8.26

A security add-
on for Windows
NT, an older
business version
of Windows, can
add sharing and
security options
to Windows XP
Home.

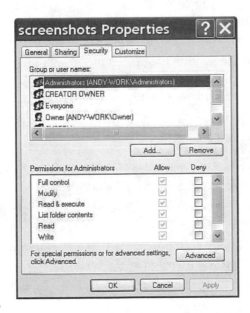

1. Click Start, and then select Control Panel.

2. Click Folder Options. If you are in Control Panel's Category View, click
   Appearance and Themes first, and then choose Folder options.

3. Click the View tab, scroll down to the bottom, and uncheck the Use Simple
   File Sharing (recommended) option (see Figure 8.27).

FIGURE 8.27

Turn off Simple
File Sharing in
Windows XP
Professional.

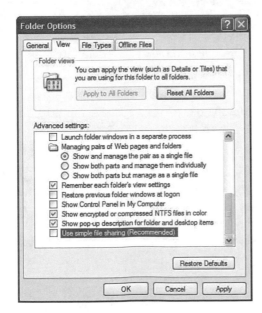

When you right-click on a file or folder and choose the Sharing or Security tabs now, you have full control over which users you allow to share files.

You can do this by choosing the Security tab and manually editing the permissions that allow people accessing your computer over the network to read the file (open it) or write to it (geekese for being able to change it and save it).

THE ABSOLUTE MINIMUM

- Get rid of unwanted programs and clean up your system startup before adding all the critical security upgrades to Windows XP.

- Install and use Firefox because it's a more secure web browser than Internet Explorer.

- Configure the security settings in Internet Explorer to medium or high to provide better security when you have to use the browser.

- Install a good antivirus program. Grisoft offers a free version of its program, AVG, and it's very good.

- Install two anti-spyware programs because just one won't protect you. Microsoft AntiSpyware, Spybot Search & Destroy, and Ad-Aware SE are all good free programs.

- Turn on real-time protection during the installation of your spyware programs to inoculate your system from spyware.

- Use a firewall to keep out worms and hackers. Either use a home network router with built-in firewall capabilities or turn on Windows firewall. You can also opt to use a third-party software firewall such as ZoneAlarm.

- Run Windows Update and download all the available fixes. Then install Service Pack 2, the big security fix for Windows XP, because it is the most significant all-in-one security upgrade to Windows you can get.

- Install an anti-phishing toolbar to alert you to scam artist emails and websites that try to steal your bank and personal information.

- Install an anti-spam program. Cloudmark Desktop is affordable and easy to use.

- Turn off Simple File Sharing in Windows XP Professional and password protect the Guest account in Windows XP Home to protect your computer from unauthorized users who can access your shared files.

In This Chapter

9

Starting from the Beginning: Wiping a Hard Drive and Rebuilding from the Ground Up

Sometimes a computer is just so infested with viruses, spyware, and other bits of computer unhappiness that it's easier to just wipe your hard drive clean and start from scratch, rather than start a prolonged search-and-destroy mission. This is especially true if you're not really sure what you're looking for. This chapter explains how to wipe an XP computer clean, re-install Windows XP, and build a more secure computer from the ground up.

Light the Fuse and Stand Back

Let's say you live in a house that keeps the rain out just fine, but it's not very pleasant to live in because it's fallen into slumlord disrepair. Mice crawl behind the walls. Roaches snack on your toast crumbs. The neighbors steal your garden tools through a broken window. And the mailbox is jammed full of furnace-cleaning flyers and pizza delivery menus. What do you do?

Well, you can call in the exterminator, patch the windows, threaten the postman, and stop eating toast. It's going to be expensive, inconvenient, and take a lot of time. Plus there's no guarantee that your defensive efforts are going to turn the house into a Barbie Dream Home.

Maybe what you need to do is drop a wheelbarrow full of TNT down the basement stairs, light a match, and run. When the smoke clears you can rebuild the house from the ground up.

That's what we're going to do to your computer in this chapter. We're going to wipe away Windows and start fresh.

Let's Get Started

You're going to need some tools to get that proverbial TNT down the stairs in order to rebuild again. Here's what you'll need:

- Windows XP install CD or system recovery CD
- Windows XP Service Pack 2 (SP2)
- Driver files for all your crucial hardware
- Install CDs for all your programs
- Internet service setup disk and settings

Let's go through the tools one by one.

XP Installation CD or System Recovery Disk

You need one of the following to reformat and re-install:

- **Windows XP CD**—This is a CD provided by your manufacturer that contains the installation files for Windows XP. You might also have bought this from a retail store. Think of it as a house kit you buy from a prefab builder—it has all the plans, materials, and instructions to build a do-it-yourself house.

- **Recovery CD**—Some computer makers provide a recovery CD. This is a CD that, when installed, wipes your system clean for you and puts the computer back to the way it was the day it was bought. Think of this as the original blueprints from a brand-name builder who first built your house years ago.

Recovery CDs for system builders such as Dell, HP, and Gateway often contain modified versions of Windows along with drivers specific to their proprietary hardware. It's important to note that recovery CDs and Windows installation CDs are not interchangeable. If you purchased a system from HP and it came with a recovery CD, you must use it and not a store-bought version of Windows to do your re-install.

Make sure you also have the Windows product key. That's the license code on the back of the CD sleeve for which the Windows installation process asks. If you don't have the key, you won't be able to complete the installation.

Windows SP2: The Mother of All Service Packs

If your Windows installation CD or recovery CD was acquired in mid-2004 or before, you also need a copy of Windows XP SP2 on CD (see Figure 9.1). This is an uber-update to Windows XP provided free by Microsoft. It has major fixes in it that patch many critical security holes in XP.

You can get this as a download from Microsoft.com after the re-installation of Windows XP, but it's very handy to have it on CD. At press time, you were able to order the SP2 CD from Microsoft at www.microsoft.com/windowsxp/sp2/, but sooner or later this service will be discontinued. Even if you plan to download it from the Windows Update site, order a CD copy anyway, if it is available. It's as handy as a pair of waterproof underpants in a hurricane.

caution

Instead of giving you a recovery CD, some PC makers put the Windows installation files on your hard drive. You need to check with your computer maker if this is the case. There should be an option to restore the system to its original configuration when you start it. If not, look up your computer make and model on the manufacturer's website to find out how to restore the system without a CD.

tip

If you have a recovery CD or Windows XP installation CD made in 2005 or later, SP2 is a part of the installation programming. Versions of the Windows XP CD that have SP2 integrated into them are marked as such. If that's the case, you can skip the sections in this chapter on installing SP2, including the "Step 8a: Install Windows XP Service Pack 2 (from CD)" and "Step 8b: Install SP2 from the Internet" sections.

FIGURE 9.1

The Windows XP
Service Pack 2
CD can be
ordered free
from the
Microsoft.com
website. At press
time, it was
unknown
whether
Microsoft would
continue offering
the SP2 CD
because
Windows Vista
(the eventual
replacement to
Windows XP) is
due out in 2006.
SP2, however,
should remain
available for
download even
if the CD is
discontinued.

Collect Your Drivers

Drivers are files that contain little pieces of programming that help Windows XP communicate with various parts of your computer. These include your motherboard (the big main circuit board inside your computer), video adapter (which runs the monitor), network card, and so on.

If you are using a recovery disk from the manufacturer, you won't need most of these because they are built into the CD. You just need the drivers for any computer parts that were added since you bought the computer.

You can usually download drivers from your computer maker's website or from the manufacturer of the add-on part (such as a mouse, video card, or network card). You should always look to see if the maker of a particular piece of hardware offers a newer driver than the one that came with your piece of equipment. If you can find a newer driver, use it instead.

note

Think of SP2 as a renovations crew that updates the original floor plan and fixes all the original design flaws of a home.

Installation CDs for Your Programs

When you wipe your hard drive clean, all your programs are deleted, so you need the programs' installation CDs for programs such as Office, Photoshop, Filemaker, and so on, to restore them to your system after the fresh Windows installation. Be sure to have their license codes handy, too.

If the programs were downloaded, you need a copy of their installation files and license codes, if applicable, on a blank CD or other external storage device, such as a USB key or external hard drive.

An external hard drive plugs into your computer (with a USB or a Firewire connector) and acts as additional storage space. It's a good place to keep installation files and backups of your data. External hard drives typically cost less than $300.

A USB key is a similar device except it has no moving parts and is about the size of your thumb (see Figure 9.2). They typically cost less than $100.

tip

You might think of drivers as servants. You tell them what to do and they go deal directly with the appliances. In a new house, you don't really need servants because you operate the appliances yourself. But for the sake of the analogy, let's pretend we're related to Paris Hilton and we can't live without a maid, a chauffeur (a driver!), and a cook.

FIGURE 9.2

A USB key is a thumb-sized storage device that can be used like a high-capacity floppy disk to store files and programs.

Internet Service Software and Settings

If you use a high-speed Internet service from your telephone company or cable TV company, make sure you have your installation disk handy (assuming your ISP provides such a disk). You also need your username and password, if applicable, and any other settings provided by your Internet provider.

If you use dial-up networking to connect to the Internet (where you use a modem to dial a phone number to connect to the Internet), make sure you know the phone number you need your modem to dial, your username, and your password.

note

You can think of your programs like furniture and appliances. They serve a specific task and they make a house functional.

Above all, keep the tech support number for your Internet service handy. If you are inexperienced with configuring your Internet service, you probably need to talk to the company's tech support people to get back online.

Security Programs

Make sure you have the installation CD and registration key for your antivirus, anti-spyware, and firewall programs. If you don't have any of these programs, I'll provide you with some places on the Web to get freebies.

Step 1: Download Drivers and Software You Need for the Re-install

The first job at hand is to go get the drivers you need for your computer from the Internet. These files allow Windows to communicate with the various parts of your computer such as the motherboard, hard drives, and peripheral devices such as printers, mouse devices, and keyboards.

Got a Recovery CD? That's Good News!

If you have a recovery disk from your computer maker, you already have pretty much all the drivers you need to proceed because they are built into the CD.

One caveat: If you have added parts to your computer, such as a better video card, a printer, or a new mouse, download drivers for all of these products from the part maker's website, unless you have the original installation CDs for the add-ons handy.

Retail Copy of Windows XP? There's Some Work to Do

If you're installing from a Windows XP CD you bought from a retail store, you need to ensure you have at hand important drivers for your system or you might not be able to finish your installation. The most important ones you need to ensure you have are discussed next.

> **tip**
>
> If you have lost your product key for Windows XP or Microsoft Office, you might be able to recover it from your computer by using a free program called RockXP available from www. snapfiles.com/get/rockxp.html.

> **tip**
>
> Your network settings and installation disks bring the outside world of the Internet into your computer. In a house, this is like cable TV and phone line service.

> **note**
>
> Antivirus, firewall, and anti-spyware programs are like the security guard, video surveillance, and alarm systems in a mansion.

Motherboard or Chipset Drivers

The motherboard is the major circuit board inside your computer. The Windows XP CD has drivers for major motherboard makers. Often, however, you'll have better system performance if you get the drivers directly from the computer maker or motherboard maker. Depending on who manufactured your motherboard, these drivers are referred to as motherboard drivers or chipset drivers.

These driver packages include INF files, network adapter drivers, and integrated video drivers, if your system uses a video adapter that is built into the motherboard. The best way to get these is by looking up your make and model on your computer maker's website.

If the computer maker is not helpful (this is often the case) and you are not sure what motherboard you have in your system, you should be able to find this information by opening your computer case and looking for the information printed on the board itself (unless you have a laptop and then this is not possible, at least not without voiding your warranty).

To download an updated version of your motherboard driver, follow these steps:

tip

Once upon a time, computer motherboards were purely circuit boards. Everything else, such as network cards, sound cards, and even mouse devices, attached to them separately using special slots called ISA, and later, PCI slots. For cost and efficiency (to the end user), motherboard makers started integrating many of the extras on to the motherboard. Today it's common to see these features built in as part of the motherboard. Also, many add-ons are now plugged into AGP, Serial ATA (SATA), and PCI-Express slots.

1. Determine the motherboard make and model by looking at the printing on the motherboard, and then look for the motherboard manufacturer's website. Google.com can be helpful here.

2. Find the Support or Download section on the manufacturer's website, and locate your motherboard model.

3. Download the system/chipset drivers (also known as INF drivers).

4. Download the Ethernet/LAN drivers, if your Ethernet adapter is on the motherboard. (An Ethernet port is sometimes called a network adapter).

5. Download the video/graphics drivers, if your monitor plugs directly into the motherboard, and not into a separate card.

6. Download drivers for your hard drive controllers (designated as SATA or IDE drivers). You probably won't need them for your installation, but it's better to be safe.

Ethernet Drivers

The Ethernet port is where you plug your network cable in. If it is on a separate adapter card (sometimes called a network interface card or NIC), you can determine the name and model number of the card by following these steps:

1. Click Start, Control Panel.

2. Click System.

3. Click the Hardware tab and select Device Manager.

4. Click the + sign beside Network adapters and look for the make, model, and manufacturer (see Figure 9.3).

Use Google.com to find the driver on the Internet. Search using the make, model, or manufacturer.

tip

Don't be confused here by various lingo used to refer to your network card. The device to which you connect your high-speed Internet cable is variously called a network interface card (NIC), a network adapter, or Ethernet port. You might also hear it called a local area network (LAN) card or adapter. It's all the same. Sometimes this is integrated into the motherboard and sometimes it's connected via a special slot called a PCI slot.

FIGURE 9.3

You can find the make and model of your computer parts in the System applet in Control Panel. The network adapter is shown here.

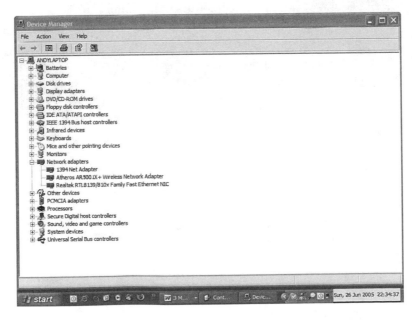

Video Drivers

If the video adapter, which makes the computer screen work, is on a separate card, you can determine what graphics card you have by opening up the Device Manager (as you did for the video card above) and clicking the + sign beside Display adapters. You can also do this as follows:

1. Right-click on any unused space on the Windows desktop.
2. Choose Properties.
3. Click on the Settings tab.
4. Click the Advanced button.
5. Choose the Adapter tab.

Security Software

Your new system needs an antivirus program, an anti-spyware program, and a firewall to round out your defenses. If you don't already have these on CD, make sure you download all of them. If you're looking for free programs, I recommend the following:

note

If any of this hardware talk is making your head hurt, don't worry, you're not alone. Although there are many people out there who live and breathe this stuff, there's far more of you out there who want to stay as far away from the inner workings of your PCs as humanly possible. That said, a little casual knowledge about these technologies can save you lots of time and money when your PC is on the fritz. Unfortunately, there's no way I can cover everything there is to know about PC upgrading and repair. For that, I recommend you pick up a copy of Que's *Absolute Beginner's Guide to Upgrading and Fixing Your PC*. It's an excellent counterpart to my book and will answer all of those hardware questions that just go beyond the scope of this book.

- **Antivirus**—Your best bet for a free antivirus program is AVG Free Edition from www.grisoft.com. Alternatively look at avast! from www.avast.com or AntiVir from www.free-av.com.

- **Anti-spyware**—When it comes to anti-spyware programs, no one program does a perfect job. You need two programs to catch all the infections. For XP users, I recommend Microsoft AntiSpyware from www.microsoft.com/spyware as your primary program. Spybot Search & Destroy from www.safer-networking.org or Ad-Aware SE from www.lavasoft.de are good second choices. For people who have older Windows versions, I recommend both Spybot and Ad-Aware. All three programs are free.

- **Firewall**—I discuss the merits of software versus hardware firewalls in Chapter 3, "Hackers: There's a Man in My Machine." If you do not have a home network router (a device that shares your Internet connection with several computers in your home), I recommend a software firewall that keeps bad people and some viruses and worms on the Internet out of your computer. Alternatively, Windows has a basic built-in firewall you can use. If you'd like to use a free firewall program, download SyGate from www.sygate.com or Zone Alarm from www.zonealarm.com.

Mozilla Firefox Web Browser

Take a few minutes to download a copy of the most recent version of Mozilla's Firefox web browser. Avoiding Microsoft's Internet Explorer web browser and using Firefox with Windows XP goes a long way toward reducing your security risks. Download it free from www.mozilla.org.

> **tip**
>
> Before you go any further, save all of the driver files and program files you need for the re-installation process to a USB key or burn them to a blank CD. Keep this in a safe place.

Step 2: Back Up!

It's time to back up your important data because you're about to wipe your hard drive clean. Are you rolling your eyes? I hate back-ups, too. But all you have to do is find your critical data files: that novel you have been working on, your family photos, and maybe your email files. You don't need to back up every file on the system, just the data that is irreplaceable, like those cute pictures of your spouse with that enthusiastic herd of goats.

You have to save all of the files you want to keep on external media, such as a USB key, DVD, CD, or external hard drive. It's best to have a CD/DVD burner in your system, or use an external hard drive. Don't do this with floppy disks unless you have a lot of time on your hands, like if you're reading this in prison.

If you're organized, you have probably saved the majority of your data in the My Documents folder. Make sure you save all subfolders in this folder to your external media. If you're disorganized like me (I found my sandals under the vanity in the bathroom the other day), it's probably not quite that simple.

> **tip**
>
> Think of this as removing all the family pictures, personal effects, and Niagara Falls souvenir snow domes from the house before the wreckers come.

> **tip**
>
> If you have a home network, you can always save your data to another computer on the network. Just be sure you back up across a wired connection because a wireless connection is slower and can sometimes be flaky.

If you have other folders on your hard disk, specifically for your photos, business files, and so forth, make sure you find and back them up, too. If you want to keep your email, don't forget to save your mailboxes, too.

The following is a series of items you should remember to back up and where you can find them on your computer. It's by no means a comprehensive list, but hopefully it will help you gather most of the important data and settings you should back up.

Outlook

Outlook stores all of its settings (including your Outlook email and your Contact and Calendar information) in a big fat file called `outlook.pst`. It's usually kept in `c:\Documents and Settings\<user>\Local Settings\Application Data\Microsoft\Outlook`, where `<user>` is the account you use to log into Windows. When it auto archives old emails, it stores those in a file called `archive.pst`, so be sure to back up that file, too.

Outlook Express

If you use Outlook Express as your email program, you'll need to back up your DBX file by following these steps:

1. In Outlook Express, select Tools, Options, Maintenance, and click the Store Folder button.

2. In the dialog box, you see the name of the folder that contains your mail files. Look in that folder to locate files named after your mail folders and news groups. They all have a .DBX suffix.

3. Make copies so you have a safe backup of your email.

My Documents

Windows creates a folder for you called My Documents where many people keep all their personal files and folders, as well as pictures, videos, and music, in some cases. If you are in the habit of keeping files here, back up the whole folder. You can find it at `C:\Documents and Settings\<user>\My Documents`.

IE Favorites and Cookies

If you keep favorites in Internet Explorer, you want to save those. Use the Import Export wizard for that and follow these steps:

1. Open IE and click the File menu.

2. Choose Import and Export to manage favorites and cookies files.

Firefox Favorites

Firefox bookmarks can be exported to a file as follows:

1. Open Firefox and click the Bookmarks menu and then Manage Bookmarks.
2. The Bookmark Manager opens in a new window. Click the File menu and click Export.
3. Choose a name for the bookmark file, select a location to save it, and then click Save.

Saved Games

If you play games, make sure you create a copy of your saved games. These files are located in a folder where your game is installed. Usually your game shows you the path where the files are saved.

Pictures, Music, and Videos

You might keep your pictures, music, and video files in the My Documents folder or you might keep them elsewhere. Either way, make sure you don't forget to back these up to a safe place.

Microsoft Office 2003 Settings

If you use Microsoft Office 2003, you can save your settings as follows:

1. Click Start, All Programs, Microsoft Office, Microsoft Office Tools.
2. Choose Microsoft Office 2003 Save My Settings Wizard
3. When the Setting Wizard box appears, click Next, and then choose Save the Settings from This Machine and click Next again.
4. It then shows you where it will put the OPS file that contains the aggregated settings. You can store this anywhere you like.

Windows Media Player

If you use Windows Media Player 10 and have licenses for music you have bought, you want to back those up. Here's how:

1. Open Windows Media Player and click the Tools menu. If the menus are hidden, click the down arrow at the top right of the WMP window.
2. Click Tools and then Manage Licenses.
3. Choose a location to put the license file and then click Back Up Now.

You can also see what folders your music and video files are kept in as follows:

1. Click WMP10's Tools menu and then Options.
2. On the Library tab, click the Monitor Folders button. The music and video folders WMP10 uses for its library are listed.

If you would also like to back up the WMP playlists you have saved, you'll find them in the `c:\Documents and Settings\<user>\My Documents\My Music\Playlists` folder. Note that `<user>` is the name of your Windows login account.

Other Odds and Ends

In addition to the items previously listed, there are a number of other items that you likely want to save. Of course, no list I can place here could be all-inclusive. Because every user is different, there's just no way I can tell you what should be backed up. My best advice: Think it through carefully and make a list. If you're not sure that you have everything, don't start the re-install. Talk to your friends or a tech-savvy co-worker. Make sure you cover all the bases because I can tell you, there's no pain quite like the one you feel when you realize that you forgot to back up irreplaceable data. Remember how Charlie Brown would look up to the sky and scream when Lucy pulled the ball away just as he was about to kick it? It's sort of like that, only worse.

Okay, here are a few other things you should nab:

- Print out a copy of your Outlook Contacts. Trust me, if something goes awry and you lose your Outlook data, you will consider a quick scamper into traffic, especially if you live and die by your Contacts list. Think about losing every email address, mailing address, cell phone number, and so on that you own. Printing the Contacts list is just some extra insurance.

- If you make software purchases online and have been emailed registration keys, make sure you print those emails so you can unlock your software after you re-install it later. This is especially important if you download music from legal online music stores, such as iTunes or Musicmatch, as your digital license for those files is tied directly to your registration key.

- Make sure you write down all of your instant messenger buddy contact info. If you chat online and have buddies with whom you chat frequently, you can save yourself a lot of heartache if you make sure you have this information so you can restore your buddy list later.

- Make sure you write down settings for connecting to the Internet, including phone numbers if you use dialup and your computer name if you use broadband (cable, DSL, or satellite). You need this info to reconnect. Make sure you know your email password. This might sound silly, but most of us tell Outlook (or whatever email program we're using) to remember our password so we don't have to enter it every time we check email. It's not unheard of to forget the password. Before you nuke your drive, make sure you remember the password because you have to enter it later to get your email.

SAVING YOUR WINDOWS SETTINGS

If you've been running Windows for some time, it's likely that you've made a bevy of custom changes (display settings, printer settings, keyboard settings, and so forth). While it isn't a huge deal to reset these manually after Windows is re-installed, Windows XP does include a File and Settings Transfer Wizard that makes the whole mess easier. Here's how it works:

1. Click the Start menu and choose All Programs, Accessories, System Tools, Files and Settings Transfer Wizard.
2. Click Next in the resulting dialog box.
3. Click the Old Computer radio button.
4. Choose how you want to save settings; you have the option of saving them to floppies, CD/DVD, or to another networked drive.
5. If you've done a good job backing up all of your personal data, you can just choose the Settings Only option. If you want to have the wizard back up your documents, too, choose Settings and Data. Just remember that Windows isn't going to be as thorough about saving your data as you can be when doing it by hand. If you save relatively few files and you trust the good folks at Microsoft to know best, go for it.
6. The wizard now gathers your settings and prompts you through the remaining steps, which vary depending on what method for saving the settings you chose in step 4.

FIND MISSING FILES

If you're not sure where all of your photos or documents are or think you're missing some, do a search for them. Click the Start button and select Search. You can search for all Microsoft Word files on the computer by clicking All Files and Folders and typing ***.doc** into the search window.

By changing your view mode to details using the View menu on the top of the search window, you can see all of the files and the locations where they are saved. This tells you which directories you can check for your files. You can open the directories from the search window by right-clicking on one of the files and choosing Open Containing Folder.

Step 3: Pull the Plug on the Network

If you are using a high-speed broadband service to connect to the Internet (from your phone company or cable TV service, for example), it's time to turn it off. Unplug the network cable from the back of your computer (see Figure 9.4). If you are using an old-school dial-up modem, unplug the telephone cable from your computer.

FIGURE 9.4

Disconnect the network cable from your Ethernet adapter on the back of your PC.

If you're connected via your wireless network, turn the Wi-Fi switch to off or disable your wireless connection in Windows. Click Start, go to Connect To: and Show All Connections, and then right-click on the wireless connection to disable it. In short, disconnect from the network entirely.

Step 4: Wipe Away Windows

Now you're ready to wipe the hard drive clean. This is called *reformatting*. The process destroys all the data on the primary partition on the hard drive. That's what you probably know as your C: drive.

One important thing to check here before you call in the wreckers is to check to see if you can boot the computer from a CD or DVD. When a computer starts up, it reads files on the hard drive and that gets the operating system running in memory. But you can also get it to start up without checking the hard drive by booting from a bootable CD or DVD.

In the case of an operating system installation, this is necessary because you don't want to be using files on the hard drive that you are going to wipe clean. This would be like ordering the demolition of a house while you are still standing inside it making a curry.

That said, here's how to configure your CD or DVD drive to boot the system:

1. Reboot your computer, and look for the option to go into your computer's BIOS. Sometimes it's called Setup. The instructions for which key you should press to enter the BIOS should flash on screen quickly during start up. Often it's the DEL key or a function key such as F2.

2. If you see your computer manufacturer's logo when the computer boots up, you might have to hit the Esc key to see information that tells you how to access the BIOS.

3. After you know which key to press, restart the computer, and hit the appropriate key. You enter the BIOS settings.

4. You see a row-looking screen with lots of weird settings. It looks like technology out of a 1980s submarine movie.

5. In the BIOS, use the cursor keys to go over to the BOOT menu. If there isn't one, look for an option in one of the menus that reads Boot Disk Priority, Boot Sequence, or something like that (see Figure 9.5). BIOSes from different manufacturers are slightly different, so it's impossible for me to tell you exactly how yours works.

6. In many cases, the computer is set to boot from the floppy first, then the hard drive, and finally the CD. You want to move the CD to the top of the list. Some BIOSes allow you to choose each item separately and set its priority. Others make you move items up and down the list.

7. Read the instructions on the screen, typically found on the right side of the screen. It tells you what keys to use to rearrange the list (see Figure 9.6). Then look for the option to save. It's often F10, but not always. Save and exit.

tip

If you are uncertain which key to tap to access the BIOS, check with your computer maker's support area on its website. Or you could just use this handy dandy little cheat sheet I've provided here:

BIOS Manufacturer	BIOS Access Key
AMI BIOS	Delete
Phoenix BIOS	F2
Award BIOS	Delete or Ctrl+Alt+Del
MR BIOS	Esc

And if that doesn't help, don't despair. I've also listed brands of computers and their BIOS access keys on my website at http://www.cyberwalker.net/faqs/reinstall-reformat-winxp/enter-BIOS.html.

FIGURE 9.5

Locate the BOOT menu in your computer's BIOS, and then locate the menu that allows you to change the order of the bootable drives.

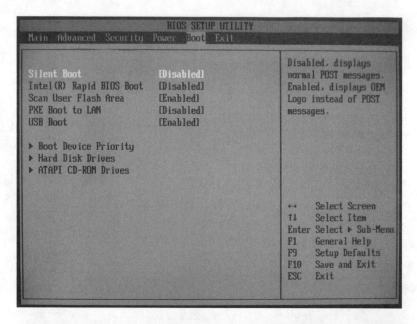

FIGURE 9.6

Change the order of the bootable drives in BIOS so the CD or DVD drive boots first.

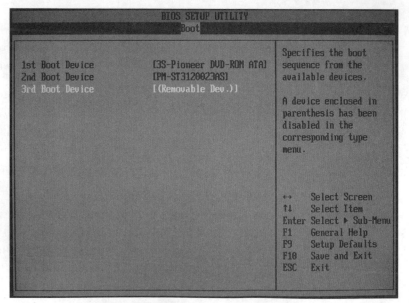

8. After the BIOS is configured to boot from your CD or DVD drive, place your Windows XP install disk or your system recovery disk into the CD/DVD drive and restart the computer.

Using a System Recovery CD

If you're using a system recovery disk when the system restarts, files are read from the CD, the system boots, and the re-install process starts. Follow the instructions as they appear on your screen. This process is different for each brand of computer as it's customized by the computer maker. It should, nevertheless, be fairly straight-forward.

When you are finished, your system should be in the exact state you got it from the manufacturer, with all Windows files and drivers already in place. If everything is working, skip ahead to "Step 7: Install Protection Against Malware," on **p. 276**.

Using a Windows XP Install CD

If you're using a Windows XP CD when the computer restarts, you are prompted to Press Any Key to Boot from CD. Note that there is no Any key. Press whichever key you fancy. However, the Enter key will do as well as the [key.

You see a blue screen, but don't panic. This isn't the typical Windows blue screen of death (as geeks are fond of calling it) that you see when the computer crashes. It's the Windows Setup screen. You won't see much for a while—just a blue screen with a white bar at the bottom. The white bar lists all of the things that the Windows Setup process is loading.

When these are all loaded, you see a screen that says Welcome to Setup near the top (see Figure 9.7). Just below it is an instruction that says To Set Up Windows XP Now, Press Enter. Ignore the items below this instruction and press Enter. The bottom of the screen reads Please Wait. So wait. Maybe go floss your teeth because you can never floss enough.

caution

Be extra careful when tinkering with your system's BIOS! If you think Windows can be ornery, you haven't seen anything yet. Because the BIOS is the heart of your computer, it's a very powerful and dangerous item. Don't toggle options on and off unless you know what they do, and for the sake of all that's good and wholesome in the world, don't save your changes unless you're absolutely certain you know what you're doing. Changing the boot order sequence is a simple task, but toying with some of the other settings is kind of like opening the hood of your car and randomly heaving bits in the lake. It can be fun at the time, but you'll find yourself helpless and stranded later.

caution

Using a copy of a Windows XP installation CD or using a recovery disk from a different brand of computer does not work. You either get an error or the system ignores the CD and tries to go to the hard drive to boot up.

FIGURE 9.7
When you first boot from the Windows XP CD, you see a blue setup screen like this one.

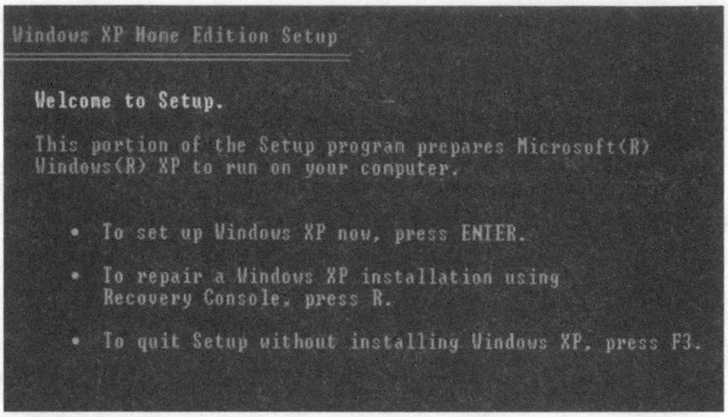

Eventually the End User Licensing Agreement (EULA) appears on your screen. This is where you click away all your rights. A lawyer would tell you that at this point you should read really carefully because not only is it a legal contract between you and Microsoft, but it's also really interesting. I'll leave it up to you. I hold my nose and press F8.

The setup program then searches for previously installed copies of Windows. A screen appears (see Figure 9.8) offering to repair previously installed copies of Windows. Ignore this offer and press the Esc key to continue installing a fresh copy of Windows XP.

FIGURE 9.8
Ignore the very nice offer to repair a previously installed copy of Windows XP.

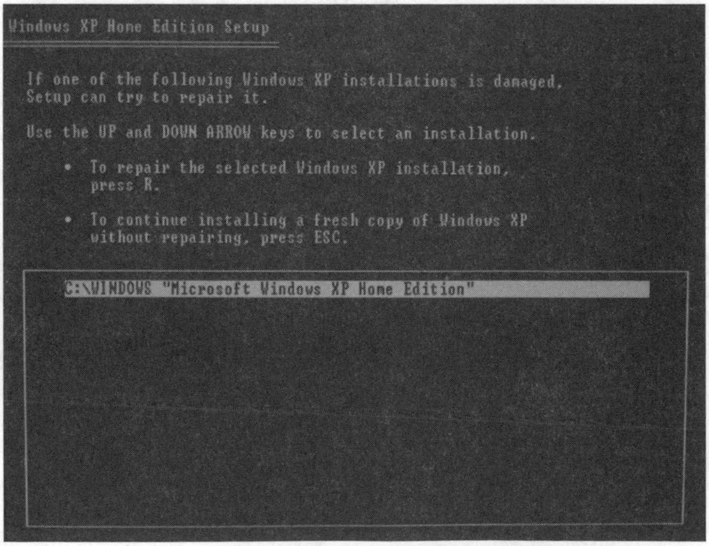

The next screen shows you the partitions on your computer (see Figure 9.9). A hard drive can be subdivided into sections called *partitions*. Each of these partitions is assigned a drive letter. So if your computer had a hard drive that was divided into three partitions and your system had a CD-ROM drive, it would look like this:

FIGURE 9.9

The installation screen lists the partitions on your hard drive.

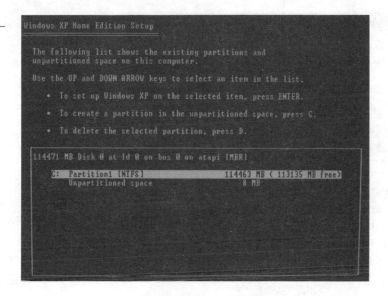

- **C: drive**—Your primary partition where Windows is installed
- **D: drive**—Your CD-ROM drive
- **E: drive**—Your second hard drive partition
- **F: drive**—Your third hard drive partition

Most hard drives only have one partition, and it is listed on this screen.

If you have more than one partition, your current Windows installation is generally the first one. Drive letters are listed on this screen, too. You generally want to choose the C: drive.

Because you want to do a thorough job of this re-installation, first you want to delete the selected partition. Press the D key. You see a confirmation screen. This might make you a little nauseated. I poise my finger over the Enter key at this point and close my eyes tightly. It helps.

So press Enter.

Just for good measure, the screen asks you if you're sure one more time. Don't chicken out. Unless you have good reason, go ahead and delete the partition. Hit L (see Figure 9.10).

Get it? D-Enter-L? D-E-L? Yes, even Microsoft has a sense of humor.

caution

Have you backed up your data? This would be a good point to hit F3 and quit the installation process if you have forgotten to back up something important. In computer terms, this is where the dry cleaner says, "Are you sure you want to clean this dress, Miss Lewinsky?" After this point, there's no turning back.

FIGURE 9.10

Press D, Enter, and then on the next screen press L. You'll DELete the partition.

```
Windows XP Home Edition Setup

You asked Setup to delete the partition

   C: Partition1 [NTFS]                     114463 MB ( 113135 MB free)

on 114471 MB Disk 0 at Id 0 on bus 0 on atapi [MBR].


   •  To delete this partition, press L.
      CAUTION: All data on this partition will be lost.

   •  To return to the previous screen without
      deleting the partition, press ESC.
```

So do it. This bit is where you push the big red button that drops the big demolition ball into the house. At this point, all the data on the C: drive is gone. Poof! Just for fun, pretend to cough and wave away the dust. Mime can be a fun part of Windows demolition.

The process now takes you back to a previous screen showing the partitions, but the partition that was previously listed now appears as unpartitioned space. This is like the smoking hole where the house used to be.

If you want to re-install Windows onto a single big partition, select Unpartitioned Space and press Enter. You can think of this as space to put a foundation for your house. If you subdivided your land into several partitions, you'd have lots to build several smaller houses.

If you want to create smaller partitions, choose C, and tell the installer program how big a partition you want (in megabytes). Don't make these partitions too small—make sure they are at least 10GB. Repeat until all your unpartitioned space is used up.

If you're uncertain, you can delete and add partitions as many times as you want. By the way, 8MB are always listed as unpartitioned. Ignore this, like you would a cat licking your hair from the back of the couch.

note

Think of partitions as individual storage bins. Hard drives can be a single bin or can contain multiple bins. Some users divide their drives into several partitions for storing different kinds of data (operating system on one partition, data files on another). Some users create more than one partition because they're really big geeks who want to run Windows XP on one partition and say, Linux, on another partition. In the end, just be sure that you install your new version of Windows in the correct partition and all will be right with the world.

After you are done divvying up the hard drive, select the first partition and press Enter. The next screen tells you to format the drive using NTFS (see Figure 9.11).

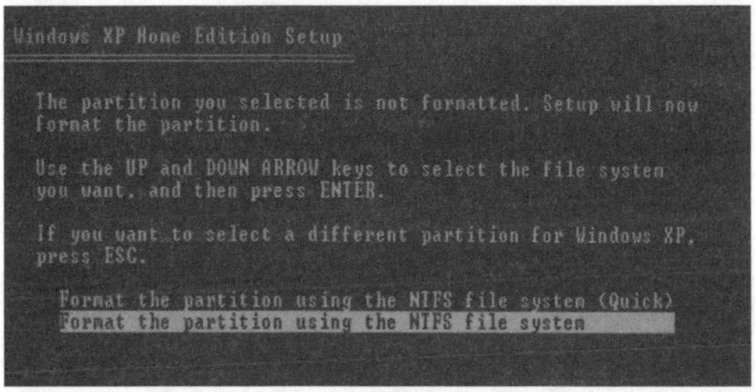

FIGURE 9.11

Choose to format using the NTFS file system, but don't cut corners by using the quick mode.

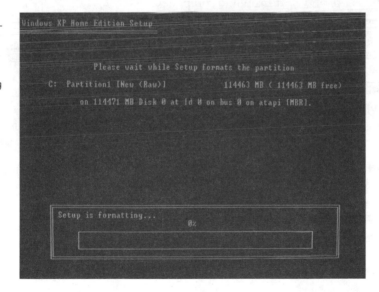

You have a quick option and a regular option. You're welcome to use the quick format option and save some time, but I like to do it right and choose the regular option. It'll take a bit longer, but it erases the drive. Go find something to do while the hard drive is formatting (see Figure 9.12). I bet there are dishes in the sink. Every time I look at the sink, I think, "I wish I had time to clean those up." This would be a good time.

FIGURE 9.12

The formatting process takes a while, but shows its progress along the way. Note that staring at it or yelling won't make it go any faster.

The formatting process takes a while, but it is worth it. Do not turn the computer off during the process, no matter what, because half formatting a drive and stopping it in the process is like half pooper-scooping the lawn. It still can't be used for sunbathing.

When the formatting process is complete, your computer does a bit more work on the drive, and then automatically restarts. Do not press any keys during the reboot process no matter how tempting it is.

Step 5: Re-install Windows

The good news at this point is that the hard part is done. Now you get to build your new house. Yep, it's time to install a fresh, squeaky clean version of Windows. Hooray! This is a good time to dance around your office chair and make victorious chicken noises.

The beginning of the Windows installation is largely automatic. Sit back and allow the computer to gather information about your system, set things up, and start installing components. You see a status bar at the bottom right reading Setup Will Complete in Approximately xxx Minutes. Keep an eye on this. If it freezes for too long, you might have to press the reset button and start this portion again, but in general, let the re-install process do its thing.

The first time you need to do anything is when the setup program asks you which language and regional settings you'll be using on the computer. The standard choice should be U.S.-based English. If you need to change this, click Customize. If you need to add other input options, click Details. Unless you have any special language requirements, you can just click the Next button.

The next screen asks you to personalize your software with a name and organization. Put in something appropriate and click Next.

caution

While your drive is formatting and you're off bathing the cat, patrolling the lawn for dog bombs, or moussing your pompadour, you should be very, very careful to not let anyone—especially children—in the room with your computer. A sudden power loss during drive formatting leaves your drive in an ugly, unrecoverable state. And we all know how much children enjoy power buttons. In fact, years ago a cover for power buttons called a Molly Guard was invented to protect power switches from little hands after the daughter (Molly) of a programmer shut down a few machines. So close and lock your office door, or if your computer is in the living area of the home, lock the children outside with a tent and a packed lunch. If you have pets, particularly cats who like to walk on the keyboard or lounge near your power strip, you're just asking for trouble. I recommend temporary detention of any furry creatures in another part of the house.

The next screen asks you for your installation key, sometimes called a *product key*. You'll find this on back of your Windows XP CD sleeve or on a sticker found on your computer case (in some instances). Type the installation key in and click Next. The key is not case-sensitive, but it must otherwise be typed exactly as it appears.

USING AN UPGRADE VERSION OF WINDOWS XP

If you are using a version of Windows XP marked Upgrade to re-install your system, you should have a copy of an older version of Windows on CD on hand. At some point during the installation, the Windows installer asks you to insert the old Windows CD into your computer to validate that you are eligible to use the upgrade. If you don't have this, you won't be able to continue the installation.

You are then asked to choose a name for your computer. By default, a seemingly random near-gibberish name already appears in the box. It's better to choose a name that you will remember. If you connect your computer to a home network, this name is used to identify the computer. You can change this later, by the way. So if you name your computer Liza-Minnelli and later change your mind, it's no big deal.

tip

Because of a weird piece of computer math, there is actually 1024MB in 1GB. So if you make your partition 10GB, be sure to use 10240MB as your partition size.

One thing you might keep in mind here is that some cable Internet companies use your computer name to validate your Internet access. So if you have a cable Internet connection and you do not use a home Internet router, you should name your computer in this process the same name as you had when you first set it up so you don't bung up the Internet reconnection process.

If you can't remember or aren't sure of your computer name, name it whatever you want and if you have trouble connecting to the Internet later, call your Internet service to resolve this issue.

When you have chosen a name, press Next.

Now make sure your date and time settings are correct. Then press Next. The install process goes into automatic mode again for a few minutes as it sets up networking.

The next screen asks you if you want to use typical or custom settings for your networking setup. Choose Typical install and press Next. The setup process configures your network, registers components, and saves your settings.

When this process is complete, your computer restarts. Again, don't press any keys during the reboot process. When it reboots, you see a message noting that Windows is about to automatically adjust your screen resolution. Click OK. Your desktop is automatically resized. If you can see the dialog box at the top, click OK. If not, don't worry. Just wait. It will fix itself. You can re-adjust these display settings later.

The Windows XP installation process is now complete. Have a sandwich, you deserve it. I like peanut butter and jelly.

ACTIVATE LIKE YOU HAVE NEVER ACTIVATED BEFORE

Microsoft is getting clever with its anti-piracy measures. The company introduced a new scheme to stop you from buying a copy of its software and installing it on all the computers within a half mile radius of your home, which is what we all used to do.

Now when you install Windows XP, Microsoft makes you activate your copy within 30 days of installation or it stops working. Office XP and Office 2003 also require activation. They get gimped (you can't save or change a document) after 50 launches without activation. Visio 2002 gets choked after 10 launches.

Activation works like this: The system takes an inventory of all the components in the computer and generates a numeric identifier that is like a digital thumbprint. It sends the thumbprint to a Microsoft server on the Internet and this is paired with the license you typed in from the back of the XP CD.

When you install the same CD on another machine, Microsoft checks the new machine's thumbprint against its database and if it the thumbprint doesn't match, the activation is rejected and the software stops working or gets gimped after the grace period.

There's a certain amount of tolerance in the system. You can activate two copies before the axe falls. And if you change a couple of parts in your computer, which changes that thumbprint, the activation process doesn't choke. But if you swap out your motherboard, add new RAM, and add a new video card, you might have a problem. If this is the case, it can be rectified with a call to Microsoft.

Step 6: Re-install Your Drivers

If you've re-installed Windows from a recovery CD, you can generally skip this step altogether, as all of the drivers for your system are loaded at the same time Windows is re-installed. You should only need to re-install drivers for hardware you installed yourself, as an add-on to your system.

Windows XP does a nice job of allowing your system to work right after an installation, by using generic hardware drivers. You might be able to use the generic drivers (the ones that come with Windows) without ever noticing anything is wrong, but it's always best to install the drivers designed specifically for your computer's components.

You can find a list of all of the drivers that need to be updated before you finish this whole process. Here's how:

1. Click the Start button.

2. Move your cursor over to the My Computer icon and right-click on it.

caution

If you realize at this point that there's data you forgot to back up, I'm sorry to say, it's too late. Like a toilet paper tube in a hamster cage, that data is munched.

3. Choose Properties.

4. Select the Hardware tab and click on Device Manager.

You see a list of hardware installed inside or connected to your computer. In most cases, all parts and peripherals should be working normally. Items that aren't yet working appear with a yellow question mark beside them, usually under the Other Devices category (see Figure 9.13).

Install drivers for all of these, but let's get to the critical ones first.

Begin by looking for the motherboard drivers in the list. If you have an installation CD for your motherboard, insert it into your CD/DVD drive and run the installation program. If not, pull out your CD with the previously downloaded drivers, and start installing.

FIGURE 9.13

Drivers not installed properly are marked with yellow question marks in the Device Manager.

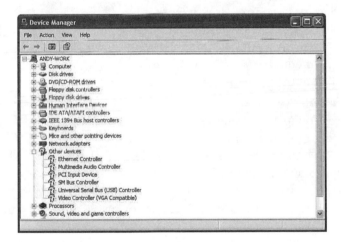

DRIVERS THAT DRIVE YOU MAD

Drivers can be sticky little critters. Sometimes they just don't work, so keep these two troubleshooting tips handy when installing a new driver.

As a precaution, you might want to set a system restore point before you install a new driver. This feature of XP (and Windows Me) allows you to roll the system back in time to the state it was in before something went wrong. Here's how to set a restore point:

1. Click Start, All Programs, Accessories, and finally System Tools.

2. Click System Restore to start it and choose Create a Restore Point and name it something such as Installation of Video Driver, and then click Create.

3. If you install the driver and it bungs the system, you can go back to System Restore, choose the restore point you created, and roll the system back to the way it was before everything exploded.

Windows XP also has a driver rollback feature that allows you to undo a bad driver installation. Here's how to do that:

1. Click Start, Control Panel, System.

2. Click the Hardware tab and choose Device Manager.

3. Find the hardware device that's not working properly. It will probably be obviously marked with a yellow circle with an exclamation mark in it.

4. Right-click the device and choose Properties, and then click the Driver tab, choose Roll Back Driver, and let the system restore the older driver.

Install the system/chipset drivers first. These are the foundation for your system. Then install the Ethernet drivers for your network adapter, if it is on the motherboard.

If your video or audio adapters are on the motherboard (meaning you don't have separate audio and video cards), install drivers for them, too. You should also install drivers for your USB controllers, if these are available. In fact, if you have the motherboard installer CD, you can safely install all of the drivers for components that appear on your motherboard at this point.

> ## caution
>
> Be aware that some motherboard manufacturers make variations of their motherboards with different components on them. So, don't just install everything that's on the installer CD. Some drivers are not applicable. Be selective.

If your network adapter isn't on the motherboard but is on a separate card, re-install the drivers for it now. Don't plug the network cable in just yet. Video and sound card drivers can be installed as well, if you have them. But because they're not essential to the rest of the process, you can always fix these later, after your system is fully up and running again.

Step 7: Install Protection Against Malware

If you've already read the rest of this book, you know what that viruses and spyware are digitally toxic to your computer. What you might not know is that an unprotected computer can be infected within minutes of being connected to the Internet after an installation. So you need to have some security software in place before you reconnect.

INFECTED IN SECONDS

My colleague, Sean Carruthers, who has good hair and a better music collection, maintains his mom's computer. One day he re-installed Windows on her system and hooked it up to her high-speed Internet connection. The machine was attacked by eight worms within three minutes of being connected. The computer got so hamstered up in those first few minutes that he had to yank the Internet connection, reformat the drive, and start again, this time installing McAfee VirusScan before connecting the network cable again.

So before you go any further, you should install antivirus software, a firewall, and anti-spyware software as follows.

Install an Antivirus Program

If you already have an antivirus program, install it as you did on your previous Windows installation and be sure to update its virus signatures. These are updates from the software publisher that recognize viruses and they are inbound to your computer and nab them.

If you don't have an antivirus program, install AVG Free Edition. It's available free from www.grisoft.com (see Figure 9.14). It updates its virus signatures once a day and scans inbound email as well.

To learn more about antivirus software, see Chapter 1, "Viruses: Attack of the Malicious Programs."

tip

Some antivirus programs offer to run a virus scan before they install. In general you can skip this during a Windows re-installation process, unless you're installing from a questionable copy of the Windows CD. If you're installing from a legitimate CD, there's no need to scan at this point.

FIGURE 9.14

AVG Free Edition is a very good antivirus program that can be used free of charge by individuals.

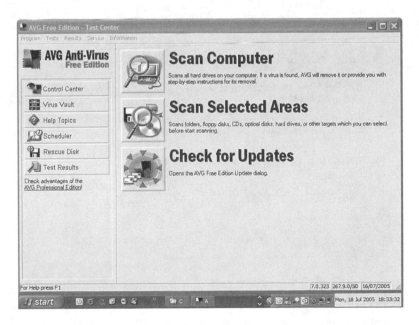

Install an Anti-spyware Program

Spyware and its nasty sister adware are worse than the virus problem because there are many more types and variations of spyware and adware than there are viruses. Spyware sneaks on to your computer and records and sometimes steals information about you. Adware watches your computer behavior and then shows you ads.

The best defense is to install at least two anti-spyware programs because one won't catch all of it. Windows XP users should definitely install Microsoft AntiSpyware and one of the following:

- Spybot Search & Destroy from www.safer-networking.net
- Ad-Aware SE from www.lavasoft.de

All three programs are free. If you run an older copy of Windows, install both of the listed programs. Microsoft AntiSpyware won't run on older versions of Windows.

During the installation of Microsoft AntiSpyware, you are asked several questions (see Figure 9.15). Be sure to agree to enable the AutoUpdater to keep the program automatically up to date. Also enable the Real-Time Protection so the program stops your computer from becoming infected with spyware (more on this in the next section).

FIGURE 9.15

Microsoft AntiSpyware asks you a series of questions when you first install it. It's important that you agree to turn on the AutoUpdater and Real-Time Protection.

You are also asked to join the Microsoft AntiSpyware community. This allows the program to send spyware it catches on your computer to Microsoft for analysis. At the end of the installation you are asked to run a QuickScan. This is not necessary at this point as your system has a freshly installed version of Windows XP on it.

To learn more about anti-spyware software, see Chapter 2, "Spyware: Overrun by Advertisers, Hijackers, and Opportunists."

Turn on Real-Time Protection

Anti-spyware programs not only remove spyware and adware, but they also block the initial infection if you turn on what Microsoft calls real-time protection (see Figure 9.16). On Spybot Search & Destroy it's called Immunize. And on Ad-Aware SE it's called Ad-Watch, but note that Ad-Watch is not available in the free version.

FIGURE 9.16

Real-time protection is a feature in Microsoft AntiSpyware that stands guard over your system to ensure that spyware doesn't sneak in.

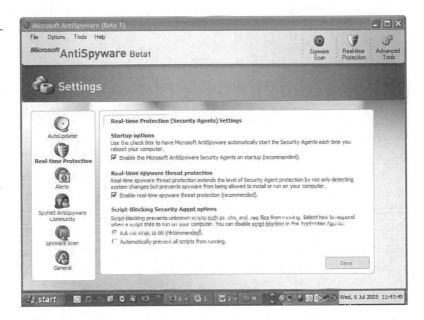

These mechanisms simply stop spyware from getting on your system in the first place. If you choose not to turn on real-time protection in the set-up, you can always activate it later. It's very important that you do activate it. Here's how:

1. Start Microsoft AntiSpyware.
2. Click the Options menu and then Settings.
3. Click the Real-time Protection button on the left.
4. Check off Startup options.
5. Check off Real-Time Spyware Threat Protection.
6. Under Script Blocking Security Agent, choose whichever option you feel is best. Personally I like Ask Me What to Do, but if you want to stop all scripts from running, choose the Automatically Prevent All Scripts from Running option.

Install a Firewall

You should also turn on a firewall, a program that protects your computer from intruders on the Internet from accessing your computer. Think of it as a large cinderblock wall between your computer and the outside world, with a beefy security guard that raises the gate only when you invite someone in. Firewalls only let data in if you initiate contact with the data source first, such as when you fetch your email or a web page, for example. A firewall also stops worms, which are network-traveling viruses that infect exposed computers.

You have several choices when it comes to a firewall. I talk about these at length in Chapter 3, "Hackers: There's a Man in My Machine." However, here's a quick summary. Choose one.

Hardware Firewall

If you have a home network where you share your broadband Internet connection from the phone or cable company, you probably have a home network router. This little junction box has a built-in mechanism called Network Address Translation (NAT) that hides your computers attached to it from the Internet. This works as a basic firewall to keep intruders out.

For most people, this is sufficient protection. It's also simple because it's a physical barrier between your computer and the Internet. It's also the least intrusive technology because it doesn't need any software installed on your computer to work.

Third-Party Software Firewall

If you don't have a home network router with a built-in firewall, you might want to install a software firewall from a third-party publisher. I recommend two free products:

- ZoneAlarm from www.zonealarm.com (see Figure 9.17)
- Wingate from www.wingate.com

Both inspect inbound and outbound data traffic to and from your computer. Inbound data inspection is important because it stops hackers and worms. Outbound data inspection stops

tip

If you are asked to activate or register your antivirus or anti-spyware program, choose the option to do this later. You are also prompted to update your virus options, but hold off on this; you'll do that later when you reconnect to the Internet.

unauthorized programs from sending data out to the Internet without your knowledge. Trojan horses, viruses, and spyware would all be stopped by outbound data inspection.

FIGURE 9.17
Zone Labs offers
a free version of
ZoneAlarm, a
software firewall
that protects
your computer
from hackers,
viruses, worms,
and spyware.

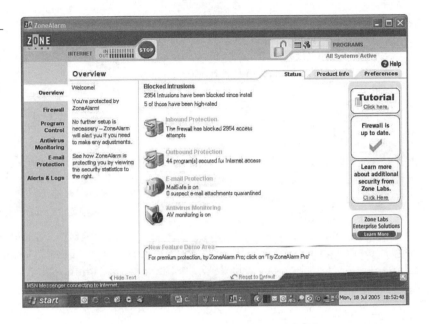

Windows Firewall

The simplest approach is to turn on your Windows Firewall, a built-in software firewall integrated into Windows XP (so long as you have one of the Service Pack updates). It is turned on for you when you install SP2 in Step 8a or 8b.

Step 8a: Install Windows XP Service Pack 2 (from CD)

Windows XP in this state is like a newly built house. It's all shiny and fresh, but it's full of building flaws. Left like this, it's a great target for all kinds of Internet nasties. So you have to fix the flaws.

Microsoft issued a great big security fix in the summer of 2004 called Service Pack 2. It has a wide-range of new features that make the paper house that is Windows XP a little more corrugated.

You can get a copy of SP2 on CD free from Microsoft (they even pay for the shipping!). It takes a month or more to show up after it's ordered, but it's worthwhile. I'm going to assume you have it in your hot little hands now. However, if you don't, go back to the beginning of this chapter where I show you how to order it.

tip

Don't forget: If you have a recovery CD or Windows XP installation CD made in 2005 or later, SP2 is part of the installation programming. If so, you can skip the installation of SP2 as it has been installed with Windows. If you're not sure whether SP2 is installed on your PC, open any folder on your hard drive, click the Help menu, and choose About Windows. The dialog box that pops up tells you whether SP2 is installed.

Insert the Windows XP SP2 CD into your CD or DVD drive. The installer program should start automatically. If not, click Start, select My Computer, select your CD/DVD drive, and double-click the icon for your drive. If it still doesn't automatically start, go to your Desktop, double-click My Computer, double-click the icon for the SP2 disc, double-click the Autoexec.exe file, and the installation should begin.

tip

If you can't be bothered to order SP2 on CD and want to forge ahead anyway, skip to "Step 8b: Install SP2 from the Internet," where I show you how to download it.

Click the Continue icon in the lower-right side of the screen to get started (see Figure 9.18). The next screen features a link that says What to Know Before Installing Service Pack 2. Clicking it launches a Frequently Asked Questions page in Internet Explorer. Don't worry; this is on the CD, not on the Internet. Read this, and then close the browser. Click Continue and the installation program begins to extract some files, though there might be a brief delay.

Eventually, another window opens to take you through the actual installation process. Click Next. The next screen is a license agreement. Make the lawyers happy and read legalese if you need a sleep aid. Then click the dot to the left of I Agree and click Next.

The installer then inspects your hardware configuration, backs up files, and updates the necessary files. A blue progress bar moves slowly from left to right, and the Details box below it tells you what's happening. Wait for this process to complete (see Figure 9.19).

The next screen tells you that you've completed the process. Click on Finish to reboot your computer, and then go to "Step 9: Configure Your Security Settings."

FIGURE 9.18

Install SP2 to fix all the security holes in Windows XP. To install SP2, insert the CD and follow the instructions.

FIGURE 9.19

The installation of SP2 is mostly automated and includes a back up of replaced files.

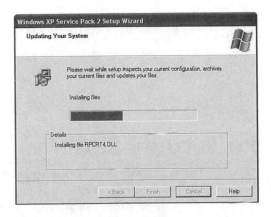

HOT NEW SECURITY FIXES ADDED BY SP2

Service Pack 2 is arguably the most important Windows service pack ever issued by Microsoft. It completely renovates XP, changing it from a skinny 98 lb. weakling to a skinny 98 lb. weakling inside an armored personnel carrier: Weak at its core, but with better defenses.

SP2 adds these key features:

■ **Windows Security Center**—This new Control Panel element monitors your antivirus and firewall programs and turns on the Windows firewall, if needed.

■ **Windows Firewall**—SP2 turns on the firewall by default. The firewall is easier to configure than before and is turned on during Windows startup.

■ **Outlook Express**—SP2 turns off images in emails and alerts you to any email-sending activity that could be virus behavior. It also warns you about potentially dangerous email attachments.

■ **Other nonsecurity features**—SP2 improves Wi-Fi and Bluetooth support, updates DirectX, and adds Windows Media Player 9 (which has since been made obsolete by Windows Media Player 10).

Step 8b: Install SP2 from the Internet

If you forgot to order the free Service Pack 2 CD or you can't be bothered because you've wasted too much time already, you have to connect to the Internet now.

It's not ideal because you're connecting a computer that is not yet secure to the Internet. That said, I'll talk you through the process anyway. You have to do a little jumping around here to prepare:

1. First, skip ahead to "Step 11: Configure Your Networking" to make sure you're ready to connect to the Internet.

2. Go to "Step 12: Update Windows with All Recent Security Patches" and download all relevant updates from Windows Update, repeating Step 12 as many times as necessary to get to the SP2 download.

3. When the SP2 installation process begins, hop back to Step 8 to finish the SP2 installation.

Step 9: Configure Your Security Settings

After SP2 is installed, your system reboots. It takes your computer a bit longer than usual to start up, as it has to configure a few things. During this process, you see a setup screen asking you if you'd like to turn on Automatic Updates (see Figure 9.20). This gives Windows XP the ability to detect and automatically download and install new security fixes from Microsoft. This means that as soon as Microsoft releases a fix, your computer fetches it. So it's a very good idea to turn this feature on.

FIGURE 9.20
After SP2 is installed, you are asked to turn on Automatic Updates. This is a very good idea.

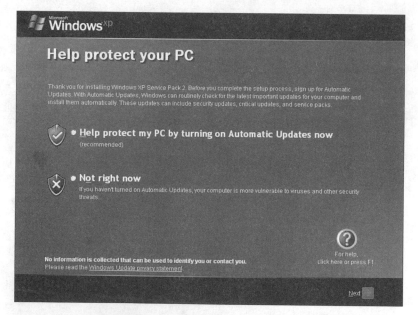

To do that, click the dot beside the green security shield, and click Next. Windows XP starts up, and you see the new Security Center (see Figure 9.21).

In the Security Center under the heading Manage Security Settings For:, note the three icons near the bottom. They are Internet Options, Automatic Updates, and Windows Firewall. If you are having problems with your automatic updates or your firewall, you can adjust them from this panel.

Next, click on the Internet Options icon. A dialog box titled Internet Properties appears on your screen, opened to the Security tab (see Figure 9.22).

FIGURE 9.21

SP2 adds a new feature to Windows XP called Security Center. This monitors your antivirus program and your firewall, and turns on automatic updates from Microsoft.

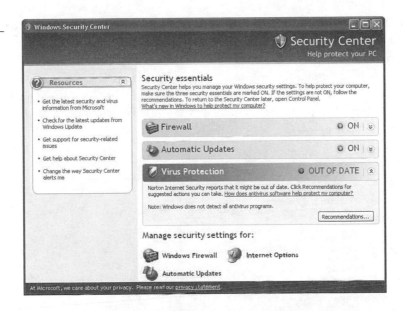

FIGURE 9.22

From the Security Center you can access your Internet Properties. These are the same settings found in Internet Explorer.

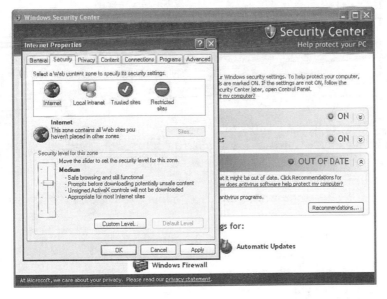

Click on the icon that says Internet. You want to create a security setting for your time on the Internet that strikes a balance between usability and safety. In general, medium is the best way to go because the high setting baby-sits almost everything you do, meaning that you'll be barraged with warnings from the firewall, asking if this application can access the Internet, if that application can act as a server, and if this one can go to the bathroom. If you're anything like the rest of us, you'll go stark raving mad and disable the firewall because it annoys you, which is a bad, bad thing. Setting the security to medium provides a solid level of security without making you want to climb out onto the roof with a rifle.

Try both security settings for a bit and surf the Internet. You'll quickly find out which suits you best. If you'd like to further tweak your settings, click Custom (see Figure 9.23) to enable or disable prompting for behaviors that are either a security risk, such as automatic scripting, or too intrusive, such as pop-up messages that ask you for permission before the browser does something. You can come back to this dialog box at any point, so don't worry if you make the wrong choice—you can change it later.

FIGURE 9.23

The Custom button in the Security table in Internet Options can be used to customize security in Internet Explorer.

Click Custom in the Security tab to override the preset security features and customize them to your own taste. For most people, these settings seem like a menu from a Bosnian-owned Chinese food restaurant. Ideally, stick to the presets.

In this same tab, there are settings for intranet (computers on the same network as you) and a list of trusted and restricted sites. If you use an Internet service via your cable TV company to connect to the network and don't have an Internet-sharing home router, you should bump your Intranet setting up to a higher setting. Otherwise the default settings should be okay.

You can come back to this dialog box later to add trusted sites—websites you visit that you know are safe but that trigger too many security warnings. You might also want to restrict websites—sites that you want to be off

tip

A message might pop up telling you that Windows Firewall is running. If you installed another software firewall in Step 7, you can turn off the Windows Firewall at this point (despite any admonishment that the good folks at Microsoft might dish out when you do). If you cheated a bit and didn't install a firewall program, leave Windows Firewall on.

limits for members of your family, including adult content sites, spyware-infested sites, or other scary content you want to block, such as Martha Stewart's home page. (Clip-art napkin rings kind of scare me.)

SP2 also adds a new feature under the Privacy tab to help you manage pop-up windows in Internet Explorer. You see a Block Pop-ups section at the bottom of the Privacy tab window (see Figure 9.24). Note the Settings button here. If you click this, you can enable pop-ups for trusted sites you visit that require pop-ups to work. Some sites, for example, pop open separate windows to enter site login information.

While on the Privacy tab, reset your Privacy setting to medium-high or high. High is a good option if you want maximum security and are willing to be pestered by your computer when surfing the Internet.

Again, note the Sites button. You can use this to change cookie settings for specific websites. Cookies are little pieces of text sent to you by a website and stored by your web browser to track your movements, populate a shopping cart, and store settings such as User IDs and passwords. To learn more about cookies, see Chapter 2. At this point, you can close your Internet Properties dialog and the Security Center.

> ## tip
>
> In case you're wondering, ActiveX is a set of Microsoft technologies that allow programs to download from the Web and run on your computer. An ActiveX control can trigger sounds, animations, or other programs that execute from the Web. It's that last item that is scary. If ActiveX is turned on, you might get an ActiveX control automatically downloading programming from a web page and installing malware such as a Trojan horse, spyware, or adware.

FIGURE 9.24

Service Pack 2 adds a customizable pop-up blocker to Internet Explorer.

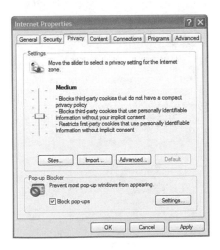

Step 10: Install Firefox

The Microsoft Internet Explorer web browser has a nasty history of being very insecure. If you surf the Web with it in its uncustomized, unpatched state, your computer is extremely vulnerable to all kinds of malware. It is about as safe as wearing pepperoni chaps in bear territory.

I have been showing you how to secure Microsoft Internet Explorer because there is no way of living without it. Some websites (such as the Windows Update site, for example) just won't work without it.

However, it's wise to access most websites with a different browser. The one that has gained the most popularity in the past year or so is Mozilla Firefox, a free web browser available from www.mozilla.org.

My dear friend and TV colleague, Leo Laporte, has been promoting the benefits of switching browsers since Firefox first appeared on the scene, and if you've heard about it before, it's probably in large part due to his influence. And for good reason: It is a lot more secure than Internet Explorer because it does not support VBScript or ActiveX, which are technologies used by malware to hitchhike onto your computer. It also avoids Microsoft's Java virtual machine, a piece of programming that enables programs written in the Java language to run on Windows. Firefox isn't without its own flaws, but it is innately more secure than Internet Explorer, which has as many security features as a fish sandwich.

Earlier I asked you to download Firefox's installation program. I hope you did because we're going to install it now. Double-click on the installer program's icon, and when the program launches, click Next (see Figure 9.25). Click the dot beside the I Agree option for the license agreement, and click Next. Choose the standard installation, and click Next twice. Then click Finish.

FIGURE 9.25

Use Mozilla Firefox as your web browser to avoid the massive security flaws in Internet Explorer.

Step 11: Configure Your Networking

Now it's time to reconnect the Internet. Here's how, using the most common types of Internet connections.

Home Network

If you have a home network, it's time to reconnect your network cable or turn your wireless back on. You should be able to reconnect instantly.

Digital Subscriber Line (DSL)

If you have a Digital Subscriber Line (DSL) available through your telephone company, install the software provided, and enter your username and password in the appropriate places. Then connect your Ethernet cable to your DSL modem.

Cable Internet

If you use cable Internet, consider getting a broadband home router, if you don't use one already. Cable Internet makes your entire neighborhood one big local network. So a router gives you extra protection against bad things circulating in your neighborhood. If not, your software firewall (installed earlier) protects you. After either of these protections is in place, reconnect your network cable.

Dial-up

If you use a dial-up connection with your phone line to connect to the Internet, re-install the connection software provided to you by your Internet provider, if any was provided. Otherwise follow these steps:

1. Click Start and select Control Panel.
2. Select Network and Internet Connections.
3. Click Setup or Change Your Internet Connection (see Figure 9.26).
4. Choose Add and then Dial Up to Private Network, and follow the setup process, entering all of the information for your Internet provider.
5. Reconnect your modem to the phone line.

tip

If you don't see Network and Internet Connections in the Control Panel, click the Switch to Category View on the left side of the window.

FIGURE 9.26

Set up your dial-up modem in Network and Internet Connections in the Control Panel.

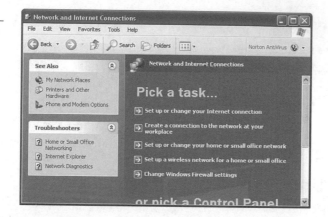

Step 12: Update Windows with All Recent Security Patches

Now that you are able to connect to the Internet, go to Windows Update and download any necessary security updates.

To get to Windows Update:

1. Click Start.

2. Select All Programs and click on Windows Update.

3. Internet Explorer launches and takes you to the update site.

At this point, your firewall software might pop up an alert asking your permission to connect to the Internet. Of course, you want to say yes. As Internet Explorer connects to the update site, you might also get a security warning. If so, click OK (see Figure 9.27).

After the page loads, you have to choose between Express and Custom install modes (see Figure 9.28). To install only the most important updates, click on the Express Install option. If you want to update other software and hardware that's non-essential, choose the Custom Install option. But don't worry about it too much, as you can come back to this at any time.

tip

You can also get to the Windows Update website by opening Internet Explorer and typing http://windowsupdate.microsoft.com. Note that it won't work using Firefox.

After choosing your installation option, a message might pop up warning you that any information you send to the Internet may be viewable by others. If it does, click Yes to continue. When the Express Install menu appears, it lists a number of items that will be installed, most of which are security updates.

FIGURE 9.27
When Windows
Update loads,
you might get a
security warning
because it
uses ActiveX
technology.

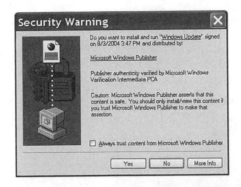

FIGURE 9.28
Windows Update
gives you the
choice between
Custom and
Express updates.
Only the most
important
updates are
downloaded if
you choose the
Express option.

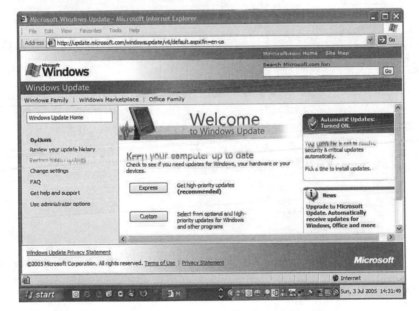

Click the Install button. An End User License Agreement appears; click I Accept to continue, and then sit back while your updates download and install (see Figure 9.29).

When this process is complete, the installation program asks you if it can restart your computer. Go ahead and wait for the computer to reboot.

After your computer has rebooted, go to Windows Update again to make sure there aren't any further updates that need to be downloaded. Sometimes installing one update makes another available on Windows Update. Repeat this step until your system is up-to-date and no more updates are available for download.

tip

Sometimes new hardware drivers are available through Windows Update.

FIGURE 9.29

You are asked to agree to the End User License Agreement again when running Windows Updates. Then the updates begin to download.

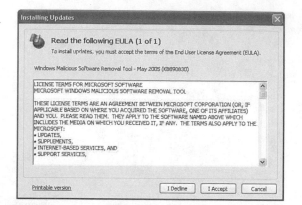

Step 13: Update All of Your Security Programs and Security Signatures

After you have connected to the Internet, some of your security programs might have started updating themselves to protect you automatically against new threats. Nonetheless, you should manually go to each security program you've installed and look for the option to update the program.

Don't forget to update the following programs:

- Antivirus program
- Anti-spyware program(s)
- Firewall program

Sometimes an update of your program might require further updates of the program. For any updates that require you to restart your computer, run the update process on that program again after rebooting to make sure you've caught all relevant updates. Just like it says on a shampoo bottle: Repeat as necessary.

Step 14: Activate Windows

After you're satisfied that everything is running properly, it's time to activate your copy of Windows. Double-click the set of keys in the lower-right corner of the screen. A dialog box entitled Let's Activate Windows appears (see Figure 9.30). You can choose to activate over the Internet or over the phone. Choose the Internet option and click Next.

If you've already activated your copy of Windows many times, you might be prompted to call Microsoft to activate your copy over the phone. Generally Microsoft is pretty good about giving you a code to activate your copy of Windows, unless your Windows key has been abused mercilessly. For this reason, you should never give your key to anyone. It might work okay for your friend in an emergency, but it could lead to you not being able to re-install your operating system later.

FIGURE 9.30

The Windows
activation
process needs to
be complete
within 30 days
or Windows XP
stops working.

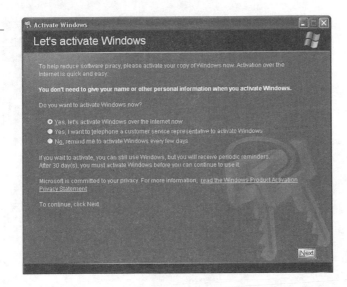

Step 15: Re-install Your Programs

After Windows is updated, back in operation, and all the security programs are running, then it's time to install all of your day-to-day programs. There is no real trick to this. If you have the original CDs or copies of the install files on a backup CD, it's just a matter of re-installing them.

After installation, though, you should check with the companies that publish the software you own to see if there are any fixes or patches on their websites. This is especially true of Microsoft Office, which, like Windows, has service packs available. Check www.microsoft.com/office/ and look for the Check for Updates link on that page. Like Windows Updates, the Office Update site scans your computer to determine which updates you need (see Figure 9.31) and these updates can then be downloaded and installed. You need to keep your Office CD handy when you install any fixes as you might be prompted to put it into the computer to show that you own a copy of the software.

FIGURE 9.31
Be sure to check
for Microsoft
Office updates
on the Microsoft
website.

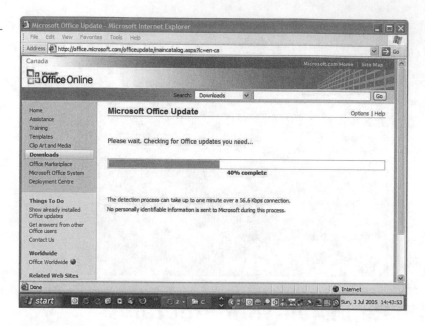

Step 16: Other Things You Can Do

If you have followed this chapter through from beginning to end, your system is
about as secure as it possibly can be given the flaws in Microsoft Windows XP. In
the future, Microsoft will integrate a lot of these fixes into the operating system and
find new ways of making it more secure.

The company has taken a lot of criticism for its lax security focus and you can be
sure that future releases of Internet Explorer will repair many of the holes in version 6.0 that was current as this book was being written. The next version of IE is
slated for release in the fall of 2005.

Moving forward, you should consider adding several more tweaks to the system:

- If a new web browser becomes available from Microsoft, hold off installing it
  until it's several months old (if you like to be conservative). A new browser
  will have new flaws. It'll take three to six months for these to be revealed.

- Add an anti-spam program to your email program. I recommend
  Cloudmark Desktop from www.cloudmark.com.

- Consider installing the Netcraft Anti-Phishing Toolbar for both Internet
  Explorer and Firefox from www.netcraft.com.

KNOW WHAT YOU'RE OPENING

One of the stupid things Windows does is hide file extensions—the bit of the file name after the dot, such as .doc or .txt—for what it considers to be familiar or known file types. These include JPG and DOC files, but also potentially harmful files such as EXE, PIF, DAT, and COM files, all of which can execute programming that can compromise your computer.

One well-known trick hackers use is to send an email with an attachment named something like sexygirl.jpg.exe, which appears in most mail programs as sexygirl.jpg when this option is turned on. You might click on it thinking it's a naughty, yet non–security-threatening file, and wind up infecting your system.

There is an easy fix, though. Double-click My Computer, choose the Tools menu from the top, and select Folder Options. Then click the View tab, and uncheck the item that reads Hide Extensions for Known File Types, if it is checked (see Figure 9.32).

If you make this change, you see the extensions for all files. All you have to do is make sure you always pay attention to what you're clicking on when you receive a file attachment.

FIGURE 9.32

Reveal your file extensions so Windows lists the whole filename, including the file type that comes after the dot in the name.

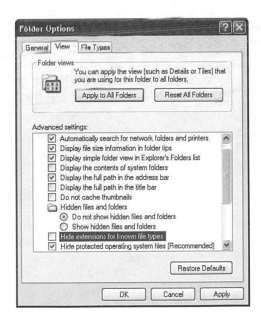

THE ABSOLUTE MINIMUM

- Be sure you have a legitimate copy of Windows XP.
- Get a copy of Service Pack 2 on CD from Microsoft.
- Collect all your system drivers.
- Get antivirus, anti-spyware, and firewall programs for your computer.
- Set your BIOS so the CD or DVD drive is the first bootable device on the system.
- Wipe your hard drive clean and install a fresh copy of Windows XP after disconnecting from the Internet.
- Install drivers.
- Install an antivirus program, two anti-spyware programs, and a firewall.
- Install Service Pack 2.
- Configure your security settings.
- Install Firefox.
- Reconnect to the Internet.
- Use Windows Update to download security fixes and updates for your security programs.
- Add extras such as anti-spam and anti-phishing programs.
- Hold off on a new web browser from Microsoft until three to six month after it launches.

10

Ongoing Maintenance: Fend Off Future Threats!

The advice in this book is going to make your computer more secure than it ever was before. But just because your system is now malware-resistant doesn't mean it will be forever. You'll need to do a little ongoing maintenance. So in this chapter I'll show you what to do on a daily, weekly, and monthly basis to keep your computer free of computer nasties.

Note to Self: Keep Computer Secure

Let's say you've followed every tiny little detail in this book (if you have, I am very proud of you!) and you're feeling much more secure about your computer because it's much more secure.

There's still a problem, though. While you're taking your kids to soccer practice or shopping for hair products, the virus writers, spyware mavens, and hackers are remaining uncoiffed and childless because they are busy writing the next genera- tion of Internet threats. Villains don't get many dates.

So your work isn't finished. You still need to fight the future—future threats that is. You can do that by taking a few minutes every day or so, 30 minutes each week, and maybe an hour every month to keep abreast of emerging security issues.

To that end, here are a series of easy security maintenance tips. One little note: The frequency I recommend is just a guideline. I don't want to schedule you into obliv- ion. If you do most of them with any kind of reasonable frequency, you'll be ahead of the game.

Daily Routines: Walk the Dog, Feed the Kids, and Secure the Computer

Here are the tasks you should do every day to keep your computer secure. They should only take a minute or two and should become part of your routine computer maintenance.

Update Your Antivirus and Anti-Spyware Signatures

Antivirus and anti-spyware programs are only as good as their signatures. You'll recall those are digital snapshots of viruses and spyware that help these programs recognize threats. Ideally, you need to check for new signatures every day. That way, if a fast, replicating virus, worm, or particularly nasty piece of spyware appears, your defenses will be able to block it when it attacks your computer.

What's handy here is that most programs auto- matically update signatures daily. So no matter which antivirus and anti-spyware program you use, make sure automated updates are turned on. If you hear about a new malware outbreak in the news, be sure to manually update your antivirus or anti-spyware program.

caution

If you use a software firewall, it might be a good idea to manually initiate an update with your antivirus and anti- spyware program to see how the firewall responds. You might get a warning from the firewall that you'll have to respond to for the update to proceed. That also allows future updates to get through the firewall automatically.

Update AVG Signatures

If you are running Grisoft's AVG Anti-Virus, you'll be pleased to know that in addition to being absolutely free, AVG virus signatures can be updated by the program daily. Here's how to ensure that this feature is turned on:

1. Start AVG's control center by double-clicking the AVG icon in your system tray (bottom-right side of your screen).

2. Click the Scheduler box and below that click Scheduled Tasks.

3. Click on Update Plan in Basic Mode and then click the Edit Schedule button. Check the boxes next to Periodically Check for Internet Updates and If Internet Connection Is Not Available, Check When It Goes On-Line. Next to Check Daily, choose the hour you'd like the program to check for updates (see Figure 10.1).

FIGURE 10.1

Set the hour in which AVG Free Edition checks for virus signatures for a time when you won't be using your computer.

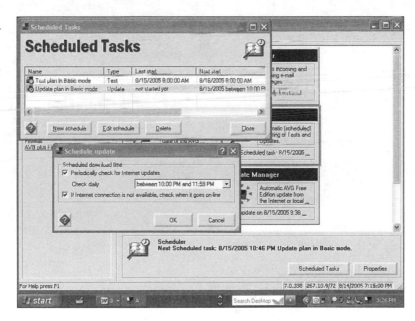

4. I like it to check for updates before I start my work day so I set it for late at night or early in the morning.

5. Click OK and click Close.

Update Microsoft AntiSpyware

Microsoft AntiSpyware can download its spyware signatures automatically as well. Here's how to check that this feature is turned on:

1. Start Microsoft AntiSpyware.

2. Click the Options menu.

3. Choose Settings.

4. If the AutoUpdater settings are not displayed, click the AutoUpdater icon on the left.

5. Make sure the box next to Enable Automatic Updates is checked and choose the frequency you like the updater to run. System startup is ideal if you reboot your computer daily. The Daily option is ideal if you leave your computer on.

6. It's also useful to check Definition Update Notifications. When checked, the program installs any updates automatically without bugging you. If you leave this option unchecked, the program does not apply updates, but lets you know when they are available so you can download and install them yourself.

7. It's also worth turning on Software Update Notifications so you're alerted when a new version of Microsoft AntiSpyware is available for download.

To run a spyware signature update manually, follow these steps:

1. Start Microsoft AntiSpyware.

2. Click the File menu.

3. Choose Check for Updates.

4. Let the update mechanism run. It downloads and installs updates if they are available.

caution

Is it okay to leave your computer on all the time? Some say yes, some say no. I do because it means my security software always has a chance to check for updates. The downside is if your computer is on all the time, it's available to be attacked. Also, it burns power and is subject to being shut down rudely and unexpectedly during power outages, which is rough on your hardware. But others argue it's better to keep a computer on and warm than cycling it on and off, warming and cooling components and subjecting them to heat stress. At the end of the day, it's your call.

You should also consider whether leaving your computer on all the time is a security risk because others in your household could have access to your data if your PC is powered on and you are logged in. At the very least, log off as the computer administrator to prevent others from being able to unwittingly damage your computer.

Update Spybot Search & Destroy

Spybot can automatically download and install signatures every time you start the program. Here's how to set that up:

1. Start Spybot.

2. Click Settings in the left margin of the main screen, near the bottom.

3. A settings list appears in the margin. Click the Settings item.

4. In the main window scroll down to the Web Update section and select by adding a checkmark to the Download Updated Include Files If Available Online item. Optionally add a checkmark to Search the Web for New Versions at Each Program Start to have the program check to see if there's a newer version of Spybot available.

tip

Being aware of the latest computer threats is a handy habit to get into. I keep my eye on News.com's security page (click the Security tab at http://news.com.com/). I also check in with Secunia.com (http://secunia.com/) to see what the latest security advisories are.

5. When you are done, click Spybot S&D at the top left to return to the main screen.

To look for signatures manually, follow these steps. Without this step you are not as well-protected as you could be.

1. Start Spybot and click the Search for Updates button (see Figure 10.2).

FIGURE 10.2

Be sure to check for updates in Spybot each week (and daily if you have time) or set the program to check for updates each time it starts up.

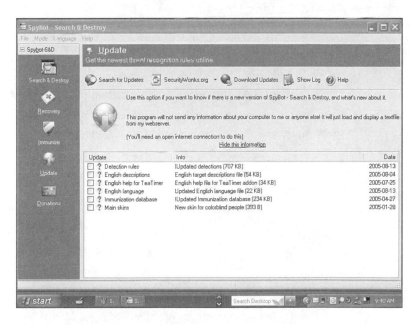

2. The updates available for download are listed.

3. Check all the items. Some will be new features available for the program, while others will be updates for the immunization database and spyware detection rules. Sometimes only Detection rules updates are available (these are the important spyware signatures).

4. At the top of the window, click the Download Updates button. A green check-mark appears after each item has been downloaded and installed.

Weekly Routines: How to Never Be Bored on Saturday Morning

Here are the security tasks you should do once a week. They shouldn't cumulatively take more than about an hour or so.

Scan for Viruses and Spyware

Use your antivirus and both anti-spyware programs to do a scan of your computer once a week. Here's how to do that with the key programs suggested in this book. If you use other products, be sure to run scans with them instead.

Microsoft AntiSpyware

1. Start Microsoft AntiSpyware.

2. Under the Run Quick Scan Now button, click Scan Options.

3. Click Run a Full System Scan.

4. Be sure to check off all the boxes provided, including Deep Scan Folders.

5. If you want to scan particular specified folders and drives, click the Select link next to Scan Selected Drives/Folders and check off the areas you want scanned.

6. Click Run Scan Now and allow the program to detect spyware. Remove the programs you don't want on your system.

Spybot Search & Destroy

Here's how to do a spyware scan with Spybot Search & Destroy:

1. Start Spybot.

2. Click the Check for Problems button and allow the scan to run.

3. If the software detects any spyware, it is displayed as an item to be removed.

AVG

Here's how to do a virus scan with AVG:

1. Start AVG by double-clicking the icon in the System Tray.
2. AVG Control Center opens. Click Test Center.
3. Click on the Scan Computer button and let the program scan your computer until it's finished.
4. If it finds anything, follow the recommendations to remove the virus.

Check for Firefox Updates

The Firefox web browser is relatively new and so browser vulnerabilities are being found fairly often. Some clever geek might find a security hole and alert the team at Mozilla.org to the problem. A fix is usually issued within a day or so.

Be sure to check every week (or two) to make sure you take advantage of these discoveries and patch the browser with fixes. Here's how:

1. Open Firefox.
2. Click the Tools menu and then Options.
3. Click the Advanced icon on the left and scroll down to the entry that says Software Updates.
4. You see two check boxes. If the Firefox box is checked, the program searches updates for the browser. If Extensions is checked, the program looks for updates for the add-in items in Firefox (found under Tools, Extensions).
5. To check for updates, click the Check Now button (see Figure 10.3).
6. Firefox checks for updates on its server and if it finds any, it prompts you to install them.

note

If you're wondering why I haven't suggested updating Internet Explorer, it's because those fixes are issued as part of the Windows Updates.

tip

If a Firefox update becomes available, a red arrow pointed up in a circle will appear at the top of the Firefox Window to alert you. Click it to access the update.

FIGURE 10.3
Update Firefox by clicking the Check Now option in the Advanced area of the Options box. You have to scroll down to find it.

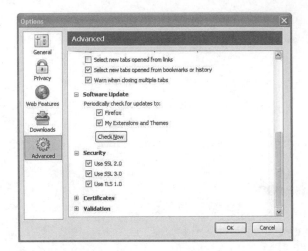

Monthly Routines: Clean the Garage, Trim the Hedge, and Update Windows

These once-a-month routines can be achieved in fewer than 30 minutes each.

Windows Updates

Microsoft issues scheduled security updates on the first Tuesday of every month. When an urgent security hole is found, however, a fix is usually issued right away. If you have installed Windows XP Service Pack 2, fixes are automatically downloaded and installed for you. You have installed SP2, right? If not, please do. To learn more about Windows Updates, see **p. 281**.

Here's how to check to make sure the automatic updates feature is turned on in Windows XP (with SP2) so you don't spend any time worrying about critical updates:

1. Click Start, Control Panel.

2. Double-click the Security Center applet.

3. Automatic Updates should show as ON.

4. To schedule the updates check, click the Automatic Updates link at the bottom of the window.

tip

It's worth visiting the Windows Update site manually every now and then because noncritical updates such as new Windows features, drivers, and other non-urgent updates are made available fairly often. On the Windows Update website at www.windowsupdate.com, click the Custom button to see what fixes are available. They are accessible via the menu on the left. Click Software, Optional and scan the list of available updates. Do the same for hardware updates.

5. Ensure the button next to Automatic (Recommended) is selected (see Figure 10.4) and that you've chosen Every Day and a time when your computer is turned on. If you switch your computer off at night, make sure you schedule the update check for a time when the computer is on and idle. Even if you're using it, the check will occur quietly in the background.

6. If you are more conservative, click Download Updates for Me, But Let Me Choose When to Install Them (see the "When Updates Bite Back" sidebar).

FIGURE 10.4

Choose to download and install Windows updates automatically. If you're more conservative, choose to download the fixes and manually install them.

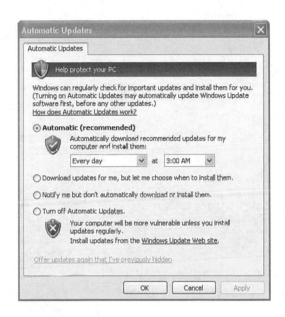

WHEN UPDATES BITE BACK

Sean Carruthers, one of my geek friends, said to me as I wrote this chapter, "You're not going to recommend in the book that Windows updates be set to automatically install, are you?" Sean worries that Microsoft occasionally issues a bad fix that can cause more trouble than it fixes.

So his recommendation is to set Windows to download the updates, but then notify you they are there so you can review the fix before installation. This is a good practice, but it adds a level of complexity. You have to not only review all the updates as they come in but you also need to be tuned into what the experts are saying if a bad fix comes along.

Personally, I choose to auto-install fixes and use the System Restore feature in Windows XP to roll back the system if there's a major problem. I've never had a situation, however, where an incremental patch has been a problem.

That said, Service Pack 2, the biggest and fattest security fix, caused huge problems. It ate my system when I first installed it. But then again, I didn't heed the very early warnings from the alpha geeks that it was temperamental at best. Hey, you can't be a pioneer without a few arrows in your back.

One excellent source for the skinny on Windows Update is Woody's Windows Watch. Woody Leonhard is a globally-known Windows and Office expert who is respected, feared, and loathed by our friends at Microsoft. He's a straight-shooter when it comes to all things Microsoft. His bimonthly email newsletter routinely discusses Microsoft updates and will help you decide which to install and which to ignore. Go to http://mcc.com.au/www/wwwsub.htm to subscribe.

GET REMINDED ABOUT WINDOWS 98 UPDATES

Although Windows 98 cannot install updates automatically, a Critical Update Notification tells you to install updates. You'll first need to install Windows Critical Update Notification by using the Windows Update website:

1. Visit http://windowsupdate.microsoft.com

2. Click Scan for Updates.

3. Under Pick Updates to Install, click Windows 98 and Windows 98 Second Edition.

4. Click Add to select the Windows Critical Update Notification Recommended Update, and then click Review and Install Updates.

5. Click Install Now.

Inspect Other Computers

Do a security check on the other computers in your home, especially if you have a home network. Even if your computer's defenses are rock solid, having a vulnerable or infected computer on your network puts your computer at risk. Viruses and spyware love to jump from computer to computer.

Router Firmware Updates

If you have a home network router, you want to occasionally check for firmware updates to repair any bugs in the router's built-in software. The firmware is the programming inside a router that controls it. Most routers have this capability. Here's how to do it in a D-Link router:

1. Access your router's control panel by opening your web browser (I use Firefox in this example) and type in its IP address.

> **tip**
>
> Mac OS X also has an equivalent auto-update feature that is turned on by default. Here's how to check. Click the Apple menu, System Preferences, and then under System click Software Update. You can set the system to automatically check for updates daily, weekly, or monthly.

2. You are asked for the router's user ID and password. Enter that information and click OK.

3. In a D-Link router, click the Tools tab, and then the Firmware button on the left.

tip

If you have an older copy of Windows (such as Windows 95, 98, or Me), be sure to check for new security updates monthly by visiting http://windowsupdate.microsoft.com.

4. Make a note of the model number of your router (it's in the top-left corner in the D-Link router setup screen), and also make a note of the firmware version on the Firmware page (see Figure 10.5).

5. Right-click the link that says Click Here to Check for an Upgrade on Our Support Site and choose Open Link in New Window. This opens the D-Link site in a new browser window.

FIGURE 10.5

Locate the Firmware update page on your D-Link router. This feature allows you to update the program-ming inside the router.

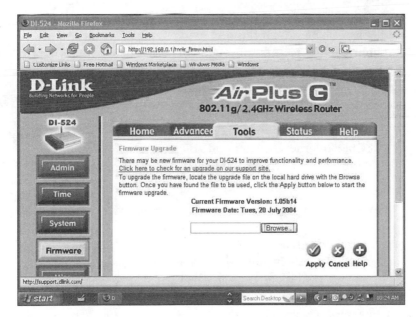

6. Enter your router model number using the drop-down boxes on the site and click Go. The website should refresh with available updates.

7. Compare the firmware update version (or release date) to the firmware version or release date shown in your router. If the website's version is newer, you should download and install it.

8. Click on the update link and choose the Save to Disk option.

9. After you have downloaded the firmware update, return to your router's setup screen, where you left off, and use the Browse button to locate the downloaded firmware file on your computer. Then click Apply.

10. When the firmware update is finished, the router restarts.

11. You have to go back into it and restore any customizations you made, including turning on WEP or WPA security, renaming the router's name (the SSID), and changing the default password.

Patch Microsoft Office

Microsoft Office should be updated as fixes become available for it because it has a scripting language (which many macro viruses are written in). It also features the email program Outlook that communicates with the outside world and is a popular conduit for mass-mailer worms. It should be updated as soon as bug fixes become available for it.

Here's how to update Office:

1. Open Internet Explorer and visit http://office.microsoft.com.

2. Click the Check for Office Updates link.

3. A bar at the top of your browser appears that reads, "The previous site might require the following ActiveX control: Office Update Installation Engine from Microsoft Corporation. Click here to install." Click it and choose Install ActiveX Control.

4. A box with a security warning that says "Do you want to install this software?" appears. Click the Install button.

5. A list of updates appears that are checked (see Figure 10.6).

6. Click the Agree and Install button. The

note

If accessing your router is new to you, I cover how to access a router's setup in great detail in Chapter 6, "Wireless Network Snoops: Lock Down Your Wi-Fi Network," starting on **p. 161**.

caution

You are warned to not update the firmware over a wireless connection. This is because if the connection fails during the update, it renders your router inoperative. It is okay to download the firmware file over a wireless connection, but when it comes to updating it, I recommend that you connect your computer to your router using a network cable and turn your wireless option off by right-clicking it in the System Tray (bottom right of your Windows screen) and choosing Disable.

updates begin to download. This takes a while, but after it's done the updates begin to install.

7. You need to restart the computer to enable the updates.

FIGURE 10.6

Make sure you update your Microsoft Office programs. A Microsoft website is used to provide Office updates.

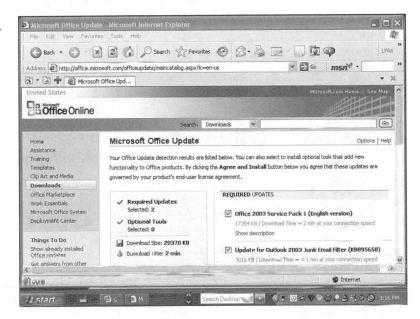

Software Updates

It's not just Windows that needs updating. You should check to see if there are updates available for all the programs you use on a regular basis because the fixes will close security holes that could make your software vulnerable to attack by malware. It's especially important that you check for updates for the following programs:

tip

During the installation of the Microsoft Office updates, you might be prompted to insert your Microsoft Office CD, so keep it and your Office license key handy.

- Email program
- Web browser
- Any program used to communicate with the Internet
- Software firewall

Every program's update process is different, but in the Help menu there is often an option called Check for Updates that automatically checks for newer versions of most programs. If not, check with the software maker's website to see if there are any fixes or patches available. These should be available under Downloads (if there is such a section on the program maker's website) or in the product support area.

tip

If you are using Zone Alarm as your software firewall, you'll see a Check for Updates button under the software's Preferences tab. Automatic product updates should be turned on there, too.

Bathe Once a Year Whether You Need It and Reformat and Re-install, Too

Once a year there's one major task you should do to ensure your computer is extremely secure. Actually, there's one major task and one minor one.

The minor one is easy. Buy an updated copy of this book because I'll keep you tuned into new developments in security. Windows Vista, the next version of Windows, is due out in late 2006 (so Microsoft says) and so that will be a whole new bunch of security fun. I also promise to write new jokes in every new edition.

That said, the major task you should do annually is to wipe your hard drive clean and re-install Windows from scratch.

Wipe Your Hard Drive and Re-install Windows

All versions of Windows are notorious for becoming unstable over time. The registry, where Windows keeps track of all of its settings, can become jam packed with garbage and this in turn can cause sluggish behavior and crashes. That's why I strongly recommend that you reformat your hard drive to wipe it clean and re-install Windows once a year. If you really work your computer hard (especially if you install and uninstall a lot of programs), you should reformat and re-install twice a year.

This ensures that you have the latest greatest Windows fixes as well as the freshest versions of all your security applications. It also eliminates any residual spyware or virus infections (should any have slipped past the defenses). If you have been visited by a hacker, the cleanse also wipes out any modifications they might have made to your computer.

To do this, simply refer to Chapter 9, "Starting from the Beginning: Wiping a Hard Drive and Rebuilding from the Ground Up," starting on **p. 249**, and follow the steps. It's a drastic measure, but it's extremely worthwhile. It keeps your computer as secure as it can be and a side benefit is that it's the best way to keep your computer running as fast and efficiently as is possible. Understandably, it is an enormous pain in the yum-yum, so take your time. Try to do it over a spare weekend when the kids are at camp or in the Alps skiing.

THE ABSOLUTE MINIMUM

- Update your spyware and virus signatures daily or several times a week and ensure that automatic updates are turned on in these programs.

- Run Windows updates once a week or monthly at the very least.

- Run a spyware and virus scan once a week. Use a deep scan if available in the software you use.

- Check for Microsoft Office and Firefox updates once a month.

- Update all your key programs as fixes become available.

- Be sure your firewall program's automatic updates are on.

- Help your Grandma with her security and check other computers in the house, especially those on your network.

- Be sure to check for firmware updates for your home network router. These updates fix programming bugs in your router's software.

- Reformat your hard drive and re-install Windows, all your programs, and all your security applications every year, and twice a year if you work your computer really hard.

PART III

Tools for Maintenance and Protection

11

SELECTING SOFTWARE: STEALS, DEALS, AND SOFTWARE DUDS

There's a lot of software out there in the market to help you make your computer more secure. Some of it's free, some of it's paid, and some is halfway in between. What's safe and what's not? This chapter helps you decide between the various offerings and tells you what features you should look for.

Security Software: Nothing in Life Is Free, Except Software

When it comes to security software, there are lots of choices, lots of features, and lots to worry about. After all, you're acquiring a program to protect your computer from malicious software, so you have to make sure the security software is safe and secure in the first place. But can you do it all with free software? Yes, absolutely. I worked really hard to provide you with free software options all the way through this book.

Leo Laporte, my co-host on the TV show *Call for Help*, taught me about freeware. He has been proclaiming the merits of free software, especially free security software, for a long time. I have to say I was a little dubious at first, but Leo sold me. Freeware is often as good as payware. That said, let's look at the difference.

Payware: Software You Pay Hard-Earned Cash For

Payware is a made-up word that I invented to define programs that you pay for. It is commercial software, the kind you see when you go to the store and buy at the checkout or download for a fee from the Internet. Typically payware is created by a for-profit company that is in the business of publishing software.

Some payware is subscription-based. For example, antivirus programs work forever, but they stop downloading new virus signatures after a year unless an annual fee is paid. Without new signatures, it's not useful against new threats.

Advantages: Payware has a company that stands behind it. That's important when it comes to security programs because you want someone to go to in the event of a problem.

The price also includes some form of help offering (often called *support*). There is usually a phone number to call where you can reach someone (if only for a limited period of time) if you have a problem with the product or need help making it work. However, sometimes this service is not that helpful. Payware also comes with the expectation that it is spyware- and virus-free.

Disadvantages: Payware can be expensive. Although some software can be affordable, often packages will cost you $30–$50 and sometimes more. Sometimes the support offering is not very good.

Trust factor: When it comes to security software, you can generally trust payware because there's a company that stands a lot to lose if its products fail, are defective, or are not trustworthy.

Freeware: Don't Pay a Cent Software

Freeware includes programs that are offered to the public free, although programmers will sometimes ask for voluntary donations or will limit free use to individuals or non-profit organizations.

Programmers distribute free programs for the following reasons:

- It's a public service and the programmer believes there's a public need for the program (see Figure 11.1). Sometimes the programmer has idealistic or altruistic motives.

- It's a marketing ploy that helps upsell users to a paid version that has more features.

- It supports other paid interests, as is the case with free software from Microsoft or Google.

- Because it's paid for with advertising or included adware or spyware.

- It supports a service, with which the programmer makes money.

- For self-promotion, to show off their programming prowess.

note

The adware or spyware model for free software is not used (to my knowledge) with free security software. It would be counter-intuitive, don't you think?

FIGURE 11.1

Patrick Kolla, author of Spybot Search & Destroy, gives away the software for a prayer and some luck sent to him and his girlfriend.

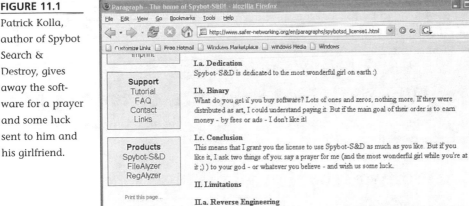

Programmers will also sometimes offer the source code free as well. The source code is the lines of programming that make up the program. This is often referred to as *open source software*.

If a program is open source, it's a good sign that nothing in it is untoward. Buried programming code in open source software that does bad things to the end user's computer would be discovered quickly by other programmers.

Advantages: It's free! It's available instantly from the Internet. It's often really great, and sometimes as good as or better than its payware equivalents.

Disadvantages: If it's not open source, you don't know if there's any dangerous code in the program. There is little support for the program from the author because he doesn't have the resources to help everyone who needs it.

Trust factor: Not trustworthy; however, if it's free and recommended by the Internet community or other reliable sources, it's pretty safe to use. If it's open source, that's even better.

note

In the license for the free Spybot Search & Destroy anti-spyware program, author Patrick Kolla writes, "What do you get if you buy software? Lots of ones and zeros, nothing more. If they were distributed as art, I could understand paying it [*sic*]. But if the main goal of their order is to earn money—by fees or ads—I don't like it!"

Weirdware: When It's Not Payware or Freeware

Some software lives in the netherworld between freeware and payware. Here are some types you might encounter.

Gimpware: Free Software, but Not All the Bits Work

Gimpware is a type of payware that has some of its features disabled. It's designed to allow you to use it to get a sense of whether it will be useful to you. In order to get the extra features unlocked, however, you need to pay the author and acquire a license key so you can unlock the full functionality of the program. Some antivirus and anti-spyware programs scan and find infections but don't remove them unless you buy a software license, for example.

Advantages: Offers a "try before you buy" experience.

Disadvantages: Doesn't give you the full experience of all the software's features.

Trust factor: Gimpware is payware, so generally gimpware does nothing to impact the trustworthiness of the end product. It is more of a marketing tactic. Using gimpware as a full solution is not a good idea from a security perspective unless all the features you need are unlocked.

Trialware: It's Free, Until It's Not

Trialware is payware that is free to use without any limitation for a set period of time, often 15 or 30 days, so you can try it out before you decide to purchase it (see Figure 11.2). After the trial period, the program no longer runs. Again, this is a marketing tactic.

Advantages: "Try before you buy" approach to software.

Disadvantages: Sometimes the trial period is not long enough to get a full sense of its usefulness.

Trust factor: Trialware tends be trustworthy and in fact can instill more trust because you see how it works before committing to paying for it.

FIGURE 11.2

Zone Labs offers 15 day trials of all its software, except for Zone Alarm, which it gives away.

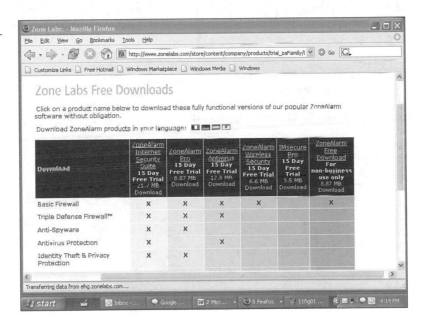

Shareware: I Trust You to Pay Me

Shareware is usually written by a small company or individual programmer. It's distributed with the understanding that if you like it and use it, you will voluntarily pay for it after a 30-day trial period, but it doesn't become disabled when this time period expires.

Advantages: The ultimate "try before you buy" software because the trial period never ends. It's often a very affordable way to acquire excellent software. Since it usually comes from a small programming shop, the support can be excellent because the publisher is close to the product.

Disadvantages: The support may be non-existent because the publisher is a small company or an individual. Sometimes the program is not well designed or amateurish, although I find this is the exception to the rule.

Trust factor: It's tough to feel secure when using shareware, unless it's a product that has been around for a while and has a good reputation. If you watch the Internet for feedback on shareware, you'll be able to avoid bad programs. Use shareware based on its reputation and look for reviews or commentary on the Internet before installing it.

What Should I Pay for My Security Toolbox?

Security problems on your computer are not your fault. So you shouldn't have pay to protect yourself. However, sometimes the responsible parties, such as your Internet provider, the software publishers, and Microsoft, fail miserably to protect you. So you have to take it upon yourself to make sure your computer, the assets on it, and your digital life is as secure as it can be.

These programs I recommend in this book are every bit as good as the payware products marketed to you. The freebies are by no means premium products and so some conveniences are not included.

If you come across payware that you like the feel of, that you learn to trust, and that makes you feel more confident than freeware, by all means pay for the software and use it.

Sometimes it's worth buying the extra-strength, coated painkillers, right? It's better than the chalky, slow-acting, and bitter tablets. But both kinds do the job. So it is with security software. Sometimes it's worth the money to get software that's a little more palatable.

So what should you pay? Usually not more than $50 per software title. Antivirus programs run $30–$50 per year (see Figure 11.3). Anti-spyware products seem to float around $30 per year. You're paying annually for the ongoing signature updates. Software firewalls and anti-spam programs are sometimes treated like services and run $30 per year or thereabouts.

BUYER BEWARE: HOW TO AVOID BAD SOFTWARE PRODUCTS

If you decide to buy software for your security needs, here are a few tips to help you buy the right program for your needs:

- Before buying, go to the publisher's website and look at the support area to see what problems have been posted. Also look at the support forums, if available, to see what other users are saying.

- Search for reviews of the software on the Internet and read a few. No one reviewer will have it all right. Look for a consensus.

■ Use the trialware version for 30 days, if available. Most anti-spyware and antivirus programs have 30-day trials.

■ If it's free, read the end user license agreement. It's boring as haddock, but the publisher will sometimes reveal advertising, adware, or spyware clauses.

■ New software always has problems. It usually takes a publisher three to six months to post fixes to their software after it is initially released.

■ If you want to be conservative, buy only mature software that's has reached version 3. Microsoft is famous for getting it right by the third time around, although I am not sure what happened with Windows XP.

■ Newsgroups and user forums are also great places to get unbiased feedback on software.

FIGURE 11.3

Big-brand antivirus payware runs around $30 to $50 on Amazon.com, which includes one year of updates and virus signatures.

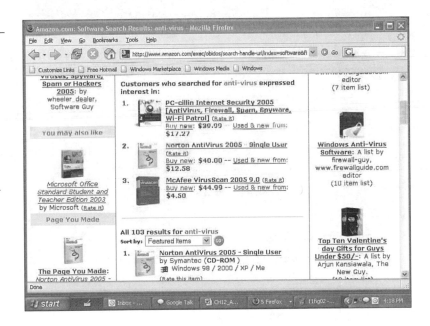

Choosing the Right Security Software

Here are the features you should look for in each type of security software.

Antivirus

All good antivirus programs should come with these must-have features:

■ **Virus signatures**—Downloadable digital snapshots used by the program to identify viruses available daily or multiple times a day.

■ **Automatic downloads**—The program should download new virus signatures once a day or more frequently as they become available.

- **Heuristics**—This is the ability for the program to learn from experience. Heuristic programming allows an antivirus program to stop a virus by detecting virus-like behavior before a specific infection is identified.

- **Automatic scans**—The ability to schedule a virus scan. Look for daily, weekly, and monthly options that allow scheduling at a specific time of day.

- **Email protection**—Most viruses arrive and spread through email so an antivirus program should at very least scan incoming email. Some also scan outbound email, although this feature can slow a system down.

caution

If you have antivirus program that has expired but is still working, is it any good? No! An antivirus program is useless if it's not protecting your computer from new threats.

- **Frugal with resources**—A good antivirus program should not use a lot of memory or processor power to protect a system. It should have little or no impact on system performance.

- **Virus cleaner**—A good antivirus program should not only stop viruses, but also clean infections quickly and on demand.

- **Redundancy**—It's nice if an antivirus program also catches some spyware or defends against other threats such as phishing emails.

Anti-Spyware

Here are the features I recommend you look for in an anti-spyware program:

- **Spyware signatures**—Downloadable digital snapshots used by the program to identify spyware adware, hijackers, and Trojan horses.

- **Automatic downloads**—The program should download new spyware signatures once a day or more frequently as they become available.

- **Hijacker removal**—Browser hijackers are difficult to remove, but some of the better anti-spyware programs deal with the nastier infections.

- **Live protection**—This is a feature that watches for spyware infections in real time at a series of entry points on a computer. Different programs use different terms. Microsoft AntiSpyware, for example, calls it real time protection. You might see it referred to as an immunization feature.

- **Effective removal tools**—The program should not only be able to defend against threats, but also remove infections. Not all anti-spyware products are created equal in this regard.

Firewall

Here are the key features you should look for in firewall software:

- **Inbound protection**—Analysis of traffic coming from the Internet into the computer.

- **Outbound protection**—Analysis of traffic out from the computer to the Internet to see if a virus, spyware, or other malware is trying to communicate with the outside world.

- **Stealth mode**—The ability to make the computer invisible even if probed from the Internet.

- **Alert suppression**—Option to turn off or minimize alerts generated by attacks or probes from the outside and the ability to set alert levels for outbound traffic. These can be frequent and annoying.

- **Downloadable policies**—Filters that can be downloaded from the Internet that keep the firewall up-to-date from certain malicious websites and new threats on the Internet. Ideally these should be automatic.

- **Malware detection**—Detection and blockage of viruses, spyware, and other malware as it travels through the firewall. Some pro versions offer this.

- **Lifestyle modes**—This is an optional feature, but a nice one if you can get it. It allows you to easily set the firewall for certain specialty uses of the firewall, such as serving a website, peer-to-peer file sharing, and gaming.

- **Low maintenance**—You should be bugged by the firewall only when absolutely necessary.

GET IT FREE FROM YOUR ISP

As part of your security software shopping spree, check with your Internet service provider (ISP). Many offer free security suites that are actually made by big-brand security companies.

For example, F-Secure makes a software suite that includes an antivirus, anti-spyware, firewall, and other security programs that are offered free or at a low cost by many major Internet providers to their broadband customers. It's branded by the ISP, but uses F-Secure technology.

The nice thing about these suites is that you can turn some components off so you can choose to only use the applications you need in concert with ones you already have.

Anti-Spam

Here are features you should find in good anti-spam programs:

- **High detection rates**—Good anti-spam programs should stop more than 90% of the spam headed for your inbox.

- **Few false positives**—Very few legitimate emails should be mistaken for spam.

- **Subscription management**—Emails that are from machines but are not spam, such as newsletters, should not be treated as spam.

- **Spam signature updates**—It's helpful to have an anti-spam engine that can be updated with spam signatures so the software can be alerted to new spam being delivered across the Internet.

- **Override**—An override mechanism that enables you to receive some mail that is tagged as spam but that you want to see anyway.

- **Undo**—A good anti-spam program should make it easy to restore email that has been marked as spam, but isn't. Look for a one-button option. Cloudmark Desktop, for example, has an Unblock button.

- **Anti-phishing feature**—Many anti-spam products catch phishing emails as well as spam.

HOT TREND: WIRELESS SECURITY SOFTWARE

Any minute now you'll see a new crop of wireless network security programs being offered in security suites. In late summer 2005, McAfee announced McAfee WiFiScan for $49, which alerts you to intruders on your network and does a security analysis to keep your wireless network secure. Expect Wi-Fi security programs to be the next big security software category. All we need now is a decent freeware version.

THE ABSOLUTE MINIMUM

- There's a lot of free security software that is as good as or better than its paid counterparts.

- You can trust freeware if it comes recommended by users on the Internet, credible reviews, or other sources you trust (like me!). Always check with multiple sources. Seeking a consensus will protect you.

- Payware, which is commercial software you pay for, is worthwhile if it offers a better experience or features not offered in freeware.

- The best kind of freeware is open source software, where the author makes the programming code available for inspection and improvement.

- Shareware software, in which the author asks for voluntary payment, is often worthwhile; just make sure it has a good reputation before you come to rely on it.

- Gimpware or trialware are versions of payware that have been crippled or have a limited free-use period to help upsell you to a full, paid version.

- Most payware security software should cost around $30 to $50. Most products are subscription based where you renew each year to continue to receive updates and signatures that identify malware.

- There are many features that an antivirus and anti-spyware program should have, but one critical one is daily signature updates.

- A software firewall should watch inbound and outbound data traffic. A bonus feature is detection and blockage of viruses and spyware as they cross the firewall.

- Anti-spam products should have a detection rate of more than 90% and a low rate of false positives, where legitimate email is marked as spam.

12

TOOLS OF THE TRADE: SECURITY PRODUCTS YOU SHOULD OWN

Because home computer security is a hot topic, many companies want a piece of the action. Products have flooded the marketplace and making a choice about which one to use can cause confusion. In this chapter I've provided a roundup of some of the most common products you'll encounter and offer some capsule reviews.

Which Security Software Is Right for You?

Marketing is an ugly business. Its mission is to highlight the good points of a product and downplay its bad features. I always marvel at how companies can turn basic products such as toilet paper or chewing gum (spanning two ends of the human spectrum!) and represent them as something more exotic that what they really are.

Marketers do the same with software. And since they can be really clever, it's hard to not be swayed by the influential messages they dangle in front of us simple apes. To that end, I've listed in this chapter some of the most common products that I think are worthy (with a couple of exceptions) that you'll likely encounter in your travels from tree to tree on the Internet. Mixed in for good measure are the freebies I mention in this book so you have a single place to reference them.

Antivirus Programs

As you no doubt know by now, antivirus programs rebuke viruses. Here are software packages you'll probably encounter, in no particular order.

Freeware

When it comes to free antivirus products, there's a decent selection of good ones. Here are three I like.

avast! Antivirus

Don't be fooled by avast!'s media player–like appearance. Under its shiny metallic skin, it is a feature-packed antivirus program. Novice users will appreciate its intuitive design. To scan your local hard drive, click on the box-like hard drive logo. Likewise, click the CD logo to select your optical drive. Then, click the Play button and avast! scans your computer for viruses. Unfortunately, avast! can only be set to perform automatic system scans when you boot up your computer. It also features email, instant messaging, and P2P scanning.

> **Price**: Free
>
> **Paid upgrade**: avast! AntiVirus Professional
>
> **Info**: www.avast.com

Grisoft AVG Anti-Virus Free Edition

Grisoft's AVG Free Edition is the best free antivirus software available. It features a scanner that constantly monitors your system for viruses. It also comes with an email scanner that can check your incoming and outgoing messages for viruses.

The software is set to automatically perform daily updates and scheduled system scans. It's nicely laid out (see Figure 12.1), but could do with some refinements in some of the submenus; still, you can't beat its ability to defend your computer, especially given the price. **Highly recommended!**

> **Price**: Free
>
> **Paid upgrade**: AVG Professional Edition
>
> **Info**: http://free.grisoft.com

FIGURE 12.1

AVG Free Edition from Grisoft is free, fairly easy to use, and effective. As free antivirus products go, you can't beat it.

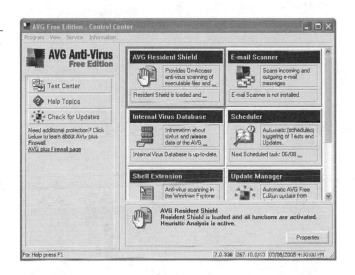

AntiVir

This antivirus program from German software developer H+BEDV Datentechnik (try saying that five times fast at Octoberfest) is another free AV product. With quirky window title names such as Luke Filewalker and menu text that doesn't make grammatical sense, AntiVir is a bit off-beat. Nonetheless, it provides simple antivirus protection to safeguard your computer with a frugal use of memory. The program can be difficult for the beginner, and note that it doesn't automatically check for updates or scan email.

tip

Grisoft also makes a paid antivirus/firewall combination.

> **Price**: Free
>
> **Paid upgrade**: AntiVir Personal Edition Premium
>
> **Info**: www.free-av.com

Payware

If you're going to pay for your antivirus program, here are two you'll definitely encounter and five more you might consider. Note that prices for antivirus products are based on an annual subscription.

Symantec Norton AntiVirus

Symantec's sleek antivirus application is an easy choice for home users because it has a basic, straightforward interface and is easy for the average person to use. Its customizable menus give advanced users the opportunity to fine-tune the way Norton AntiVirus works. However, the program is a little bloated and slows your system down, especially with the email scanner on. Put this program on a diet and it would come recommended.

> **Price**: $49.95
>
> **Info**: www.symantec.com

caution

AntiVir's website is often sluggish or down, so if you can't access it, try again a little while later.

McAfee VirusScan

Aimed at the beginner, McAfee's antivirus software is easy to use and particularly competent. The program automatically checks for updates on a daily basis to keep you as protected as possible. Unfortunately, the program isn't configured to automatically perform scheduled scans—you must set up scheduled tasks on your own. It might also be too basic for advanced users' tastes.

> **Price**: $39.99
>
> **Info**: www.mcafee.com

tip

There are three good, free online virus scanners that work from the Web. Check out TrendMicro's Housecall at http://housecall.trendmicro.com and Panda Software's ActiveScan at www.pandasoftware.com/products/activescan.htm. Also check out Kaspersky Lab's Online Scanner at www.kaspersky.com/virusscanner.

None of them work with the Mozilla Firefox web browser. You'll need to use Internet Explorer.

Eset NOD32

NOD32 is a very comprehensive antivirus product capable of detecting and removing some spyware and adware as a bonus. Unfortunately, it's somewhat difficult to use. However, it can be customized nicely and lets users control how each part of the antivirus program works. However, you'll first have to figure out the modules, each of which have been given an acronym: AMON, DMON, EMON, IMON, and

NOD32 (see Figure 12.2). If you can figure it all out, it's a nice program that's easy on system resources and a precise product. **Highly recommended!**

> **Price**: $39
>
> **Info**: www.nod32.com

FIGURE 12.2
NOD32 is an
excellent
antivirus product
that is lean on
system resources
and customiz-
able, though not
a good choice for
new users.

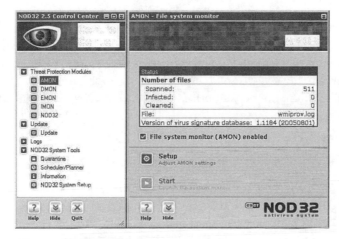

F-Secure Anti-Virus

F-Secure's antivirus product is a pricey, yet solid choice because it's easy to use, relatively light on memory, and is highly customizable for advanced users. For example, the scanning engine can be set daily, weekly, or monthly. It retrieves signature updates on demand several times a day as they come available. As paid products go, this is my first choice for new users and second choice for geeks, behind NOD32. **Highly recommended!**

> **Price**: $64
>
> **Info**: www.fsecure.com

Kaspersky Anti-Virus Personal

The Moscow-based Kaspersky Lab makes a competent antivirus software package that you'll be very happy with. I like that it can be set to check for virus signatures as frequently as hourly through once a week. It's pretty much a fire and forget product, which is nice, although advanced users will want to explore its settings menus for gems such as the Quarantine Maximum Size setting and the option to auto-scan every time the virus database is updated. This product has come a long way from its origins and is as good as any of the better-known antivirus products.

> **Price**: $39.95
>
> **Info**: www.kaspersky.com

PC-Cillin Internet Security Suite

TrendMicro is one of these up and coming security software companies that seems always to be in the news because it is buying this company or that one. It takes security products seriously and so I think it's worth taking a look at its software. PC-cillin Anti-Virus is its flagship offering that comes in a suite of tools that includes spyware, spam, and Wi-Fi protection, as well as a firewall. As suites go, it's well rounded and relatively unobtrusive. That said, its glaring red interface gives me a headache. Its settings menus are a bit scattered and it will take some patience to find key settings, tweak them, and master this software. The back-end virus scanning engine, however, is solid. PC-cillin is not high on my list as an antivirus product, but if you're after a well-priced and competent security suite, take a look at it.

> **Price**: $39.99
>
> **Info**: www.trendmicro.com

Panda Titanium Antivirus

How often do you get a panda's head sitting in your Windows system tray? That's the icon that represents Panda Software's Titanium Antivirus. Warm and fuzzies aside, this antivirus product is well designed, easy to use, and frugal with system resources. I like that it does what it calls a Periodic Self Diagnosis. Every 15 minutes the product ensures your system is properly protected and will only warn you if there's a problem unless you turn on the Always Show the Result option. Curiously, the program comes with a two-way software firewall, which is unusual in a security product that's not billed as a suite. But this makes sense because it's one of the best protections against worms. And the firewall is rarely bothersome. It self-configures really well. Symantec could learn a thing or two from Panda Software. If you're looking for a really well-designed antivirus payware product, install this product's 30-day trial to get a feel for it. It's worth a closer look.

> **Price**: $39.99
>
> **Info**: www.pandasoftware.com

ARE SECURITY SOFTWARE SUITES A SWEET DEAL?

You'll definitely encounter security software suites in your travels. They are bundles of software that try to offer a one-stop solution for all your security problems. I have never been a fan of these products because they usually include one or two great tools mixed in with a couple of duds.

I'll say up front right now that you should stay far away from Norton Internet Security Suite, which time and time again proves to be more trouble than it is worth. It bogs down your system and antagonizes the entry-level user with its complexity. It also has a nasty habit of causing as many system problems as it solves. On the TV show *Call for Help*, Leo

Laporte and I often solve problems for callers by recommending that they uninstall Norton Security Suite. So stay well away.

If you do like the idea of a security suite, however, the one to look for is Trend Micro's PC-cillin Internet Security ($39). See the capsule review in this chapter.

Anti-Spyware

Anti-spyware software is a huge category. You'll need more than one program to catch and remove all the possible infections. My optimal configuration includes PestPatrol (payware), and two freeware products: Microsoft AntiSpyware and Spybot Search & Destroy.

Freeware

Here are the key free anti-spyware products I have mentioned in this book. Use two or more together for optimal spyware detection.

Spybot Search & Destroy

Spybot is one of the best free anti-spyware applications for home users (see Figure 12.3). The program will automatically check for and fix any problems when installed, and can be set to clean and perform updates every time you start the program. The resident system blocker protects you against spyware installed through Internet Explorer. Spybot also features advanced system tools to stop unwanted programs from starting up when your computer boots up. Its myriad menus and settings can be daunting if you dig down into the program, but it's a solid application that everyone should own. **Highly recommended!**

> **Price**: Free
>
> **Paid upgrade**: None
>
> **Info**: www.safer-networking.org

Ad-Aware SE Personal Edition

Like Spybot, Ad-Aware SE Personal Edition is another anti-spyware program that's completely free. When prompted, the application scans your PC for spyware and adware. If anything is found, you're given the option to quarantine or remove the problems. Sometimes, Ad-Aware's thorough scan might indicate problems that are just normal system files. If you use Ad-Aware, be careful not to accidentally remove *wanted* files. Ad-Aware prompts you to update every two weeks so your software stays up-to-date. The paid version features pop-up blocking. Not my personal favorite program because in tests, its ability to catch key pieces of spyware was lacking, but lots of people would poke me in the eye for saying that. It is a much-loved program.

> **Price**: Free
>
> **Paid upgrade**: Ad-Aware SE Plus & Pro
>
> **Info**: www.lavasoft.de

FIGURE 12.3

Spybot Search & Destroy was one of the first free anti-spyware products and is still one of the best.

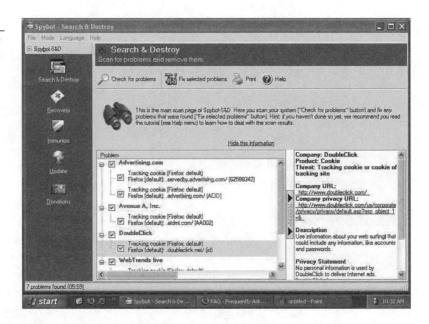

Microsoft AntiSpyware

Even though the name Microsoft isn't synonymous with computer security, the company's anti-spyware program is an exception. Of course it was written by someone else and acquired. But good for Microsoft for buying it and making the program free. It is excellent. The program is set to automatically scan your computer for spyware and adware daily. It also monitors Internet, system, and application activity for anything unusual, fixing problems as they arise. At the time of this writing, the program was still in Beta testing, but was still very functional. Because most features are automated by default, the average user shouldn't have any problems getting Microsoft AntiSpyware up and running. And my tests show of all the free anti-spyware programs, it catches the most infections. **Highly recommended!**

> **Price**: Free
>
> **Paid upgrade**: None
>
> **Info**: www.microsoft.com/spyware

Payware

Here are some paid anti-spyware products I think are worthy of mention. Not all the reviews are good, but at least two come recommended.

McAfee AntiSpyware

McAfee AntiSpyware offers basic protection against spyware and adware threats. Along with an always-on component that monitors your PC for spyware, AntiSpyware features the ability to schedule system spyware scans when desired. The application's user interface is basic and to-the-point. This is great for beginner users, but advanced users might want a program with more bells and whistles. At times, the software can become tedious and overwhelming with the deluge of pop-ups alerts it delivers. Also, its detection rates are fairly poor. In my tests, it didn't find lots of infections that free anti-spyware products did.

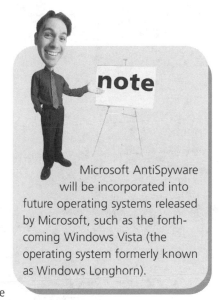

note

Microsoft AntiSpyware will be incorporated into future operating systems released by Microsoft, such as the forthcoming Windows Vista (the operating system formerly known as Windows Longhorn).

> **Price**: $39.99
>
> **Info**: www.mcafee.com

Webroot Spy Sweeper

Spy Sweeper is a solid anti-spyware product that often gets rave reviews. Along with a system scanner and a resident shield that watches points of entry (see Figure 12.4), it can also block ads in web pages, prevent browser hijacks, and protect your system settings from being altered by spyware. Novice users will like the program because it is very helpful. For example, when looking at an option menu, text explains what different settings are for. There's also a built-in news service that keeps you informed of new spyware activity. It includes a feature that allows you to disable programs from starting up when your computer loads. Plus, it makes editing your Windows startup area easy by filtering out required Windows startup components. In my tests, its detection rates were not as high as I had been led to believe, but nevertheless it's a decent program that you'll enjoy using.

caution

McAfee is new to the anti-spyware business, and so there will be a learning curve for the company to come up to speed with more mature anti-spyware products.

> **Price**: $29.95
>
> **Info**: www.webroot.com

FIGURE 12.4

Webroot's Spyware Sweeper gets rave reviews, but is not as good as the very competent PestPatrol.

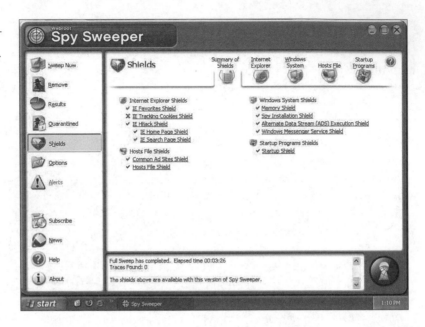

Norton Internet Security AntiSpyware Edition

Norton Internet Security AntiSpyware Edition is a comprehensive package that aims to protect you from many Internet threats. It includes anti-spam, anti-spyware, and personal firewall components. I am not a fan of the suite because it's fat, sluggish, and annoying to use. It merits mention in this section because Symantec played catch-up by adding an anti-spyware component in 2005, but didn't release it as a standalone product. Its spyware detection rates are disappointing, ranking it really low against all other anti-spyware programs.

> **caution**
>
> Symantec was late to the anti-spyware game and so its spyware detection rates in the first version of its spyware component released in 2005 are extremely disappointing. Expect better performance in its next generation of product.

Price: $79.95

Info: www.symantec.com

eTrust PestPatrol

PestPatrol is perhaps the best anti-spyware product on the market. It's not perfect (by default, Active Protection is turned off), but its plain user interface makes it easy to use (see Figure 12.5) and updates are fetched automatically by the software. The key to its success is that it has remarkably high spyware detection rates. In my tests it caught substantially more infections than most payware and freeware products and removed them all. **Highly recommended!**

> **Price**: $39.99
>
> **Info**: www.pestpatrol.com

FIGURE 12.5

PestPatrol is easy to use, catches and removes many infections, and is a nice complement to free anti-spyware programs.

PC Tools Spyware Doctor

This Australia-based anti-spyware program is an extremely strong contender. It features both quick and full system scans. It has good detection capabilities that outpaces most of its competitors, except perhaps PestPatrol, and even comes with a pop-up blocker. It also automatically searches for signature updates. You can't really go wrong with this program. **Recommended!**

> **Price**: $29.95
>
> **Info**: www.pctools.com

Firewalls

Software firewalls that are payware are a hard sell because a basic two-way firewall that watches inbound and outbound traffic on a computer is all you need. So the freebies cover this category quite nicely.

ZoneAlarm Free

The free edition of Zone Alarm firewall is a great choice for home computer users with some Internet experience. Although it's not as streamlined as some other firewall applications, it keeps things basic and easy to use. The paid version of ZoneAlarm automatically decides which programs can access the network. With the free version, users must permit or deny a program's access to the Internet. This might be tedious if you're unfamiliar with which programs access the Internet on a regular basis. It can also be dangerous if you unknowingly permit access to an untrustworthy program. Free is good; the Pro version, as you would expect, is better, especially since it also offers virus and spyware protection. **Highly recommended!**

> **Price**: Free
>
> **Paid upgrade**: ZoneAlarm Pro
>
> **Info**: www.zonelabs.com

Sygate Personal Firewall Standard

This free firewall is geared more towards experienced users. So steer clear if you're new to computers. If you're familiar with home networking, this application might be for you. The program interface is very technical. A graph shows you how many attacks your computer has received and the level of network traffic. It does not configure itself automatically, so you'll often be prompted to permit or deny network access.

> **Price**: Free
>
> **Paid upgrade**: SyGate Personal Firewall Pro
>
> **Info**: www.sygate.com

McAfee Personal Firewall Plus

Yet another component of McAfee's many security applications, Personal Firewall Plus is a software firewall aimed to keep intruders out. The application, which is available as a standalone product, automatically determines which programs are allowed to access the Internet. At the same time, network ports are closed so intruders can't gain access to your files. You're rarely prompted to deny or permit Internet access to an application because the software configures itself quite well. You also manually open ports using the System Services utility, which is a helpful tool for advanced users.

> **Price**: $49.99
>
> **Info**: www.mcafee.com

tip

If you have a home network router, you already have a firewall built in that stops dangerous inbound network traffic. Software firewalls are useful because they watch outbound traffic for malware as well.

Norton Personal Firewall

This product, sold alone or as part of Norton Internet Security, is a competent firewall that bugs you a lot about outbound traffic, though perhaps just as much as Zone Alarm and McAfee Personal Firewall. But it's not so smart. For example, it detected F-Secure Anti-Virus trying to communicate with the outside world and recommended that it always be blocked. If I pay for a firewall, I want decent accuracy on recommended actions by the software. F-Secure is a Symantec competitor so I have to wonder about Symantec's motives on this. I am not a fan of Symantec's security products in general, and while Norton Personal Firewall isn't completely offensive, it rubs me the wrong way.

> **Price**: $29.99
>
> **Info**: www.symantec.com

Anti-Spam

Besides the built-in junk mail filtering in Microsoft Outlook 2003, I have never found a free anti-spam program worth keeping, so all that follows in this category is payware.

McAfee SpamKiller

With five levels of filtering available, McAfee SpamKiller (see Figure 12.6) is designed to keep junk mail out and let legitimate email messages in. It works well with most popular email programs (note for geeks: all POP3 clients), such as Outlook Express. Rules can also be set to tell SpamKiller how to deal with different types of spam messages. You can add people to your friends list to ensure you receive their emails, or you can add addresses to your blocked senders list to keep spam out. It's a decent solution, but lets some spam through and sometimes blocks legitimate emails.

> **Price**: $34.99
>
> **Info**: www.mcafee.com

Cloudmark Desktop

Everyone who uses Cloudmark Desktop helps guard against spam. If a commercial email slips into your inbox with this program installed, you use the program to mark it as spam and it tells the Cloudmark server. Everyone benefits. When enough people mark a piece of spam, the program starts to automatically filter inboxes for that message for all Cloudmark users. The program is a plug-in available for Outlook or Outlook Express. It has a high hit rate and rarely marks a legitimate email as spam. **Highly recommended!**

> **Price**: $39.95 per year
>
> **Info**: www.cloudmark.com

FIGURE 12.6

McAfee SpamKiller is a decent anti-spam product with five levels of automatic spam filtering.

Spam Arrest

This spam blocker works through an online web service rather than through an application installed directly on your computer. Your inbound email is filtered through the service and your email program in term fetches the cleansed email from the service. Setup is difficult, and many web-based email accounts are not compatible with Spam Arrest. It works with a challenge/response system. If an email sender is not known to the system, he gets an email asking him to type in a code. When he does, the system recognizes him as a human (spam is sent by machines so they can't respond to the challenge) and the sent email is passed on to the recipient. It stops all spam, but tends to block newsletter subscriptions and other legitimate automated emails. You have to manage those manually.

> **Price**: $34.95 per year
>
> **Info**: www.spamarrest.com

THE ABSOLUTE MINIMUM

- The best freeware antivirus product is Grisoft's AVG Free Edition.

- If you choose to buy an antivirus product, consider F-Secure Anti-Virus or Eset's NOD32.

- Microsoft AntiSpyware and Spybot Search & Destroy are great free anti-spyware products. Ad-Aware is much loved, but I don't think it is as good.

- In payware, I like PestPatrol and PC Tools Spyware Doctor in the anti-spyware category.

- My favorite free firewall is ZoneAlarm. Take a look at ZoneAlarm Pro if you want a good payware upgrade.

- In the anti-spam category, there are no free software products that I recommend. However, there's no better product than Cloudmark Desktop. It's payware, but worth every penny if you are deluged with spam.

APPENDIXES

Glossary

A

ActiveX   A grouping of Microsoft technologies that allows programs to share information. However, ActiveX is most obviously encountered when using the Microsoft Internet Explorer and appears as a miniprogram that downloads and executes to provide some extra function.

advance fee fraud   A scam in which the target receives an email, often concerning an overseas nation that contains a money-laundering proposal. At some point, the target is asked to provide a fee in return for a cut on the profits of the scam. Of course, the target never sees a return.

adware   A type of spyware that snoops on a computer user and then pushes unwanted advertising at them. Sometimes, simply advertiser-sponsored software.

ASCII   American Standard Code for Information Interchange. A set of codes for representing English characters as numbers, with each letter assigned a number from 0 to 127. Computers use ASCII codes to represent plain text.

autocomplete   A software feature that makes suggestions as a user types in a web browser's address bar, a web page form, or a username or password box on a web page. An autocomplete feature also appears in Microsoft Word.

B

backup   A spare copy of a file or files that have been created in case the original data is damaged or lost.

bandwidth   An Internet connection's capacity to carry data.

bandwidth bandit   A person who accesses a network and uses its Internet connection without permission.

beets   Sugary turnip-like vegetables that are often pickled. The author of this book's least favorite food.

BHO   Browser Helper Object. An add-on program that provides extra functions to Microsoft's Internet Explorer web browser.

black hat   A hacker whose intent is malicious.

bomb   A synonym for a virus payload, the part of a computer virus that does bad things.

boot virus   A type of computer virus that hides in the boot sector of a floppy disk or hard disk. The boot sector is read as part of a disk's startup routine and this activates the virus.

broadband   An Internet connection that's multiple times faster than a 56Kps dial-up modem.

browser hijacker   A program that changes the homepage on a web browser, making it difficult to change it back. See hijacker.

Brussels sprouts   Small cabbage-like vegetables that children generally don't like. Also one of the most comedic vegetables on the planet.

bug   A defect in the programming code or routine of a program.

C

cable modem   A device that uses cable TV lines to connect a computer to the Internet at high speed.

cache   A holding area that contains information so it can be accessed faster than retrieving it from where it originates.

cheese   A dairy product made from fermented milk. Also an excellent topic to make jokes about.

cookies   Tiny text files from a remote website stored on a computer that contain data used to help identify a user to the website or useful for completing a web-based task.

cracker   What people who break into computers call themselves. Synonymous with the mass media term *hacker*.

cyber   A prefix used to indicate that something is computer- or Internet-related. Derived from the word *Cybernetics*, which is the discipline that, according to wikipedia.org, studies communication and control in living beings or machines.

cyberspace   A term used to describe the nonphysical, virtual world of computers.

D

DDoS   See Distributed Denial of Service.

default   Settings as they were originally configured by a manufacturer or programmer.

DHCP   Dynamic Host Configuration Protocol. A protocol for assigning dynamic IP addresses to devices on a network.

dialer   A computer program that underhandedly dials a remote computer via a modem incurring long distance charges or toll-line fees.

dictionary spamming   Programs that combine random words and common names in an effort to come up with valid email addresses.

Digital Subscriber Line   A broadband technology offered by telephone companies that connects a computer at high speed to the Internet.

Distributed Denial of Service (DDoS)   An electronic attack perpetrated by a person who controls legions of hijacked computers. On a single command, the computers simultaneously send packets of data across the Internet at a target computer. The attack is designed to overwhelm the target and stop it from functioning.

DNS   See Domain Name Server.

Domain Name Server (or System)   A computer (or series of computers) on the Internet that translates domain names (web addresses) into numerical Internet addresses called IP addresses.

drive-by download   A program that automatically downloads to a computer without the computer owner's consent or knowledge.

dropper   A file that conceals malware such as a virus or Trojan horse in an attempt to evade antivirus programs.

DSL   See Digital Subscriber Line.

E

email header   Address information attached to the top of an email message.

email scanner   A feature in an antivirus program that checks incoming and outgoing emails for viruses.

encryption   Scrambling of data to prevent it from being seen by unauthorized people.

End User License Agreement   Legal text that a user has to agree to before installing a software package, usually in a scrollable box.

Ethernet   A common method of connecting computers together to form a network.

EULA   See End User License Agreement.

exploit   A program that takes advantage of a known security weakness in a computer.

external media   Any storage device that can contain a computer file, such as a floppy disk, DVD, or CD, that can be connected to a computer or inserted into a reader attached to a computer.

F

false negatives   Spam that is mistaken for legitimate email.

false positives   Legitimate email messages that are mistaken as spam.

farming   See pharming.

file infector virus   A type of computer virus that attaches itself to a program file. It executes when the file is run.

filename extension   A three-character suffix that is part of a computer file name (for example, .jpg and .doc). Common to files on a PC.

firewall   A device or program that blocks outsiders from accessing a computer connected to the Internet. Some firewalls also monitor data traffic outbound from a computer or network.

firmware   Programming stored on a chip inside a device (such as a network router) that controls it.

fishing   See phishing.

freeware   Software offered to the public free.

G-H

gimpware   Software that does not provide full features until it is paid for.

greyhat (grayhat)   A hacker that sometimes acts legally and with altruistic motives and sometimes doesn't. Think of this type of person as a thief who sometimes steals and sometimes calls you to let you know a window is open.

hack   A clever modification of hardware or software.

hacker   1. In the mass market, this is a bad person who illicitly gains access to a network or computer to which they do not have permission to connect. 2. Among programmers, a hacker is an accomplished programming guru. 3. In some circles, the term can also refer to a programmer who has no finesse. 4. In hardware, a hacker is someone who makes modifications.

hacktivism   A form of vandalism or electronic civil disobedience that serves a political agenda. Usually hacktivists have altruistic motives.

heuristics   Programming code that learns as it goes. A common feature of antivirus or anti-spyware programs.

HEX Hexadecimal. A base-16 number system often used to visually represent computer bytes.

hijacker Short for browser hijacker. A program that forces a web browser to open to a specific web page and makes it difficult to change it.

home network A group of two or more computers within a user's home that are linked together and share resources such as an Internet connection, printer, or files.

HTML Hypertext Markup Language. A tagging language used in web pages to format them for display on the World Wide Web.

HTTP Hypertext transfer protocol. A mechanism or series of rules by which information is transferred across the World Wide Web.

HTTPS A secure version of HTTP, whereby data transmitted across the Web is scrambled so it can't be viewed by unauthorized eyes.

I-J

identity theft The illegal use of an individual's personal or financial information to apply for credit by a criminal without the owner's permission or knowledge.

immunization See live protection.

initialization vector The part of a security key that helps scramble information differently each time a chunk of encrypted data is transmitted.

Internet Service Provider (ISP) A company that provides access to the Internet.

intranet A private network that uses web technology to distribute information. Usually used to make information available inside a company among employees.

IP address Internet Protocol address. A numerical address consisting of four sets of numbers separated by dots ranging from 0 to 255 that is assigned to each computer on the Internet or closed network.

IP spoofing A bit of high-tech trickery that makes an email (or some other piece of transmitted data) look like it came from somewhere it did not. It's like sending a letter to your friend and changing the return address on the envelope to make it appear like it came from George Bush's vet or Oprah's dry cleaner.

ISP See Internet Service Provider.

K-L

key logger Software or hardware that captures everything typed into a computer. This data is saved for later analysis by a third party.

LAN Local area network. A computer network that spans a relatively small area.

live protection A feature common to anti-spyware programs that watches for spyware infections in real time at a series of entry points on a computer. Different programs may call this feature by other names, including *real time protection* or *immunization*.

M-N

MAC address Media Access Control address. A unique identifier given to each network device by its manufacturer. The MAC address is a series of codes separated by dashes.

MAC address filtering A router feature that allows only computers with authorized MAC addresses to connect to it wirelessly.

macro   A programmable language embedded in a large program, often used to automate tasks.

macro virus   A type of virus that is created in a macro language and embedded in a document. Macro viruses are the most common type of computer virus.

malware   Malicious software. A generic term for software that has been written for malicious or illicit purposes, includes viruses, spyware, and other damaging programming.

memory-resident virus   A type of computer virus that sits in a computer's random access memory (RAM).

modem   A device that connects a computer to an Internet provider or another computer over conventional telephone lines at low speeds.

motherboard   The main circuit board in a computer to which the system's components, including the microprocessor and memory, are attached.

multi-partite virus   A virus that attacks several parts of a computer including programs, files, and boot sectors.

NAT   See network address translation.

network address translation (NAT)   A technology that provides a built-in firewall feature on home network routers by hiding internal IP addresses. It is also known as natural address translation.

O-P

open source software   A program made available for free that includes a copy of the lines of programming code that makes it work.

P2P   See peer to peer.

passphrase   A sentence or set of words that can be used in lieu of a password. Passphrases are often used in wireless security.

patches   Fixes or security updates issued by software makers.

payload   Part of a virus that does bad things, such as deleting files, deploying spam, or vandalizing data.

payware   Software created by a publisher that is sold commercially.

peer to peer (P2P)   A network comprised of individual participants that have equal capabilities and duties.

pharming   An attack on a domain name server (DNS) that poisons it with incorrect information so web surfers are redirected to sites posing as banking and financial sites that steal their information.

phishing   Email or web pop-ups sent by a crook that attempt to fool an individual into sending her personal and/or financial information.

plug-in   Add-on software that adds features to an existing program.

polymorphic virus   A virus that rewrites its own code to evade detection.

pop-up ad   A type of window that displays an advertisement. A pop-up ad can appear on a computer desktop or during a web-surfing session.

port-scanner   Software that looks for holes in a firewall.

potentially unwanted programs (PUPs)   A term coined by security software company McAfee to describe programs, such as spyware, adware, Trojan Horses, and other malware, that can compromise your privacy and that you might not want on your computer.

PUPs   See potentially unwanted programs.

Q-R

real time protection   See live protection.

root kit   A programming toolkit that is used to program a virus, spyware, or other piece of malware from being discovered by a security program.

router   A junction box with data traffic cop capabilities that connects computers together so they can share files, access the Internet, and share printers.

S

salad cream   A tasty British condiment made by Heinz.

script kiddies   Electronic intruders who use freely distributed software designed by others to engage in computer vandalism, break-ins, or electronic theft.

secure web page   A web page that can only be accessed through a secure connection. All personal information entered into a secure web page is encrypted (scrambled) before it is sent across the Internet.

security key   A security code that can lock and unlock encrypted data as it moves between two devices, usually a computer and a home network router. Sometimes just referred to as a key.

security software   A program designed to protect a computer from malicious software.

Service Pack 2 (SP2)   A major security update issued in the fall of 2004 by Microsoft for Windows XP.

Service Set Identifier (SSID)   A router's name that it broadcasts via a wireless signal that can be viewed by wireless computers or devices.

share name   A name used to identify a printer or folder from another computer over a network.

shareware   Software that is created by a programmer who asks for payment on the honor system.

signature   An electronic thumbprint used by an anti-spyware or antivirus program to identify a threat.

Simple File Sharing   A Microsoft technology that allows you to share your files and folders with other computers on a local network.

snack   Food that is not part of a meal. Also a reward for a job well done when following instructions correctly in this book.

snoopware   Software that watches your computer habits on behalf of someone else—usually someone you know such as a parent, employer, or spouse.

social engineering   Using trickery and charm to extract security information such as passwords from an individual.

software   A computer program.

software suite   A number of programs bundled together and sold as a package that do related tasks.

source code   The lines of programming that make up a program.

SP2   See Service Pack 2.

spam   Unsolicited commercial email or electronic junk mail.

spoof   To electronically fool. For example, a spoofed email is an electronic mail message that looks like it has arrived from someone who hasn't sent it.

spyware   Software installed on your computer that collects information about you as you use your computer and delivers it to a third party. Spyware is often installed without your knowledge.

SSID   See Service Set Identifier.

SSL   Secure Sockets Layer. A data transfer method, developed by Netscape, used to move files across the Internet between two computers using a secure connection. A secure connection provides protection from hackers or snoops by scrambling data as it moves between two points.

stateful inspection   A process by which a router checks that data arriving has been requested by a computer on its network. This is also known as stateful packet inspection.

stealth mode   This feature makes a firewall and the computers behind it invisible to the Internet.

subnet   A subnet is a subdivision of a network, just as a neighborhood is subdivision of a town.

subnet mask   A subnet mask breaks down a network address into regions or neighborhoods acting as a filter for a router that is trying to send data. The mask says to ignore all the addresses in the world except the ones in this neighborhood, town, or state.

system tray   A collection of icons for easy access to tools, special Windows functions, and programs already running in memory. It's located on the bottom-right side of the Windows screen.

T-U-V

tombstone shopping   A type of identity theft in which a thief researches deaths at a public library or by visiting a graveyard and then applies for a birth certificate in the dead person's name.

trialware   Software that is free to use for a set period of time so as to allow a user to try it before purchasing.

Trojan horse   A program posing as a harmless piece of software that can contain malware such as viruses or spyware.

UDP   User Datagram Protocol. A method of sending simple messages across a network connection that allows one computer to talk another to exchange information. You'll see it often referenced in a home network router setup.

USB   Universal Serial Bus. A computer port used to attach external devices such as keyboards, mice, joysticks, or digital cameras.

video adapter   A chipset integrated into a computer motherboard that gives it graphics display capabilities.

video card   A circuit board that plugs into a personal computer that gives it graphics display capabilities.

virus   A malicious program that replicates when deployed by a human, usually unknowingly.

virus hoax   An email, usually sent by a well-meaning friend, that contains alerts about a fictitious virus. Virus hoaxes are more of an annoyance than a real threat.

virus signature   A digital snapshot of a virus issued by a software publisher that is used by the publisher's antivirus program to detect a virus.

VPN   Virtual private network. A secure connection used to access a company's servers from home across the public Internet. It can also provide a secure connection between a company and a customer's or satellite office.

vulnerability scanner   A program that checks a computer for known weaknesses such as programming errors or security holes.

W-X-Y-Z

war chalking   The practice of tagging pavement near an open Wi-Fi network to alert others that wireless access is available at that location.

war driving   The practice of probing wireless networks and cataloging them for possible future use by a third party.

web browser   A program used to retrieve and display magazine-like information pages from the World Wide Web.

web server   Computers that contain websites and make them available to computers on a network such as the Internet.

website harvesting   Programs that scan the Web seeking emails for inclusion in lists that are sold to purveyors of spam.

WEP   Wired Equivalent Privacy. One of the most common security features on wireless routers. WEP is a way of scrambling information as it flies through the air between a computer and a router.

white hat   A computer hacker with altruistic motives who breaks into computers to test their security and reveal vulnerabilities to the computer's owner.

Wi-Fi   Wireless Fidelity. A wireless technology that enables a computer to connect to a network using radio waves.

wireless hackers   People who connect to a wireless network and steal banking access information, identity, or other valuable data on a personal or corporate network.

wireless home network   A number of computers and other devices with wireless capabilities that are connected together so they can share files, access to the Internet, and printers.

worm   A self-contained computer virus that can sometimes spread across a network without human intervention.

WPA   Wi-Fi Protected Access. A wireless network security measure that is much more secure than WEP, yet is simpler to use.

Index

inform**IT**

Your Guide to Information Technology Training and Reference

www.informit.com

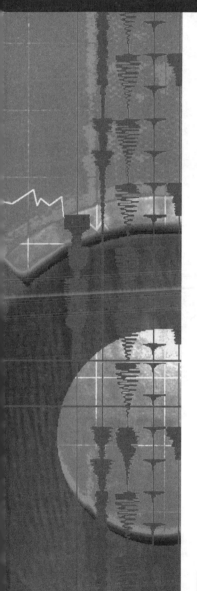

Que has partnered with **InformIT.com** to bring technical information to your desktop. Drawing on Que authors and reviewers to provide additional information on topics you're interested in, **InformIT.com** has free, in-depth information you won't find anywhere else.

Articles

Keep your edge with thousands of free articles, in-depth features, interviews, and information technology reference recommendations – all written by experts you know and trust.

Online Books

Answers in an instant from **InformIT Online Books'** 600+ fully searchable online books. Sign up now and get your first 14 days **free**.

POWERED BY
Safari

Catalog

Review online sample chapters and author biographies to choose exactly the right book from a selection of more than 5,000 titles.

As an **InformIT** partner, **Que** has shared the knowledge and hands-on advice of our authors with you online.
Visit **InformIT.com** to see what you are missing.

que®   www.quepublishing.com

Wouldn't it be great

if the world's leading technical publishers joined forces to deliver their best tech books in a common digital reference platform?

They have. Introducing
InformIT Online Books
powered by Safari.

POWERED BY **Safari**

InformIT Online Books

informit.com/onlinebooks

- **Specific answers to specific questions.**

  InformIT Online Books' powerful search engine gives you relevance-ranked results in a matter of seconds.

- **Immediate results.**

  With InformIt Online Books, you can select the book you want and view the chapter or section you need immediately.

- **Cut, paste, and annotate.**

  Paste code to save time and eliminate typographical errors. Make notes on the material you find useful and choose whether or not to share them with your workgroup.

- **Customized for your enterprise.**

  Customize a library for you, your department, or your entire organization. You pay only for what you need.

Get your first 14 days FREE!

InformIT Online Books is offering its members a 10-book subscription risk free for 14 days. Visit **http://www.informit.com/onlinebooks** for details.

LEOVILLE PRESS

NEW FROM LEO LAPORTE AND QUE PUBLISHING

LEO LAPORTE'S 2006 GADGET GUIDE

By Leo Laporte and Michael Miller

$19.99, 240 pp

ISBN 0-7897-3395-1

LEO LAPORTE'S PC HELP DESK

By Leo Laporte and Mark Edward Soper

$29.99, 790 pp

ISBN 0-7897-3394-3

LEO LAPORTE'S GUIDE TO MAC OS X TIGER

By Leo Laporte and Todd Stauffer

$24.99, 400 pp

ISBN 0-7897-3393-5

LEO LAPORTE'S GUIDE TO TIVO

By Leo Laporte and Gareth Branwyn

$29.99, 432 pp

ISBN 0-7897-3195-9

> *"Age only matters when one is aging.
> Now that I have arrived at a GREAT AGE,
> I might as well be twenty."*
>
> **—Pablo Picasso**

Welcome to This Great Age!

Like Picasso, millions of people today have reached a Great Age in their lives. Not only are we at a Great Age; we also live in a Great Age. Technology offers many solutions to make our lives better and to make living easier.

Sandy Berger's Great Age Guides reveal those solutions and show how to make the best use of them. Readers of Great Age Guides can continue their learning journey with Sandy on the Internet at **www.greatagebooks.com**.

Sandy Berger's Great Age Guides...They're more than just books. They open the door to understanding a whole new world, a world of Better Living in this Great Age.

It's a Great Age why not enjoy it?

Interested in purchasing a Great Age Guide? Please visit us at **www.greatagebooks.com** or **www.quepublishing.com** where shipping is always FREE!

NOW AVAILABLE
Sandy Berger's Great Age Guide to Better Living Through Technology
ISBN: 0-7897-3440-0
US $19.99
CAN $27.99 UK £13.99

Sandy Berger's Great Age Guide to the Internet
ISBN: 0-7897-3442-7
US $19.99
CAN $27.99 UK £13.99

Sandy Berger's Great Age Guide to Gadgets & Gizmos
ISBN: 0-7897-3441-9
US $19.99
CAN $27.99 UK £13.99

...COMING Soon!

Sandy Berger's Great Age Guide to Online Health and Wellness ***Coming Spring 2006!**
Sandy Berger's Great Age Guide to Online Travel ***Coming Spring 2006!**
Sandy Berger's Great Age Guide to Computer Basics ***Coming Summer 2006!**
Sandy Berger's Great Age Guide to Online Finance ***Coming Fall 2006!**